# Bed & Breakfast goes Hawaiian

a DIRECTORY AND GUIDE BOOK

*by Al Davis and Evie Warner*

1986-1987 edition

*Bed & Breakfast Guide*

Copyright 1985, 1986
Island Bed & Breakfast

**ISBN** 0-9615970-1-1

All rights reserved
including the right of reproduction
in whole or in part in any form

Printed by
Consolidated Printers, Inc.
2630 8th St. Berkeley, Ca. 94710

Every effort was made to ensure
the accuracy of prices and travel
information, but the authors do
not bear responsibility for
price increases

## CONTENTS

    Introduction ................................................V
    Acknowledgements..........................................VII

1. General information ........................................1
    When to Visit
    Booking B & B
    Staying B & B
    Preparing to Go
    Getting There
    Inter-Island Transportation
    Time Difference
    Hawaii's Critters
    On Island Transportation
    Weather
    Food
    Language
    Crime in Hawaii
    Ocean Safety

2. Restaurant Guide ..........................................  7

3. MOLOKAI
    Introduction ............................................  9
    Molokai ................................................. 10

4. LANAI
    Introduction ............................................ 19
    Lanai.................................................... 20

5. HAWAII
    Introduction............................................. 22
    Hilo .................................................... 23
    Kilauea Volcano ......................................... 35
    South of Hilo ........................................... 37
    North of Hilo ........................................... 42
    Waimea-Kameula .......................................... 44
    North Kohala ............................................ 49
    Kailua-Kona ............................................. 51
    The Belt Road ........................................... 61
    South of Kailua ......................................... 63

*Bed & Breakfast Guide*

6. OAHU
    - Introduction .................................................. 67
    - Downtown Honolulu ............................................. 69
    - Waikiki ....................................................... 77
    - Kaimuki/Kapahulu .............................................. 83
    - East of Honolulu .............................................. 88
    - Pearl City .................................................... 95
    - Around the Island ............................................ 100
    - Kaneohe-Kailua-Lanikai ....................................... 110

7. MAUI
    - Introduction ................................................. 121
    - Kahului ...................................................... 123
    - Wailuku ...................................................... 128
    - Upcountry .................................................... 134
    - Hana ......................................................... 143
    - Kihei ........................................................ 146
    - Lahaina ...................................................... 153
    - Kaanapali .................................................... 158

8. KAUAI
    - Introduction ................................................. 161
    - Kauai's Luau's ............................................... 164
    - Lihue ........................................................ 165
    - Wailua-Kapaa ................................................. 174
    - Hanalai ...................................................... 185
    - Poipu-Koloa .................................................. 196
    - Kalaheo ...................................................... 205
    - Hanapepe ..................................................... 209
    - Waimea-Kekaha ................................................ 212

# INTRODUCTION

Bed & Breakfast Hawaii started as an idea when we first visited Kauai in the winter of 1977-1978. Until that time neither of us had entertained the thought of living in Hawaii let alone starting a new business which we knew little or nothing about. But as so many visitors to Hawaii discover, a vacation in Hawaii seems to stir up a longing to live in the Islands.

One day, while hiking along the Na Pali Coast on the way to Hanakapai Beach, experiencing more beauty than we had ever seen in one place, we began toying with the idea of finding something to do that would allow us to live in this tropical splendor. What better thing could we do than have a home, take in guests, and share Kauai with them? Two or three days later we bought a home we felt was perfect for our needs.

From that point on starting the business was simply a matter of returning home and getting everything ready for the big move. That simple task took about twenty months, and by August of 1979 we were settled on Kauai. By then we had even contacted a B & B organization out of Princeton, New Jersey, which we felt sure could supply us with plenty of guests. We anxiously awaited their answer. We did not have to wait long, and by September of 1979 we knew that neither they nor anyone they knew of was interested in bed & breakfast in Hawaii. Keep in mind that in 1979 bed and breakfast was a relatively new thing springing up in the U.S., and when we told people what we were doing they envisioned we were serving breakfast in bed!

Yes, necessity is the mother of invention. In October, 1979, we formed our own Bed & Breakfast group by running an ad in the Kauai paper asking people to become members of . "an island network of homes." The "network" at that time consisted of one home, ours. Now it is 1985, we have five years experience behind us, and our network has grown to over one hundred, with homes on all the Islands except Lanai. We have met hundreds of fascinating people and are more convinced than ever that B & B is a great way to travel, especially in Hawaii.

At first we believed that the main benefit of going the B & B way was cost. Guests can stay in a home for anywhere from $25 to $60 a night, whereas most hotel prices start at $60, with many well over $100. But cost is only one factor. As people become more and more experienced with B & B travel, cost becomes less and less important. The prevailing opinion has become that B & B is more personal and more enjoyable. A visitor gets a first hand chance to see what living in Hawaii is like and receives a more informed idea of what to see and where to go, or not to go, from a B & B host than from someone working in a hotel. After all, what can they say if asked about the best restaurants in the area, or where the best beaches are? Right at the hotel, naturally.

*Bed & Breakfast Guide*

Also, staying in a private home can be more enjoyable. Many B & B guests and hosts have become friends, and though the guests may not return as often as they like, many keep in touch. One guest who experienced Hurricane Iwa on Kauai in 1982 and spent Thanksgiving with a local group of around twenty people calls each year on the anniversary of the hurricane.

Admittedly, bed & breakfast is not for everyone. Some people just do not feel comfortable in someone else's home. They feel it is just too personal in spite of the fact that most hosts are very experienced at making people feel at home, and many of the accommodations are separate from the main home and can be very private. Bed & breakfast is for people who are open and adventurous, people who are tired of the hotel/motel experience and are looking for an alternative way of travel.

But this book is about more than bed & breakfast. It is our opinion that Hawaii is the best tourist value in the U.S. Where else can you get good accommodations with a continental breakfast (which we like to call an Aloha breakfast since our hosts emphasize Island fruits) for somewhere between $25 and $60 a night? Or rent a car for as little as $69 a week, unlimited mileage? And in spite of what you have heard, eating in Hawaii, at restaurants or at home, is not much more expensive than on the mainland if you know where to go. Also, in Hawaii entertainment isn't necessarily expensive since the main attractions, swimming, snorkeling, hiking, relaxing on the beach, cost nothing at all.

The ultimate purpose of our book is to encourage people to visit Hawaii. Many people who have never been to Hawaii have distorted ideas. First, many think you have to be well off, if not rich, but budget travel is possible. Then, some think there is nothing to do in Hawaii but lie on the beach and bake in the sun. This is also a falacy. There is much to do and much to see, and we hope our book helps more people realize that.

First and foremost this book is a guide to our host homes. We have tried to be accurate in our descriptions of the homes, hosts, and locations. We also want to help our guests in other things such as restaurants, points of interest, beaches, sports activity, and night life where there is any. No guide book that we have seen covers everything and this one is no exception. We do not cover hiking trails, although we realize that hiking can be an important part of a trip to Hawaii. For information on hiking we recommend Robert Smith's *Hawaii's Best Hiking Trails*, published by Wilderness Press, Berkeley, Ca. Nor do we have much to say about shopping, which is an important part of vacationing. We say nothing at all about other accommodations in Hawaii, and we want everyone to know that there are many small, and some not so small, **hotels** and **motels** that offer very attractive rates. We intend to update our guide each year, and we urge guests and readers to supply us with tips and ideas about travel in Hawaii. We hope the homes described in our book appeal to you and that the information presented will be useful. We hope to see you in the Islands soon.

# ACKNOWLEDGEMENT

When we started Bed & Breakfast in 1979, we had the idea for a guide for our guests. At that time we had only Kauai in mind, and our thoughts ran more to a few pages of helpful hints than a book. As Bed & Breakfast has grown, so has our concept for a guide. No longer could we be satisfied with one Island and a mention of a few special things a guest should not miss. This growth did not occur without some big boosts from some very special people.

Our first big boost came from Jerry Hulse, the Travel Editor of the Los Angeles Times. In November of 1981 Jerry did a feature story on our new B & B Venture. That article changed our lives. Until that time we had about twenty hosts, and we worked out of our home. Four days after Jerry's article we received 184 letters. We had a policy then, as we still do today, of answering our mail the day received. Some time around midnight we sealed the last envelope. Then, last year Jerry was kind enough to review our book favorably, which gave us another big boost. Jerry, a big mahalo nui loa for your support.

About a year later we met Al Borcover of the Chicago Tribune, and he subsequently wrote an article about us and B & B took another big step forward. In 1983 we had a guest from the East Coast, Nancy Shute. After staying in several B & B homes, Nancy wrote about her bed and breakfast experience and her article was published in the Philadelphia Inquirer. So a special thanks to Al and Nancy.

Also to be thanked is Ruth Ann Becker of Hawaii Business Magazine. When she interviewed us for an article for her magazine, she asked what our next venture might be. We assured her our guide book to Hawaii would soon be complete. That was back in 1983, but that promise has been haunting and pushing us ever since.

We would like to thank all the many travel writers who have written about us over the years. Many times we were unaware of being mentioned until one of our guests sent us word of it. Please forgive us if we have failed to mention everyone.

Bed & Breakfast, obviously, would not exist were it not for all of our wonderful hosts, and it is to them we owe the greatest debt. Our hosts have also been helpful in providing us with information about the Islands. Since it is our policy to inspect every home in our organization, we have come to know our hosts and consider the relationship to be more than a business connection. Hosts, mahalo, not only for all of your support, but also for taking such good care of the thousands of visitors that have selected the Bed & Breakfast way.

*Then there are the people who so diligently helped in the proofing of the book and encouraged us to continue when the end seemed so far away. Thanks to Bev, and to Fran, and to Lorri for some valuable editing. And our apology and thanks to Janie, who proofed the Kauai section first time around and we failed to mention it in our first edition. Thanks to Michael for not only being supportive but for helping to set the format. And a very big thanks to Rocky, who spent his two week vacation making sure the details were right.*

*Last, but certainly not least, thank you, Elvrine Zeevat-Chow, our very dedicated office manager, who kept things going over a busy tourist season and allowed us to work on this project.*

# GENERAL INFORMATION

**WHEN TO VISIT HAWAII**

We once asked a Hawaii resident, "When is the best time to visit Hawaii?" He paused for a few seconds and then queried, "When is it cold where you are?" Without a doubt most people visit Hawaii during January, February, and March, and then secondly during June, July, and August. Many people would not dream of coming to Hawaii in the summer months, thinking it might be too hot. Summer months tend to be warmer, averaging a little over 80. When the trade winds blow, summer days are comfortable. There are advantages to visiting Hawaii in the off season. There are fewer people and prices are less. Off season does not mean dead season as is true in many Mainland tourist areas after Labor Day.

**BOOKING BED & BREAKFAST**

Once you've decided when to visit Hawaii, the next step is to decide where to stay. Let us know as soon as possible which homes you choose, giving more than one choice as some may have prior bookings. When you have made your selections, send 20% of your total lodging to B & B Hawaii, Box 449, Kapaa, Hi 96746 to confirm reservations. Should you need to cancel, your deposit less a $10 handling charge will be refunded, provided cancellation is made one week prior to arrival.

When we receive your deposit, we will send you a reservation form with the name, address, and phone number of your host. This form will also have the date of your arrival, departure and the balance due the host. At the same time we will send your host a copy of the reservation form with your name, address, and phone number. You should then receive a letter from your hosts giving you directions to their home. You should write to the host letting them know the time of your arrival. Our experience has been that the more communication between host and guest the better.

We do accept phone reservations. Call 808-822-7771. The best time to call is between 9 a.m. and 4 p.m. Hawaii time. Remember that it is always earlier in Hawaii than on the Mainland. When we receive a phone booking, we hold that reservation for about a week, time enough for the deposit to arrive in the mail. When the office is closed, please leave a message on the answering machine and your call will be returned the next day.

*Bed & Breakfast Guide*

## STAYING BED & BREAKFAST

B & B hosts accept in rare occasions serve a continental breakfast, or what we like to call *an Aloha breakfast*. This consists of fresh Island fruit, juice, toast or some kind of roll or bread that the host might prepare, coffee or tea. In order to serve a full breakfast, ie., bacon and eggs, kitchens would have to be certified by the Board of Health. Now comes catch 22. Kitchens could not be certified since homes are not commercially zoned. Now, if your host serves you more than we have stated, keep it quiet, at least until you get back home and can tell your friends.

If you have specific health needs or certain food allergies, let us know as we will take that into consideration in the booking. Also, let us know if you are allergic to animals as many of our hosts have pets. Some hosts permit use of the washer and dryer; however, since energy costs are highest in the nation, compensation is expected. Use of the phone is permitted and there is no toll charge for on-Island calls. All off-Island calls are toll calls and should be made on a credit card or charged to ones home phone. Hawaii has a 4% excise tax on all purchases including lodging and most hosts add that to their balance. Some hosts request one night's deposit payable to them and refundable if cancellation is one week in advance.

## PREPARING TO GO

The biggest mistake any first time visitor makes when visiting Hawaii is bringing too many clothes. Adhere to the travelers' motto of, "Half the clothes and twice the money." Dress in Hawaii is very casual. Day wear consists of shorts or swimsuits, a light shirt or blouse, sandals or thongs. It is a good idea to bring a light sweater, especially in the winter months, as at higher altitudes it is almost always cooler in the early morning and in the evening. If you intend to dine at the higher priced restaurants, men need to bring a light jacket. Most restaurants could care less what you are wearing, and residents of Hawaii give much less thought to their attire than they would on the Mainland. Cotton clothes, long pants for men and women can be comfortable. Ladies may want to buy a muu muu and gentlemen an aloha shirt. Sun glasses, sun screen, mosquito lotion are important items. A plastic bag for wet swim suits is an excellent idea.

## GETTING THERE

While flying to Hawaii is not the only option, it is by far the most popular. No single airline consistently has the lowest rate; shop them all to see who is the lowest at any particular time. If stand-by flights are available, take advantage of them, especially in the off season. At the present time, United Airlines has direct flights to all the neighbor islands except Molokai. In the future other airlines will undoubtedly also fly direct. If the airline you book flies only to Honolulu International and your destination is one of the outer islands, be sure to check your luggage through to your final destination. This may not be possible, however, if you are flying stand-by on the connecting flight.

## INTER-ISLAND TRAVEL

There are three major inter-island airlines: Hawaiian, Aloha, and Mid-Pacific. Fares are by no means constant, but vary with the number of tourists on the islands. The cheapest way to fly is stand-by. We recommend this since the planes are seldom full. If you have doubts, call the airline and ask them how the flight looks. If they tell you it is

*General Information*

wide open or looks good, fly stand-by. With all the inter-island flying we have done, we have never missed a flight. For more information call the toll-free numbers listed below.

    Hawaiian:    800-367-5320
    Aloha:    800-367-5250
    Mid-Pac:    800-367-7010

## TIME DIFFERENCE

Keep in mind that it is always earlier in Hawaii than on the Mainland. During the winter the time difference from Pacific Daylight is two hours and from Eastern Daylight it is five hours. In summer the difference is three and six, respectively.

## HAWAII'S CRITTERS

While we consider Hawaii to be nearly Paradise, we must admit that even in Paradise we have some unpleasant little critters. The most annoying is the mosquito, which was unknown in Hawaii before the white man appeared. You may not see them, but you will feel their presence. One critter you will hopefully not see is the centipede. Most centipedes have been eaten by the buffos, the big frogs you are bound to see, or at least hear. Also, alas, there is the cockroach. Do not run in panic if you happen to see one, just give him a second and he will panic and disappear. Another little critter that bothers some people is the gecko, a tiny lizard around two inches long that makes a clicking sound at night. We never disturb them; they eat a considerable number of mosquitoes. The important thing to remember is that Hawaii has no creatures that will do you serious damage: no snakes or poisonous spiders. You can hike on any trail with out fear of being bitten. We always tell our guests that the biggest threat to their well being is the monstrous mai tai or the creeping chi chi.

## ON ISLAND TRANSPORTATION

It is possible on Oahu to travel by public transportation. In fact, it is possible to tour the entire island by public bus at very little expense. Having a car, however, is a pleasant alternative. On the neighbor islands a car is close to a necessity. If you do not drive, there are a few B & B locations that might do; without transportation, one is very limited, and tour buses are expensive.

Since 1982 we have been working with National Car Rental, which has agreed to give our members a reduced rate. When conditions are at their most competitive, National has gone as low as $69 a week, unlimited mileage. National has been in business for nearly fifty years and are very reliable. At times there are rental companies which offer cheaper rates, but we feel that knowing National's cars will all be first rate makes paying a little more worth it. Arrangements should be made before arrival in the islands. Special events and peak travel times can cause car shortages. When that happens rates rise, or worse, cars are not available.

## WEATHER

We think the weather in Hawaii is ideal, but since reaction to weather is subjective, we will attempt to describe the weather and let you decide if it sounds ideal. Daytime temperatures at sea level average between 70 and 85, with the summer months having the highs and winter months the lows. Nighttime temperatures seldom fall below 65 and are often in the low 70's. Normal winds, called trade winds, come from the northeast. From around March through October trade winds are usually between 5 to 15 miles an hour, just strong enough to act as natural air-conditioning. At times, usually from November through February, trade winds get a little stronger, but many days in December rival July days. Winds from the south, Kona winds, usually occur in the winter months and often bring foul weather. Rain on some part of every island is almost a daily occurrence. It usually rains at night or in the early morning hours and simply serves to freshen things up a bit. Humidity is a factor, but trade winds tend to mitigate against a high humidity. It is far more humid and muggy in New York in the summer than in Hawaii at any time of the year. Where else can you find summer days that stay between 75 and 85? Winter is another thing. Most of us who live in Hawaii long for the cold winter snows and freezing conditions found on the Mainland and pine for winter activities such as shoveling snow and putting chains on tires. Oh, sure! And if you believe that we have some diamonds we found on Diamond Head we would love to sell you, cheap.

**FOOD**

When most people think of Hawaiian food, probably fruit first comes to mind. As the song in *South Pacific* says "...We have mangos and bananas we can pick right off a tree..." and many more fruits could have been included. Hawaii is abundant with fruit, not only mangos and bananas, but papaya, pineapple, coconut, guava, passion fruit, and lychee nut. Some of the more unusual fruits are: mountain apple, Kokee plum, surinam cherry.

Hawaii is distinctive for other delicacies you may not be familiar with. If any food is distinctively Hawaiian it is saimin, which some Mainlanders call Top Ramen. It is sort of a chicken noodle soup with leafy vegetables. Some restaurants in Hawaii serve nothing but saimin. Hawaiians say it is great for a hangover. We are unsure of the origin of saimin; whenever we ask at a restaurant that specializes in it, they end up telling us how it is made. Some say it is originally Japanese, some say it is Chinese, while others say it was first made in Hawaii.

There is, of course, traditional Hawaiian cuisine. If you have been to a luau you know about kalua pig, chicken hekka, lomi lomi salmon, and poi, a few of the dishes you will get at a luau. One need not attend a luau to sample these dishes since each island has restaurants that serve Hawaiian food.

Then there are the multi-ethnic influences in Hawaii, for the most part Oriental (Japanese, Chinese, Filipino, Korean) but there is also the Portuguese and American influence. Few restaurants are exclusively one or the other. There is a restaurant on Kauai that has Chinese, Japanese, Korean, American, and even a Mexican dish or two. This wide ethnic influence is best illustrated by one of the local favorites, Loco Moco, which is a plate of rice, the Oriental influence, topped by a hamburger patty, the American influence, crowned by an egg, the Universal influence, and all of this covered with a heavy gravy.

We could go on and describe the sashimi, the sushi, the kimchee, the manapua, the malasadas, but we will let you discover these by yourself. If none of the foods above appeal to your taste, you can dine in restaurants just like those you find at home.

*General Information*

## LANGUAGE

Most guide books to Hawaii present the reader with a fairly full discussion of not only Hawaiian words and their pronunciation but also a discussion of the much more often heard *Pidgin English*. While our discussion will not be as complete, we feel it is all one really needs to know to understand what is happening.

Pronunciation of Hawaiian names can present problems to first time visitors, not because they are hard to pronounce, but because a first time visitor is unfamiliar with the words. Pronouncing Hawaiian words is simple once you get the hang of it. The language contains only seven consonants: h,k,l,m,n,p, and w, and the vowels a,e,i,o,u. A is pronounced *ah* as in ma; E is pronounced *eh* as in bay; I is pronounced *ee* as in key; O is pronounced *oh* as in no; U is pronounced ou as in too. Now, with this in mind if you run across the word PI PE LI NE, you will have no trouble pronouncing it. Easy, isn't it. Or you could put the letters together and just say pipeline.

The first words you will hear on your Hawaii excursion will be *aloha* and *mahalo*. Mahalo means thank you. Aloha, however, is not easily defined. Simply it means hello, welcome, or goodbye, but underneath it means much more. People talk of the *aloha spirit* which suggests a caring for people that makes them welcome whoever they are. There is never too much *aloha* anywhere in the world, but it is plentiful in Hawaii.

Two valuable words that are much used in Hawaii are *mauka* and *makai*, which mean respectively, toward the mountain and toward the sea. In this book we use them almost exclusively in giving directions. It is much easier to say "go mauka" or "turn makai" than "go east" or "turn south." Just remember, mauka means toward the mountain and makai means toward the sea.

Another strange sounding word you might hear or see written is *pupus*. Do not get alarmed when you see this on the menu, or a local person asks you over for pupus. It just means hor d'oeuvres. It is also helpful to know *kane* and *wahine* in case you need the men's or ladies' room. Another one you will hear often is *pau*, which means all done.

The most common Pidgin word you will hear is *da kine*, which is used to mean anything the speaker wants it to mean. The extensive use of da kine in Hawaii must have some profound comment on the use of language, for it is possible for a meaningful conversation to take place with da kine as the main word: noun, verb, adjective, or if needed, interjection. For example try this conversation.

> *"Hey, Brah, you goin' da kine?"*
> *"Sure. When da kine get here wit da kine,*
> *we pick up da kine and see you bum bi at*
> *da kine."*
> *"O.K., Brah, da kine da beer or we da kine*
> *you lader."*

Then there is the expression *Hawaii Time* which means "whenever we get around to it." If you stay in Hawaii long enough, you will come to know the meaning of *Polynesian paralysis*. When that sets in you may have passed from being a *malahini* (Mainlander) to a *kamaaina* (a child of the land.)

So, aloha all you malahinis, kanes and wahines both. Mahalo for choosing to vacation on our beautiful Islands. We hope your travels both mauka and makai are most pleasant. Fill your *opu* with many delicious pupus, and when your stay is all pau, may your spirit be on Hawaiian time, and the next time you come da kine, may Polynesian paralysis so infect your psyche that one and all will declare you a true kamaaina.

## CRIME IN HAWAII

Several years ago much media space was given to a few unfortunate incidents where visitors to Hawaii were attacked by some local thugs, and people began to question how safe Paradise really was. As in all of America today, crime is a problem in Hawaii, yet, to keep things in perspective, if visitors avoid certain places we mention and take normal precautions, most likely they will experience no problems. There is one area of Oahu we would just as soon stay out of and that is the Waianae/Makaha area. For whatever sociological reasons, many of the people who live there do not like tourists, or to put it more bluntly, they do not like "haoles" (a word used to denote a Caucasian). Some of our guests have told us that they did not feel safe when they ventured onto the beach at Makaha. We asked several of our Oahu hosts what they thought and they said they would not go there. Waimanalo is another place where visitors are not always welcome. (see Waimanalo section for more complete explanation). No matter where you are in Hawaii, it is not wise to leave valuables in the car, locked or not. Thieves can open locked cars as fast as if they had a key.

One other area of concern to tourists is the marijuana (pakalolo) growers. If you are hiking, stay on the trails, and you will not have a problem. Growers, like rattlesnakes, get as far from human activity as possible. Hikers would have to be far off the trail to find their patches.

## OCEAN SAFETY

While this is the last item in this section, it is not last in importance. Throughout the book we urge caution in swimming in certain areas on each Island. In reality there are certain safety measures that should be observed whenever one is near the ocean. First, never turn your back on the ocean. On Kauai a woman was having her picture taken on the water's edge when suddenly a big wave knocked her off the rocks and she was drowned. Had she been looking she would have seen the wave coming. Second, never swim where there are signs posted no matter how calm the water looks. There may be a rip tide at that spot that will not be obvious to you. Third, never swim alone. Be sure others are around just in case something goes wrong. Last, do not think that because you see surfers way out in the water that the water is easy swimming. Surfers may be able to handle water that could take even a pretty good swimmer half way to Midway. On every Island there are plenty of safe beaches for swimming, so there is no need to risk ones life in any water that is marginal.

# RESTAURANT GUIDE

In order for our guide to make sense to you, it is necessary that we explain our method. First, we visited almost every restaurant mentioned and tried to eat in as many as possible over the seven year period we have been researching this book. Where we were unable to do this, we consulted with our hosts who have tried the restaurants. We are not taking the critic's point of view, feeling it necessary to make comments about the culinary arts of the various chefs, cooks, or hash-slingers, whichever the case may be. This year we have included the phone numbers of most of the restaurants except in those places where there is no need at all to make a reservation.

We feel it is more important to describe the type of restaurant and the food served rather than evaluate their culinary ability. While we know what we like, we do not pretend that our tastes reflect other's tastes. However, at times we will lavishly praise a place we think is special and perhaps damn with faint praise a few others. We will star restaurants that we think offer something special. For example, on Kauai there is a little place in Waimea that serves tasty, fresh baked turnovers. In some cases we will give a spot several stars if we think it should not be missed. We have divided the restaurants of Hawaii into five categories: 1.) fast food, 2.) tourist spots, 3.) **LOCAL STYLE**, 4.) local style, 5.) local/tourist.

Of type 1 we say nothing. They differ little from Mainland fast food spots. Of 2 we say little as they are obviously located in the hotels and resort areas and are generally good places to eat and very predictable. Our concentration is on the other three.

First, let us define **LOCAL STYLE**, or what we like to call *two scoop rice* restaurants from their inevitable habit of serving two ice-cream scoops of rice. These restaurants are always low in price, and the food is cooked to please local people. Some might call it good stick-to-the-ribs stuff. For example, if you see loco moco (see Food in General Information section) on the menu, you are probably in a **LOCAL STYLE place.** Another **LOCAL STYLE** would be the places that specialize in saimin. If you have never tried saimin, do so, for nothing is so universally Hawaiian as saimin. Then there are the places that specialize in the typical Hawaiian food. We urge you to try one of the **LOCAL STYLE** places we mention, and if you take a liking to it, you can save a considerable amount of money on food to use on other pursuits, perhaps a helicopter ride, or a sailboat ride to watch the whales.

Then there are the local style restaurants. If you are looking for bargain prices and food that is not as foreign to your palate, these, in our opinion, present the best value. For the most part these are ethnic restaurants, Japanese, Chinese, Korean, Filipino, or a combination of the above, or they are small independently owned short order places that residents of Hawaii use frequently and tourists tend to shy away from, either because they are off the beaten path, or they do not look too inviting from the outside. If we define a place as local style, for breakfast you will have a choice of rice or potatoes. If **LOCAL STYLE** you will have a choice between rice or toast, or no choice at all. Also, local style, unless specifically ethnic, will usually have a combination of local and Mainland dishes. They will have chicken teriaki, but also southern fried chicken.

Last are the local/tourist spots. Most of these are modestly priced places, basically depending on residents, with a brisk tourist trade also. In these the food will be more familiar to you; ie., chicken, steak, seafood, fish, and plenty of salad bars. Some do not offer much in the way of atmosphere, but the food is good and priced lower than hotel and resort restaurants. In some you can get a good fresh fish dinner for around $8.00, while the same meal in a hotel/resort restaurant would run around $15.00-$18.00.

We realize there are times when price is not the object. You may be looking for more than just a good meal, perhaps a memorable experience. We will not fail to give our opinion on which of the tourist restaurants we think are the best. Many we will not mention, but if you try them, you probably will be pleased. After all the hotels and resorts make it their job to please people or they would not be in business long. Also, keep in mind that the categories are artificial, and while meaningful and helpful, distinctions are sometimes hard to make.

*Chapter III*..........................................................MOLOKAI

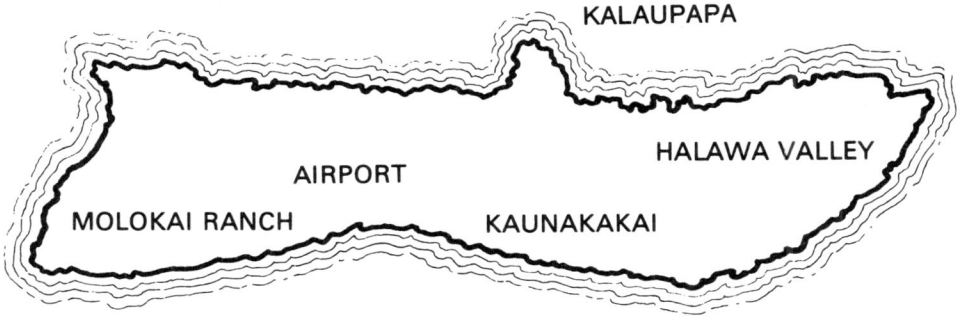

# MOLOKAI.....THE FRIENDLY ISLAND

.....DRIVING TIMES.....

From Molokai Airport: (approximate)

Kaunakaikai...............................6 miles, 15 minutes
To Host Homes....................................8 to 20 miles
Maunaloa (west side)...............10 miles, 20 minutes

# MOLOKAI

An often heard complaint about the Hawaiian Islands is that there is too much commercialism and that a place that was once peaceful and serene has been covered with too much concrete and far too many condos. People talk longingly about the *good old days* when one could walk on a beach and the only footprints seen would be theirs. While we know there are still some idyllic spots like this on all the Islands, nowhere are things more peaceful and serene than on Molokai. Also, it is not without reason that one of the names for Molokai is *the Friendly Isle*, for people there are not so hurried that they have no time to smile and chat. We like to think there is Aloha Spirit throughout Hawaii; on Molokai it is very much a way of life.

Obviously one is put in a quandary about recommending Molokai to visitors. It is a little like seeing your very favorite little known restaurant get a write up in a major paper. While you want everyone to know about it, you want it to stay special and not to become just like every other place. But we are writing for a select group, B & B travelers, and it is this adventurous group that should not miss the special treat of Molokai.

In Hawaiian tradition there are several explanations for the origin of Molokai. The one heard most today is that the god Maui pulled her from the sea as he was fishing. An older myth says that Molokai was born from the mating of the goddess Hina with the sky god of ancient Polynesia, Wakea, father of all the Hawaiian Islands. Since the arrival of the white settlers, Molokai has had several appellations, the Forsaken Isle, the Lonely Isle, and now the Friendly Isle, first called that by the late Senator Harold W. Rice.

Molokai is the fifth largest of the Hawaiian Islands and has a population of just over 6,000. For most of this century the main crop has been pineapple. In years past there were two major plantations, one located on the west end at Maunaloa which was started by Libby, Mac Neil, and Libby, and then taken over by Dole, and one in the center of the Island at Kualapuu, run by Del Monte. At the present time only Del Monte is in operation and no longer is pineapple canned on Molokai but just fresh fruit is shipped off the Island. There is, however, much experimentation of crop growing taking place and they have had some success with both corn and bell peppers. Independent farmers are doing well with such various crops as watermelon, sweet potato, string beans, onions, potatoes.

Most of the action of Molokai takes place in and around the picturesque little town of Kaunakakai, made famous in R. Alex Alexander's song the *Cokeyed Mayor of Kaunakakai*, sung by the famous Hilo Hattie. In fact, since Molokai has no daily paper, local residents find out what is happening and what good buys are to be found by checking the Bulletin Board beside the Bank of Hawaii. Nowhere in Hawaii is there more local color than in Kaunakakai. Then from the center of town it is just a short walk out to the wharf where everything shipped to Molokai arrives. Local folk use this as a kind of gathering place or a good place to catch a cool breeze when days are hot.

A visit to Molokai is a journey through time and our last visit there so relaxed us that when we returned to Kauai we found the pace almost too fast. We cannot imagine a better place for those whose wish is to experience the *Old Hawaii*, to just kick back, perhaps do a little fishing, and talk story with the local folk.

## HOSTS

### MO-2

This five acre park-like property lies at the foot of Molokai's highest mountain, on the Island's east end where cascading waterfalls and rainbows are often seen. Surrounding the charming cottage are lawns, flowering trees and shrubs, and a variety of tropical fruit trees. The cottage is fully furnished with everything from frying pans to a Scrabble game and is far enough from the hosts' home to provide total privacy. Breakfast items, including unlimited fresh home-grown fruits, are supplied for do-it-yourself whenever-you-feel-like-it morning meals. The kitchen is fully equipped so guests can have all meals at home if desired.

There are lawn lounges for sunning, snorkels and masks and a small cooler for days at the beach, books and magazines for lazy hours, and a good selection of Hawaiian records to put on the stereo.

The accommodation is ten miles east of Kaunakakai and eighteen miles from the airport. There are many coves and beaches nearby, with the beautiful Halawa Valley at the end of an intriguing drive through the truly Hawaiian area called Mana'e.

The hosts, Herb and Marion, are long time Hawaii residents, originally from Santa Rosa, California. Herb looks after their commercial lime orchard and is always happy to take interested guests on a guided tour, sharing his knowledge of the more than 100 species of flora and the ancient heiau on the property. Marian enjoys working in her small plant nursery and always has a Hawaiian-style quilting project going. Naturally outgoing and friendly, these hosts often invite guests to join them when there is a luau or other special event going on. They enjoy their guests, but happily respect the privacy of those who just want to be left alone.

The *children of this home* are two friendly outdoor dogs and two seldom seen cats; the dogs become seldom seen, too, when their company does not seem to be appreciated.

RATE: $45 single or double, two night minimum.

### MO-3

It would be hard to imagine a place more suited to the person who really needs to get away from it all and enjoy a peaceful, relaxing vacation, right at the ocean's edge. This home is located sixteen miles east of Kaunakakai, situated on a three and one half acre mini-farm. Since the accommodation offered is a fully furnished apartment with a kitchen, with a beach just steps away, with a small sail boat (a prindle) or a paddle boat available at a small fee, there would really be no need to leave the grounds once one was supplied with grub. The apartment could easily accommodate four since there are twin beds in the bedroom and a queen sized sofa bed in the living room.

What Larry and Diane have here is a producing coconut farm, and coconuts are gathered and shipped to Honolulu. Other fruit also grows in abundance so if you like you can pick your papaya the night before and have it cold for breakfast the next morning. Just up the beach a way is an ancient fish pond.

Just as fascinating as the location of this home are the hosts, Larry and Diane. At the present time Larry is very much involved working with a Molokai land developer, but we are sure he still finds time to sail his boat, since sailing is one of their great passions. Diane is the author of two cook books ( one specializing in pineapple the other in coconut) which she very graciously gave us and we found the recipes excellent.

RATE:   $50, single or double, $66 for four.

### MO-4

This accommodation is a very attractive separate apartment in the lower story of a large pole house just fifty yards or so from the beach. The apartment is really spacious and could easily accommodate four people, as it has twin beds in the bedroom and a futon (Japanese folding bed) in the living room and the couch opens up to a bed, also. There is a fully furnished kitchen so meals could be fixed at home. A crib and a high chair are available for a family with a small child. The home is just five miles from Kaunakakai and the hosts, Richard and Nadine, are happy to provide bikes for those who would rather bike than drive to town.

When we first visited here, Richard, who is a retired Air Force pilot, was hard at work on his sail boat which he was anxious to finish as sailing is one of the things Richard and Nadine love to do. Well, things haven't changed much for when we visited this year we again found Richard hard at work on their Cal 2-10 sailing sloop. Who knows, next time we might even get him to take us out for a sail, weather and time permitting. No smoking in the house, please.

RATE:   $40 single or double, $5 extra for child, two night minimum.

## RESTAURANTS

**LOCAL STYLE**

OVIEDO'S
At the east end of Kaunakakai on the mauka side of the main street. If you like Filipino food, you should like this. Everything was priced around $5., which we felt was a little high for what you get. The ice cream was good.

RABANG'S
This used to be right in Kaunakakai, but has recently moved out to Kualapuu. This seems to be the more popular with the local folk and the prices were a tad lower.

**local Style**

**MID-NITE INN**
In the center of Kaunakakai. Don't be turned off by the appearance because this is a clean, efficient little restaurant and very low priced. They are open for breakfast from 6-10, lunch from 10:30-1:30, and dinner from 5:30-9. The most expensive entree was New York steak at $9.75. Every other entree was $5 or under. The food is fixed mostly for local taste, but they serve hash browns for breakfast.

**KANEMITSU'S BAKERY**
While we realize that breakfast is of no concern to our readers, we mention this spot for those of you who are forced to stay in other accommodation on Molokai since we hear this is the best breakfast spot on Molokai. It is across the street from the Mid-Nite Inn.

**HOP INN**
If this place were cleaner, we would give it high marks because the meal we had was very tasty and not too high priced, a little higher than the Mid-Nite Inn. We have talked to several people who think Hop is great.

**JO-JO'S CAFE**
Located in Maunaloa Town on the west end of Molokai. Last year we starred this as being of particular interest. This year we tried it for lunch and found the food to be very LOCAL style. The price was very reasonable, $5.75 for Korean style ribs and around $1.75 for saimen. We still recommend it for anyone fond of local style food. The place is clean, there is a nice atmosphere, and it is obvious the owners take pride in how the food is presented. Fresh fish is available for under $5. The art work displayed was done by Perry, who we think is one of the owners, and is for sale at moderate prices. They are open from 11 a.m. until 7:30 p.m., closed Sunday.

**local/Tourist Style**

**HOTEL MOLOKAI**
The best thing about the Holoholo dining room is the location, right on the water's edge with a view of Lanai. The food is fair and the prices are just over moderate, $8-$15. It is located two miles east of Kaunakakai.

**PAU HANA INN**
Located on the ocean right in Kaunakakai. Prices are a little lower here than at the Hotel Molokai, $6-$12, and the food is just as good. If you go for lunch, don't be late or they'll be closed. We had dinner there and certainly could not complain about the amount of food served, since soup and salad is served at the salad bar and one can eat as much as desired.

**SHERATON MOLOKAI**
This is the splurge restaurant of Molokai and some say the only place to dine on the Island. Lunch prices are from $5-$8, dinner from $10-$20.

*Bed & Breakfast Guide*

## POINTS OF INTEREST

### KALAUPAPA
One of our hosts described her trip to Kalaupapa as a *spiritual experience* and this feeling is not uncommon. The story of the *leprosy problem* in Hawaii is a sad and fascinating one. It was late in the 1800's that the Hawaiian Government began rounding up people with leprosy and isolating them on the Kalaupapa Peninsula. Little thought was given to their needs until 1873 when Joseph Damien de Veuster, Father Damien, arrived on Molokai and devoted the rest of his life to those afflicted people. That Father Damien died of leprosy some sixteen years after his arrival attests to his devotion. While Father Damien is the most famous of those who labored at Kalaupapa, he was by no means alone; there are a host of other unsung heroes and heroines.

Since 1946 Hanson's Disease has been controlled by sulfone drugs and patients are free to leave. However, Kalaupapa has been home to these people all their lives and there would be little reason to leave.

Today there are three ways to get to Kalaupapa: walk, ride a mule, or fly. If you choose to walk, you must make prior arrangements for a guided tour as no independent exploring is allowed. To make arrangements for walking or mule riding contact Damien Tours, 567-6171, or Molokai Guided Mule Tour, 567-6179 or 800-367-5140. To fly call Polynesian Airways, 5676647 or Royal Hawaiian Air, 553-5317.

### KUALAPUU
This is an excellent example of a company town, where all of the homes were once owned and maintained by the Del Monte Company and rented to pineapple workers. Since Del Monte has cut back on pineapple production, they have been selling these homes to those who worked at the plantation. You will go through Kualapuu on your way to the Kalaupapa Lookout. The most impressive thing in town is the 104 acre Kualapuu Reservoir, which holds 1.4 billion gallons of water. Years ago C. Montegue Cooke, the first owner of the 45,000 acre ranch on the west end of Molokai, predicted that Molokai would feed the rest of the Islands. The University of Hawaii is doing extensive research, attempting to grow corn and bell peppers. Perhaps one day with their efforts and the water at Kualapuu, Molokai will be called the Pepper Island.

### KALAUPAPA LOOKOUT
To find go four miles west of Kaunakakai on Route 46 and turn right at Route 47 and go to the end of the road. The first time we visited here the fog was so thick visibility was around ten feet and it was hard to believe there was any view at all. But dutifully we walked through the dripping ironwoods to the lookout. As we stood there the clouds suddenly lifted and the experience was beautiful beyond our ability to describe. We have been there several times since and while the experience was different, the view is always spectacular.

### PHALLIC ROCK
When you park to go to the Kalaupapa Lookout you will see the sign pointing to the trail which leads to Phallic Rock. Hawaiian legend says that women who were having trouble getting pregnant could bring offerings and spend a night here and they would have no problem from then on. There is a sign there which tells the legend. Magical stones are located in other places throughout Hawaii but none we have seen is as impressive as this or as suggestive.

## MAUNALOA
This little town at the west end of Molokai was once the home of Libby, McNeil, and Libby, housing their pineapple workers. Later it was taken over by Dole. Most of the land used for Pineapple was leased from the Molokai Ranch so when Dole ceased their pineapple operation, Molokai Ranch took over and now the homes are rented to some of their workers as well as the people who work at the Sheraton Resort or elsewhere. One can see how workers were stratified by viewing the different styles of homes. Highest on the hill were the homes of the managers of the Plantation. At the bottom of the hill are the homes of the field workers. Some might find the gallery and the kite factory interesting.

## MOLOKAI RANCH WILDLIFE SAFARI
One would hardly expect to see African wildlife on Molokai but for the price of $12 for adults and $6 for kids they can and will be seen out on Molokai's west end. A small Grayline bus leaves from the Sheraton Hotel four times a day: 9:30 a.m., 11:30 a.m., 1:30 p.m., 3:30 p.m. We barely missed the last bus so failed to make the trip so we do not have first hand knowledge. Second hand information has convinced us to be more punctual next time.

## **EAST OF KAUNAKAKAI**

## ST. JOSEPH'S CHURCH
Just past the ten mile marker on the makai side of the road. Father Damien did not restrict his ministry to Kalaupapa but circled the Island. This little church was built by him in 1876.

## HALAWA VALLEY
Whatever you do, do not miss this drive. Halawa Valley is located about 30 miles from Kaunakakai and is one of the most beautiful drives anywhere in Hawaii. For the first twenty miles the road is very good and for the next ten it is rough, but absolutely manageable unless the weather is really bad. Do not be discouraged by a sudden shower as these are common on this side of the Island and go as quick as they come. At about the 22 mile marker the road turns inland and rises slightly, going through meadowed ranch land as lush and green as can be seen anywhere in the world. At about 26 miles you get your first glimpse of Halawa Valley and we encourage you to stop at one of the overlooks and enjoy the view. The road from here on down is narrow and caution is needed. However, there is so little traffic that you should have no problem. Once you see the Valley we feel sure you will feel the trip was worth while. Recently, because of some vandalism to rental cars, a security parking lot has been established. Also, it is possible to rent horses and ride part way to the falls.

## MOAULA FALLS
Located a little over two miles into Halawa Valley. While this hike is not as easy as some make it sound, it is worth the trip. As you start up the trail you will be on a dirt road that is driveable and you will pass by several little houses. As you pass the last house, the trail will narrow but it is still good. Not far beyond this you will cross the stream. One tourist we talked to said the book he read said to follow the water pipe and when he did the trail ran out after about a mile and a half and he had to turn back. Once you cross

the stream, the trail will be obvious. The water at the base of the falls is cold and refreshing after the long hike. Legend has it that you should throw a ti leaf on the water and if it floats you are safe, but if it sinks, the lizard who lives at the bottom of the pool will get you if you try to swim.

Be sure to take insect repellent as the mosquitoes here are fierce. Also, be careful crossing the stream if the rains have been heavy. When the river is up it is best to wait it out.

## BEACHES

### WEST OF KAUNAKAKAI

#### MOOMOMI BEACH

This is a big favorite with the local folks who assured us getting there was no problem. Well, it all depends on what you are used to. Because there had just been a storm and the last half mile of the road was washed out, we didn't quite make it by car. To get there take Farrington Rd., which runs parallel to Route 46, starting at Kualapuu Town, until it becomes a dirt road. After a little over two miles of dirt road, the road will fork. Take the right fork and go about one half mile to the beach. This area is somewhat protected making swimming easy unless the surf is high.

#### KAWAKIU BEACH

Plenty of seclusion here if you don't mind driving down seven or eight miles of dirt road. To find watch for the beach access road on Route 46 just after you pass the 12 mile marker. If you are coming from Kaunakakai turn right. This is one of the few places in Hawaii that mauka and makai do not work.

#### SOUTH OF THE SHERATON

To get to these beaches, take the turnoff from Route 46 to the Sheraton but don't turn in when you reach the Sheraton. You will drive past the golf course and shortly after that you will see several beach access roads. The first beach past the Sheraton is called Papohaku and is an excellent beach for visitors since there are picnic facilities and restrooms. Swimming on these beaches must be done with extreme care, in fact in winter we would not swim here. During the summer, if the ocean is calm, swimming is possible, but remember the advise in the introduction.

### EAST OF KAUNAKAKAI

Highway 45 runs from Kaunakakai along Molokai's south and east shore for around 30 miles ending at Halawa Valley. Most of this road is along the waters edge but you will not see many beaches since the south shore of Molokai is scalloped with ancient fishponds, some in very good repair and others barely visible. An especially good example of what these ponds once were is to be seen directly across the highway from Our Lady of Sorrows Church (another Father Damien church) at about the 14 mile marker. After you pass mile marker 18 you will come to many little beaches, very safe for swimming or snorkeling. Right at mile marker 20 you will find a little park, Maui Beach, also called Morris Point, which is an excellent place to snorkel. The water is shallow and the bottom rocky so swimming is not great. Further along you will come to some little coves where swimming is safe and the water is a little deeper. After the 23 mile marker the surf gets a little rougher and this is where the surfing starts. From here the road goes inland and the next place to take a dip is at the mouth of Halawa Valley.

## NIGHT LIFE

As would be expected, there is not an abundance of night life on Molokai. People looking for lots of action would be happier some place else. However, Hawaii's top entertainers bring their shows to Molokai but not on any established dates. Basically there are three places where folks congregate after dark: the Hotel Molokai, the Pau Hana Inn, and the Ohia Lounge at the Sheraton. At the Holoholo Dining Room of the Hotel Molokai there is Hawaiian music every Friday and Saturday night. Local folks seem to prefer the Pau Hana Inn, where people mostly just talk story. The best place to find out what is happening at any given time is to check the Bulletin Board at the center of town.

## SPECIAL EVENTS

May Day is Lei Day all over Hawaii, and it seems to be an extra festive day on Molokai. Kilohana School, on the east end, entertains hundreds of people every May Day with lei-making contests; a special Hawaiian show is put on by the students, and there is a Hawaiian plate supper in the evening. This is a rare treat for the visitor.

*The Great Molokai Mule Drag* has gained a lot of publicity in the last year or two. This event usually takes place in September, but keep *usually* in mind. Teams of people, each team assigned a mule from the Mule Ride Stables, try to see who can pull the mule a block or two through the center of town in the shortest period of time. After the contest, it is party time, Molokai style.

*The Molokai-Oahu Canoe Race* is probably the best known event, taking place each year at the end of Aloha week, usually in October. It is a unique and stirring experience to stand on the beach at dawn and watch as the canoes are blessed, then carried into the water by their respective crews and maneuvered into place for the start of the race. The paddlers have competed in many races during the summer months, but this is the big one, the real test of strength and endurance. The race across the Molokai channel has become so prestigious that teams come from the Mainland and the South Pacific to participate, some bringing their own canoes and others using borrowed craft.

## SPORTS AND ACTIVITIES

### IRONWOOD HILLS GOLF COURSE
This nine hole course was built by Del Monte to provide more recreational activity for their employees. It is located in Kualapuu. Since Del Monte has cut back they have turned the course over to the membership who maintain it. It would be hard to find without the following directions. As you drive up Highway 470 toward the Kalaupapa Lookout, .6 of a mile past the 3 mile marker you will see a dirt road going to the left. Turn here and .3 of a mile later the road will swing left up to the course. The fee for visitors is $5. There are no power or hand carts provided. The course is not fancy but very picturesque and looks like a fun place to knock around.

### KALUAKOI GOLF COURSE
Located at the Molokai Sheraton. We once had to chase wild turkeys off the green so we could putt out. This is a great place to practice your wind game.

### TENNIS
There is tennis at the Sheraton, in Kaunakakai, and at Kualapuu. The two courts in Kaunakakai are lighted.

### HORSE BACK RIDING
Horses can be rented from Ekahania Stables for $12.50 an hour for one or two hour rides. They also provide overnight trips to a rustic mountain cabin for $150 a person. For more information call 558-8981 or 558-8377.

### WINDSURFING
We are a little afraid that when the windsurfers discover Molokai it will no longer be sleepy old Molokai since windsurfing on Molokai's south and east shore looks to be ideal. Already there is a small company that will rent equipment and/or give lessons on any level desired. for information write to G.S. Enterprise, Star Route, Box 179, Kaunakakai, Molokai, or call 558-8253.

### HELICOPTER TOURS
Royal Helicopter offers three different tours: 1. a 30 minute tour over Kalaupapa Settlement and the secluded valleys of Molokai's north shore for $75, 2. a shuttle trip to Kalaupapa which departs from the airport at 9:30 a.m. and returns from Kalaupapa at 2:30 p.m. for $45, 3. a one hour full Island tour for $150.

*Chapter III*..................................LANAI

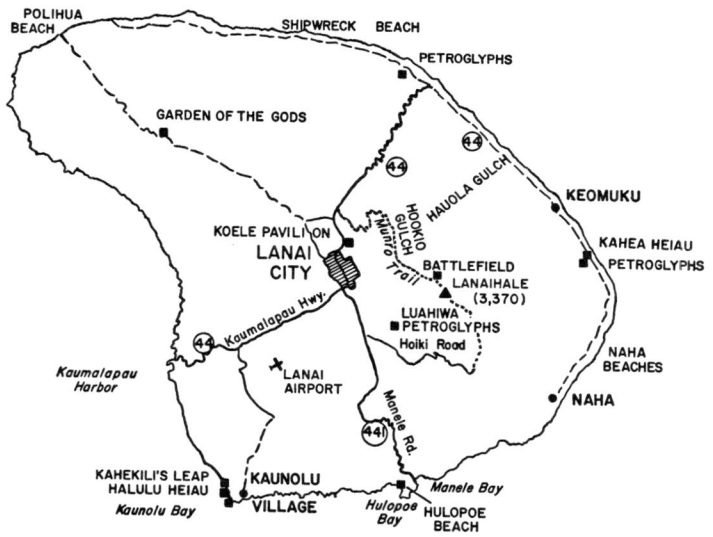

*Bed & Breakfast Guide*

# LANAI

Just as this book was being completed we obtained a new host home on the Island of Lanai. We can now say we have host homes on all of the Hawaiian Islands where it is possible for visitors to go. There is a small Hotel on Lanai, but not many tourists take advantage of it. B & B travelers, are more adventourous than most, so we feel sure that our having a host home on the litle Island of Lanai will be much appreaciated. In our next edition we will have a full section on Lanai. At the present time we must content ourselves with a description on the accommodation offered.

### L-1
Lucille has recently retired from her profession as a Registered Nurse and now finds time to devote to guests so has decided to offer two of the bedrooms in her home to B & B travelers. Both of the bedrooms are large and well furnished. Also, Lucille also owns a new Toyota Tercel 4 wheel drive wagon, well equipped to show guests the interesting places on Lanai. This spot could be ideal for those really anxious to get away from it all. After all, not many tourists get to Lanai.
RATE:   $25 single, $30 double, $10 extra person.

Chapter V.................................................................HAWAII

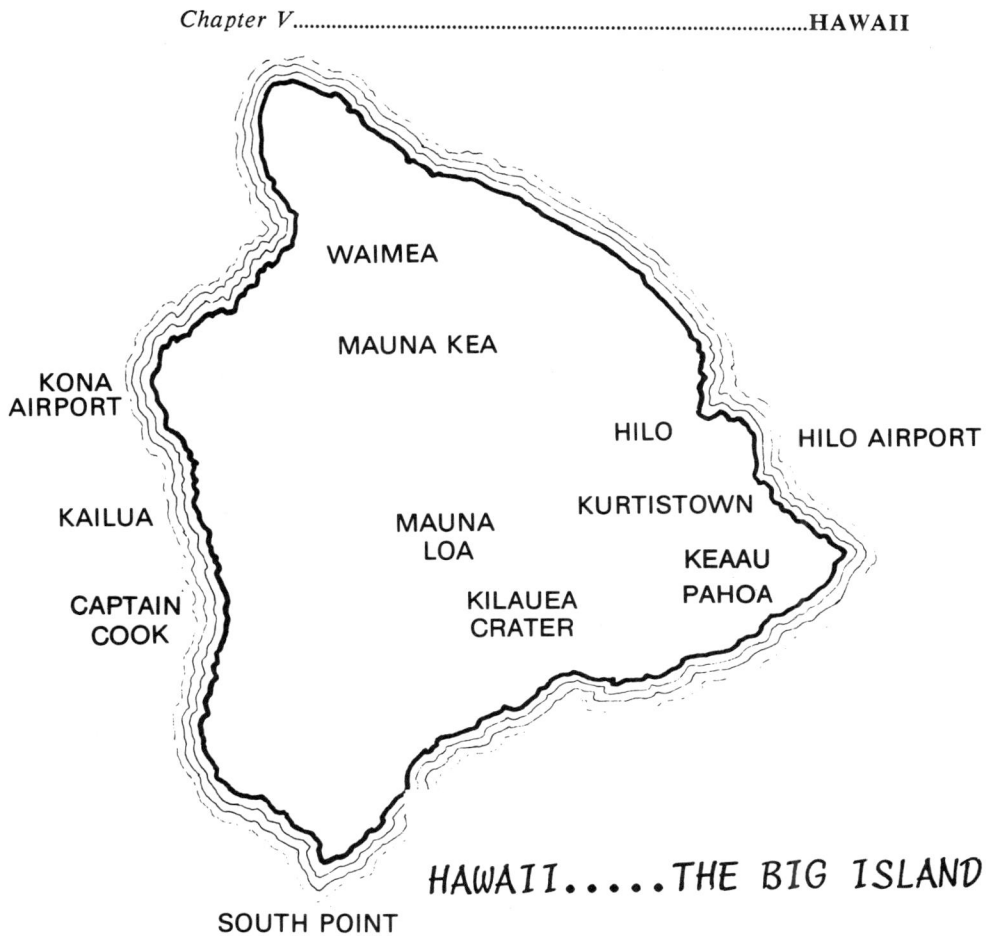

HAWAII.....THE BIG ISLAND

.....DRIVING TIMES.....

From Hilo airport-South: (approximate)

    Kurtistown.........................12 miles, 20 minutes
    Kilauea Volcano................40 miles, 60 minutes
    Kailua-Kona......................120 miles, 3.5 hours

    From Hilo North:
    Waimea..............................63 miles, 1.5 hours
    Kailua-Kona.......................98 miles, 2.75 hours

# HAWAII

Sometimes called the Orchid Isle or Volcano Island, but always referred to by residents of Hawaii as The Big Island, the island of Hawaii has about as much land mass as all of the other Islands combined. In some ways it is unfortunate that the State and the Island have the same name, since tourists sometimes confuse Big Island with Main Island, which residents of Hawaii use to refer to Oahu. The Big Island has so much to offer that it puzzles us that it has not become the main destination point for tourists. A possible explanation for this is that the Big Island does not have as many white sand beaches as the other Islands. What often gets overlooked are the beautiful black sand beaches that abound on the Big Island and nowhere else in Hawaii. Yet, how often the comment is heard, "I could care less about going to Hawaii. Who wants to sit on a beach in the blazing sun and get skin cancer?" Too bad these people don't know about the Big Island that offers beaches but oh so much more.

As said above, Hawaii is the largest Island in the chain, and it is still growing. Two active volcanos, Mauna Loa and Kilauea, still spew out molten lava, which flows to the sea, building yet more land mass. When one stands above the main caldera of Kilauea, even when the volcano is not at full steam, the view can be described as awesome. When the lava is soaring thousands of feet in the air, the experience is unforgettable. Volcano National Park is truly one of the wonders of our Nation, and no visitor to the State of Hawaii should pass it by.

The Big Island is also the agricultural capital of the Islands, growing more sugar cane, papaya, macadamia nuts than the rest of the Islands combined. South of Hilo grows almost all of the anthuriums and orchids that Hawaii exports around the world. One need not go to a nursery to see orchids since fields of them grow wild in this area. On the Kona Coast, above Kailua Town, coffee grows in profusion, in fact, this is the only place in the U. S. where there are coffee plantations. Up at the north end of the Island there is the huge Parker Ranch, which is the largest privately owned cattle ranch in the U.S.

Nowhere in the State is color more profuse and brilliant than on the Big Island. Stand on any tee at the Mauna Lani Golf Course to see jet black lava abut emerald green fairways dotted with white sand traps, and all of this along the bluest water imaginable, and if it is winter and the sky is clear, turn back to majestic Mauna Kea with its mantle of snow.

There are few places in the State where hiking is more spectacular, whether Volcano National Park, the gorges along the Hamakua Coast, up the slopes of Mauna Kea or Mauna Loa, through the Waipio Valley or Pololu Valley, or on the many trails behind Hilo Town.

However, it is not the size of Hawaii that makes it special. Maybe it is its diversity, for surely the contrasts are dramatic, from lush tropical rain forests to arid deserts, from rich fertile valleys to lava covered hillsides where pili grass and kiawe trees struggle to exist. We feel the Big Island is waiting to be discovered. Do yourself a favor, and no matter what you conceive Hawaii to be, set your course for the Big Island.

# HILO

One of the lines a travel writer used to describe Hilo was that it was more a place for travelers than for tourists. We are of a different opinion. Our experience has been that our stay in Hilo is never long enough, and this year was certainly no exception, for every time we are there we make new discoveries.

Hilo, located on the east coast of the Big Island, serves as the County Seat for the Big Island as well as the focal point of major transportation facilities into and out of the Island. With a population of around 40,000, it is the biggest city on the outer islands, and it is the banking and commercial center for Hawaii. It is also the oldest continuous city in Hawaii, having been founded by a religious revival in the 1840's when thousands of natives came to the Hilo bayfront to be baptized into the Christian faith and stayed to found a town. But in spite of Hilo's population, it lacks entirely the hustle and bustle of a city, clinging rather to older plantation traditions and slower Hawaiian ways.

Much of Old Town has been given a face lift, and a stroll up and down the streets of *Old Hilo Town* brings many pleasant surprises. There are several small shops worth a visit. A few we were particularly impressed with were the Most Irresistible Shop, the Chocolate Shop, the Futon Connection, and new this year, the Pottery Gallery. All of these shops are on Keawe St. The street above, Kinoole, has several interesting shops: Bamboo Garden, Pink Elephant Thrift, and to us the most interesting Hale Manu Craft Shop, which specializes in lauhala products. Across from the Kaiko Mall where Penny's is located is the Hawaiian Handcraft Store where visitors can watch artisans at work. New this year is the very modern Prince Kuhio Shopping Center, one of the largest in the outer Islands. It is located a mile or so out of town on the Volcano Highway.

Hilo is also the home of the Merry Monarch Festival, held every spring. It is here that all the Helaus, Hula Schools, come to display their talent in the hula and maile chant. No where in the world can one see as authentic or accomplished hula dancing. An interesting note: during the 1986 competition there was a huge thunder and lightning storm over Hilo while the dancing was in progress. One of the Helaus took this as a sign and would not dance and some of the spectators also left.

Another discovery we made this year (our fault for not discovering it last year as it is not new) was the East Hawaii Cultural Center just across from Kalakaua Park in the center of Old Town. This former police station is being restored as a cultural center. Eventually the upstairs will be used for plays and concerts while the downstairs will house various art exhibits. They even hope to have a small restaurant on the upper level overlooking the park. During the last three weeks of July Shakesperian plays are performed on the steps of the building, no charge, of course.

Using Hilo then as a home base, there is much to explore in the surrounding area. Since it is only about thirty miles from the Volcano and only a little over forty miles to Waipio Valley, day trips to these and all the sights in between are really no problem. Is Hilo then more for the traveler than the tourist, a spot better just to pass through? That can really only be answered by you, but remember, to answer properly, you should plan to spend time there. We cannot imagine you will be disappointed.

*Bed & Breakfast Guide*

## HOSTS

### H-1A
This spectacular home, located just two miles north of Hilo, is perched on the seacliff and is surrounded by a colorful garden. Guests are welcomed in true Hawaiian style as they enter Suzanne's home by a bridge over the koi pond. The peaceful atmosphere is enhanced by the decor and the sliding glass doors open to the view. The guests enjoy the tropical foliage: bougainvillea, plumeria, hibiscus, ginger, gardenia, banana, papaya, coco palms and more. But most exciting is the view of all of Hilo Bay and the Pacific Ocean. On Tuesday and Wednesday the cruise ships slide by at breakfast time. At all times there are fishing boats, barges, and sailboats to watch. Early morning risers can catch the tropical sunrise from the front lanai. A short stroll brings the guest to a black sand surfing beach and a river with two waterfalls. The guest room with double bed has its own private shaded lanai and private entrance through an orchid and anthurium garden. A private bathroom is located around the corner from the room.

Suzanne, the hostess, has time to spend with her guests and has lived in Hilo for many years. Although she was raised in San Francisco and Beverly Hills, she and her husband lived all over the western U.S. while raising their four children. Her interests now are in the Hawaii Concert Society, Arabian horses, and children's books.

RATE: $30 single, $35 double, two night minimum.

### H-1
A large Hawaiian type home about two miles north of Hilo on the cliff overlooking Hilo Bay, this home has a yard so private that if you decide to take a swim in the lovely pool, only the birds will know. There are two bedrooms available, each with twin beds, one of which converts to king if desired, and for the B & B guests there are one and a half baths. Not only is the yard beautifully landscaped around the pool, there is also a charming tea house which the guests can enjoy.

Amy, the hostess, came to Hawaii in the middle 1970's from Pennsylvania, where she raised purebred Angus cattle along with five children, multitudes of cats, dogs, etc. Amy likes to say she came to Hawaii via Africa, since it was when she was there on a cattle project and met cattle raisers from Hawaii whom she liked so much she decided to make Hawaii her home. In spite of this being quite a move, she has never looked back and has no regrets. Now out of the cattle business, Amy devotes some of her time to the East Hawaii Humane Society. She is also president of the Navy League and keeps a sharp eye on the ships as they glide in and out of Hilo Harbor.

RATE: $35 single or double, plus 4% State Excise Tax.

### H-2
Semi-country living. In the hills above Hilo, in a peaceful macadamia nut orchard is a stunning, beautifully landscaped chalet with two bedrooms, private bath, and separate entrance for guests. Close to the airport, town, and ocean, there are lovely parks, black sand beaches, and many scenic places to visit before one even starts exploring the Volcano or coastline of the Big Island.

Our hosts, Chuck and Joan, have been with B & B since we started. They have lived in Hawaii since 1966 and can give assistance in planning your trip. They serve fresh baked goodies, island preserves, and fresh island fruits, many from their yard.

RATE: $30 single, $35 double, $50 for three, $60 for four.

### H-3
Relax on a grand scale in this large, modern, Hawaiian style home, surrounded by nearly four acres of park like setting, on an ocean front bluff with a spectacular view of Wailea Bay. This is the perfect spot for anyone desiring a peaceful haven away from the cares of the world, yet close enough to everything to be convenient. A tennis court and a municipal beach park is within walking distance and the world famous Akaka Falls is just a short drive away. The accommodation is a 1,008 square foot private guest quarters with a separate entrance. It includes a large bedroom, a private bath, a fully equipped kitchenette and bar, a large living room with a 25 inch cable TV, a radio, piano, and two day beds. This is a perfect accommodation for a small family or possibly even two couples traveling together. There is a bedroom in the main house, twin beds, private bath, which is available when the guest quarters are rented to accommodate the person in the family who needs more privacy.

The host and hostess have lived in Hawaii all their lives and can offer valuable information on where to go and what to see on the Big Island.

RATES: $45 single or double, $55 for three, $65 for four. Room in home $30, no children under 8.

### H-3A
This large, architect designed home, flanked by sugar cane fields, is located six miles north of Hilo very close to Akaka Falls and the Onomea Botanical Gardens. The home, in a very tropical setting with a creek passing by, has a great view of the sometimes snow capped Mauna Kea, Hilo Harbor, and when Kilauea Volcano erupts it can be seen clearly from this home. The accommodation offered is a very pleasant spare room with its own wash basin, twin beds, and guests share the bath with the hosts, Claire and Jim, who are pleased to have travelers share their home. The downstairs is unusually decorated with stained glass windows and a handsome art collection.

RATE: $35 per night.

### H-5
Twenty thousand square feet of tropical plants surround this bungalow located in the Hilo hills near Rainbow Falls. Not only is the home filled with curios the hosts have collected from their years of living and traveling in the Far East, but even the lanai space is used for display. Pearl and Dick, the hosts, hail originally from Pennsylvania and Illinois. However, they have been in Hilo for thirty years and feel like natives. Their interests include books, needlepoint, mahjong, crafts, baking bread using tropical fruits, giving performances with handicapped puppets, and taking classes at the University of Hawaii at Hilo. Not even all this activity has kept them from keeping in touch with the many friends they have made abroad and befriending various travelers to Hawaii. They are well acquainted with the hidden beauty spots and are anxious to help visitors discover Hawaii.

RATE: $25 single, $30 double, two night minimum.

## H-5A

B & B at its finest in your home away from home. This totally furnished 1350 sq. ft. duplex not only includes breakfast, but comes with a fully equipped kitchen. Also included are color TV, phone, washer and dryer, patio and barbeque. This custom home will accommodate six people, making it perfect for a large family or two or three couples traveling together. Located three miles above Hilo Harbor, this lush one acre vacation setting has a view of the ocean, volcanoes and Mauna Kea. There is also a secluded waterfall and swimming pond up the street.

The hosts, BJ and Rick, live in the adjoining duplex so there is always good company when you want it.

RATE: $75 up to four, $10 for each additional person, 2 night minimum.

## H-6

This home is located five miles north of Hilo on a twenty-one acre ranch, pretty good size by Hawaii's standards, and is ideal for the guests who enjoy horses, cattle, chickens, dogs, and cats and all that goes with life in the country. If anyone wants to spend time horseback riding, this is perfect, since Pudding, the hostess, keeps horses and rents them out for riding. She accompanies the riders and shows them the really interesting trails to ride, making sure all are safe. A big bonus on this farm is a waterfall with a pool where one can swim in the refreshingly cool water. There are two bedrooms available for families or for couples traveling together, but only one is used normally. One bedroom has a queen sized bed, the other has twin beds. The bathroom is in the hall and for B & B use.

RATE: $35 single, $38 double.

## H6-A

Towering coconut palms and an acre of tropical foliage and plants frame this spacious old home located on the water overlooking Hilo Bay. Since this home is less that 1/2 mile from downtown Hilo, a vacation here without a car would be possible. There are two bedrooms available, one with a queen sized bed, the other with twin beds. There is a bath between the rooms for the exclusive use of the guests.

Kapua, your hostess, is Island born and can tell many tales of old Hawaii as well as many places to visit. She does beautiful quilting and has made quilts for her eight grandchildren. She also raises fancy chickens.

RATE: $30 single, $35 double.

## RESTAURANTS

### LOCAL STYLE

**HILO SEED AND SNACK**
Located at the foot of Wainuenue Street on the left going up. If all you want is a snack and the budget is tight stop here and get a ham sandwich for $1.00 or a hamburger for $.99 or four sushi for $1. The real specialty of the house, though, is their shave ice; they make a coffee flavor by soaking Kona coffee with a vanilla bean in a syrup. On top of this they put cream. Our mouths water just thinking about it. Since our visit last year the whole place has been spruced up.

**KK'S PLACE**
At 413 Kilauea Avenue is a little shopping center. This is real local chow down cafeteria style, with low down prices and plenty kau-kau. We were told by those in the know that the food was pretty good, not real ono, but o.k.

**KAWAMOTO TAKE OUT**
On Kilauea Avenue across the street from Penny's. Strictly takeout and Oriental with low prices. All the food is prepared ahead, and you can just pick and point to your heart's or stomach's content.

**KOW'S WUN TON & NOODLE**
In the Penny's Shopping Center. Like KK's Place, low down prices, Oriental, cafeteria style. We have eaten here and while it is not gourmet it is not bad.

**SUMIDA'S**
At 399 Kawili in Hilo. Breakfast, lunch, dinner: weekdays 7a.m. to 10p.m. Cheap and good service, no atmosphere. Interesting dishes.

**CAFE 100**
On the makai side of Kilauea Ave. just south of the main part of Hilo. This is interesting because it is here that the Loco Moco originated, an invention of the 100th (Nisei) Infantry in W.W. II

-----------------------------------------------------------------
local Style

***DICK'S COFFEE HOUSE***
In the Hilo Shopping Center on the makai side of Kilauea Avenue. Open seven days a week for breakfast, lunch, and dinner, locals consider this just about the best deal in town. There is little or no atmosphere, slightly reminiscent of a roadside diner, but there are few places anywhere that give so much for so little. Dinner comes with soup and salad and most entrees run around $6.00. They have a cocktail lounge where you can dine if you want drinks or wine with your meal. Master Charge and Visa accepted.

### SACHI'S GOURMET
Located on the mauka side of Keawe Ave. We had lunch here and were pleased. The owners are from Japan so authentic Japanese dishes are available, but there are dishes to please those not used to Japanese food. Lunch is from 11-2 and dinner is from 5-9. Prices are not high.

### KAWAKA'S DELI
A few doors from Kawamoto Take out, a good place for sandwiches most of which run a bit under $3.00. Mostly takeout, there are a few tables outside. We were told that the name "Kawaka" is the Hawaiian equivalent of George; this year we were told it was David, and that, we discovered, is correct.

### SUN SUN LAU
Located at 1055 Kinoole in the center of Hilo. Cantonese food at modest prices, closed Wed. 935-2808.

### *LEUNG'S CHOP SUEY*
On the mauka side of the main highway that goes to Volcano about a mile past Banyon Dr. in a sort of industrial area. We have been assured that this is the best Chinese food in town and the prices are low. It does not look like much, part of it is an old quonset hut, but those who know say do not judge by outward appearances.

### MUN CHEONG LAU
At 126 Keawe Street in the center of Hilo. Again not much to look at. We asked all of our hosts and many of the shop keepers their opinion but nothing was confirmed. A few said lots of food, low price.

### ROY'S GOURMET
On mauka side of Kilauea Avenue, across the street from Penny's. You might be fooled by the name, but once you walk in the cat is out of the bag. At Roy's *Chowdown* you can get American, Hawaiian, or Japanese grub at low-low prices. Open from 6 a.m. until 2 p.m. for breakfast and lunch and from 5:00-10:30 for dinner. Lunch will run around $4.00 while dinner (prime rib) can go all the way to $8.00. There are many dinner entrees under $5.00.

### *TING HAO*
In the Puainako Town Shopping Center. This is the only place we have found in Hilo that served Szechaun/Hunan cuisine. We ate there when they were located in the Lanikai Hotel and have not been to this new location. We liked the food and the price. No credit cards.

---

**local/Tourist**
### **ROUSSELS**
This is Hilo's newest restaurant and considered by most of our hosts as Hilo's best. The chef is from New Orleans; the cuisine is creole style. We went there with a party of six and with one exception, all thought it was very good. One voted fair on the duck. It is not inexpensive but it is worth it. Located on Keawe Ave. just north of Wainuenue Ave. 935-5111.

## RESTAURANT FUJI
Located in the Hilo Hotel in the center of town at 142 Kinoole. The food is good and the prices are moderate. This has long been a favorite with locals and tourists alike, closed Monday. 961-3733.

## *KK TEI*
AT 1550 Kamehameha Avenue on the mauka side. If you try to find this at night it can be a bit tricky since the area and the restaurant are not well lighted. If you like Japanese style food that is not "to da max" authentic, you should like this. Prices are moderate to low. For example, a combination of tempura and tiriaki chicken with miso soup, rice, and several pickled vegetables, proceeded by a serving of sashimi was only $8.00. The atmosphere is nice. Liquor is served and Master Charge and Visa accepted. 961-3791.

## HILO BAY HOTEL/UNCLE BILLY'S
On Banyon Drive. As its counterpart in Kona, Uncle Billy's is somewhat of an institution on the Big Island and a definite favorite with the locals. Along with your meal, which is moderately priced around $8.00, you will get a free Hula show from 6:30-7:30. If you have never seen a Polynesian show, here is your chance and because it is free it is worth the money. 935-4222.

## KEN'S HOUSE OF PANCAKES
On Kamehameha Avenue at Kalanikoa intersection. Are you getting homesick and lonesome for some good old Mainland grub? Or are you a person who occasionally in the middle of the night has to have a snack? Do not raid your hosts refrigerator, just drive on down to Ken's and load up on blueberry pancakes or country fried chicken, 'cause Ken's is open 24 hours a day and in Hawaii that is rarer than a frog hair. Ken's will make you think you are right at home, until you look a little closer and see Loco Moco on the menu. The prices are low to moderate, the atmosphere is stainless steel clean and the food is pretty good. We think Dick's is better, but it could be a toss of the coin.

## *NIHON CULTURAL CENTER*
(JAPANESE RESTAURANT)
On the north end of Banyon Drive. If you like Japanese food, this is the place to go. Local people who ate here when it first opened in late 1983 might put the knock on Nihon, but those who have tried it lately sing a different tune. We tried it for lunch and really enjoyed both the food and the price, and also a nice view of the harbor. Lunch is served from 11-2 and dinner from 5-9, closed Tuesday, and Sunday is dinner only. Liquor is served. Master Charge and Visa accepted. 969-1133.

## ROSEY'S BOAT HOUSE
This can be tricky to find. Located on the mauka side of Piilani Avenue between Manono Street and Laukapu. Manono is the extension of the north end of Banyon Drive. So from Kamehameha Avenue go mauka on Manono to Piilani and turn left to Rosey's. To many in Hilo Rosey's is reserved for "dinning out," while Dick's is where you go to eat. We were a little disappointed in the atmosphere since the name had us thinking we would be on the water. The food is good but a bit high priced.

### NORBERTO'S EL CAFE
At 11 Wainuenue Street. Owned and operated by the same people who own the El Cafe on Kauai. You will get lots to eat at moderate prices and it is acceptable Mexican fare. They are open only for dinner from 5:00-9:30. Liquor is served.

### BEAR'S COFFEE
If all you want is a cup of coffee and maybe some great dessert, stop by this little coffee shop, located on Keawe St. in the center of town. You can get espresso, capachino, or good old Kona coffee.

### HUKILAU
At 136 Banyon Drive. Open for dinner only from 7:00-9:00 Monday through Saturday and until 10:00 on Sunday, this is a big favorite with the residents of Hilo. Nice atmosphere and food for a variety of palates and prices in the moderate range; i.e., $8.00 to $10.00. Be sure to see the Tidal Wave marks recorded on the windows as well as the large koi pond. Liquor is served and Master Charge and Visa are accepted. 935-4222.

### REUBEN'S MEXICAN RESTAURANT
At 336 Kamehameha Street in downtown Hilo and open for lunch and dinner from 10 am. to 11 p.m. Monday through Saturday and from 4-9 p.m. on Sunday. Mamo Street, just a few doors away from Reuban's, is mentioned in one guide book as the sin center of Hilo. But be not dismayed, local folk assure us that it is perfectly safe here. At any rate, we tried Reuben's in Kona and found the food good and the prices low. Liquor is served and Diners, Master Charge, and Visa accepted. 961-2552.

### *HARRINGTON'S*
When last year's book came out we had not yet tried this. Now we have and were very pleased. It is located on Kalanianiole just past the Hukilau on Hilo's Ice Pond. Does that confuse you. It did us until we were told that the little pond in front of the restaurant was fed by underground springs, hence the water is very cold. It's a great place to cool off when the temperature is up. Dinner only from 5-10, 5-9 on Sunday. 961-4966.

---

**Special Category**

### UNIVERSITY OF HAWAII
To find go south on Kilauea Avenue to Kawili and turn mauka and you will see the University on your right as you drive up the hill. Open for lunch Monday through Friday, this is a good place to get an inexpensive, unimpressive, cafeteria style meal.

## **COMMUNITY COLLEGE**
To find go south on Kilauea Avenue to Kawili and turn makai and you will see the college on your right as you drive down the hill. This year we did get a chance to try this and we recommend it highly. The menu is creative and the food is well prepared and the prices are very reasonable. The facilities are not large so lets hope not everyone discovers it. They are open for lunch from 11:00 a.m. until 12:10. The school trains cooks who to show their skills operate a restaurant for the public. Prices are low and the food can be great.

## POINTS OF INTEREST

### IN HILO

**LYMAN MISSION HOUSE AND MUSEUM**
At 276 Haili Street which runs mauka off Kamehameha Avenue. We strongly urge you not to pass this up, for at $2.50 we found this a real bargain. Built in 1839 by the Reverend and Mrs. David Belden Lyman, and recently restored by the Lyman/Baldwin family, this home once served as a gathering place for Hawaiian Royalty as well as visiting foreigners. In the museum you will learn much of early Hawaiian history and later if someone tries to tell you that the Tedeschi Winery is the first in Hawaii you will know better.

**KAUMANA CAVES**
On Kaumana Avenue about five miles from downtown Hilo. To get there take Wainuenue Avenue mauka and stay to the left as Kaumana Avenue branches off. These are lava tubes formed by one of Mauna Loa's eruptions. The lower cave is safe for exploring, but the other is considered dangerous.

**RAINBOW FALLS**
Several miles from downtown Hilo up Wainuenue Ave. The trick in finding the falls is that Wainuenue goes to the right and Kaumana Ave. to the left. The total distance from downtown Hilo is a little over two miles. Morning is the best time to see the rainbow as the falls cascade to the pond below.

**BOILING POTS**
About two miles beyond Rainbow Falls. The "pots" are a series of deep, round pools cut in the lava beds.

**SUISAN FISH MARKET**
An auction is held every morning on the north end of Banyon Dr. While there are bigger fish auctions in the world, we doubt they are as interesting or as easily seen as this one. The Honolulu fish auction is *pau* (over) by 5 a.m., while this one does not start until 8 a.m. and the day we visited that was Hawaii time, in other words 8:30. Here every day but Sunday local fishermen bring in their catch of the day or night before, ahi (yellow fin tuna) for the most part, but also a sprinkling of akule, opakapaka, mahi-mahi, ono, ulua, and papio. All of this is auctioned off to the owners of restaurants and fish markets. Ahi brings the best price not only because it is served in all the better restaurants but also because it makes the best sashimi. When you live in Hawaii, learning to like sashimi is almost inevitable.

**LILIUOKALANI GARDENS**
On Banyon Dr. You can't miss it. You can spend minutes here just passing through or you could spend all day just lounging and watching the life of Hilo pass by. While we were there, we watched several men catching small shrimp in little nets which they used as bait to fish in the harbor across the road.

### COCONUT ISLAND
Located via a footbridge from Banyon Dr, in Hilo harbor. A great place for a picnic or just to sit and view Hilo and the Harbor and on a clear day Mauna Kea.

### HILO TROPICAL GARDENS
This is located about 1/2 mile down Kalanianiole, which is the road to Hilo's beaches. It looks like a Mon and Pop market at first, but behind the store is an exquisite two-acre garden of natural beauty. The bountiful orchid blossoms, colorful tropical flowers, shrubs and trees, together with natural tidal pools create a picturesque atmosphere. Visitors are welcome to wander through. The owners, who were most helpful, ship flowers to the Mainland and Canada.

## SOUTH OF HILO

### ORCHIDS OF HAWAII
Several miles south of Hilo at 2801 Kilauea Ave. It is free to visit this but like most "free" things you could end up spending a bundle since they do ship orchids all over the world. The day we visited they were working diligently on an order for Ceasar's Palace in Las Vegas: 1000 vanda orchid leis. Each lei consisted of 35 orchids, the smallest made. We asked if all the flowers used came from their nursery or whether for such a large order they had to call on other nurseries. The lady in charge, who was most helpful in answering all our questions, assured us their gardens were sufficient to fill the need. We urge you to visit here.

### KUAOLA FARMS
About seven miles south of downtown Hilo, mauka off Kilauea Ave. To really learn about anthuriums, be sure to stop here. Once again, no charge, but you can have the flowers shipped anywhere in the world. Anthuriums though not native to Hawaii thrive in the Islands and to many people are synonymous with Hawaii.

### MAUNA LOA MACADAMIA NUT FACTORY
About six miles south of Hilo on Highway 11 you will come to the road which runs makai for about three miles to the Visitors Center and the factory where you can sample and purchase Mauna Loa's various products. Keep in mind, though, that when it comes to buying, it is hard to beat Long's Drugs or Pay and Save's prices. Mac nuts are grown all over the Big Island, replacing much of the sugar cane fields. From the time the tree is planted (actually grafted) seven years pass before fruit appears. Open Monday-Friday, 8 a.m. to 5 p.m., Saturday 9 a.m. to 1 p.m. Recently they have added an ice cream/juice stand.

## NORTH OF HILO

### AKAKA FALLS
Several miles north of Hilo, past the scenic road, watch for the sign to Honomu where you turn left and proceed up the mountain through Honomu for about 3 and 3/4 miles to the end of the road. From the parking lot it is about a half an hour walk to Hapuna Falls and on past Akaka Falls back to the parking lot. Along the trail you will see most of the flora of Hawaii including coffee and golden bamboo. Akaka Falls with a vertical drop of 400 feet makes the trip worthwhile, but as one guest told us, "Send me back to Waikiki 'cause if I see another water fall I'll go bananas." Well, that's what makes horse races and why, thank goodness, not everyone wants to live in Paradise.

### HAWAII TROPICAL BOTANICAL GARDEN
Located five miles north of Hilo on the four mile scenic road. The admission of $6.00 is tax deductible and is a bargain anyway. About 1/2 mile down the scenic road you will see a church on the left. From here a mini-bus takes you into the garden, 17 acres of unspoiled beauty where you will view not only most of the Hawaiian flora but also lily ponds, cascading water falls, streams and picturesque Onomea Bay.

## BEACHES

While the Big Island is not noted for its white sand beaches, do not conclude that Hilo is not a great place for beaching, snorkeling, and swimming. Most tourists fail to find what we found to be one of the loveliest spots in Hawaii. Access to this area is easy once you know where to go. As you come around Banyon Dr., Kalanianiole Dr. goes off to the left. Along this road are a number of parks (Onekahakaha, Kealoha, Leleiwi, and Richardson's Beach) all with picnic tables, where access to the water is easy and swimming is very safe. At Richardson's Beach there is a small museum, no charge and closed on the weekends, that has displays dealing with aquaculture. On the weekends this area is crowded with local families but during the week it is not that heavily used, for as said above, not many tourists have found it.

### REED'S BAY BEACH PARK
Located at the foot of Banyon Drive this is a good spot for picnicking and swimming is safe.

## NIGHT LIFE

### ROSEY'S BOAT HOUSE
(for directions see Rosey's under Restaurants) On Thursday, Friday, and Saturday night there is dancing here after 9 p.m.

*Bed & Breakfast Guide*

### BANYON HARBOR DRIVE
All of the hotels are along Banyon Drive and at times there is something going on there, especially at the Crown Room of the Naniloa Surf Hotel.

### MOVIES
In the Waiakea Shopping Plaza there are three theaters which show first run movies. There is also a theater in Mt. View, south of Hilo. For more information call (in Hilo) 935-9747, (in Mt. View) 966-6110.

## SPORTS

### GOLF
There are two courses in Hilo, both open to the public. Hilo Country Club (935-7388) on Banyon Dr. is a nine hole, flat course and fairly short. The green fee is $3 for nine and $5 for eighteen, $6 on weekends. One can walk or take a cart. Hilo Municipal Golf Course (959-7711), at 340 Haihai St., is an eighteen hole regulation course. The green fee is $3 on weekdays, $4 on weekends and carts are $12.50 but not mandatory. Another course considered in the Hilo area is Volcano Golf and Country Club at Volcano, some forty miles from Hilo. The daily green fee is $14.50, carts are $8.00 on share basis. For more information call 967-7331.

### TENNIS
There are at least twenty-two (22) courts in Hilo located in nine different parks. Around half of these are lighted and indoor, located at Hoolulu Park.

# KILAUEA VOLCANO

In the first edition of our book we listed Kilauea Volcano as a point of interest under the section South of Hilo. This displeased our Hilo hosts who felt we were not as enthusiastic about Volcano National Park as we might be. Since our intention is to make sure that all of our readers visit this National treasure, we have decided to give it more emphasis.

Volcano National Park is thirty miles, about a forty-five minute drive on excellent highway, from Hilo Town. If you simply make this a stop along the way you will miss much and end up wishing you had planned differently. It is our suggestion that you plan to spend at least one day visiting here. Of course, if you are lucky enough to arrive at a time when an eruption is in progress, we don't think you will need any special encouragement.

One word of advice we would give is to bring along some warm clothes, long pants and a sweater will do, since the Park is at a higher elevation and at times can be chilly. Remember, it is easy to take a sweater off, but if you don't have one on, your stay might be a short one. That is just the mistake we made on our first visit here.

The amount of time spent here is up to you, it can be long or short, but it is hard to exhaust the wonders of this region. If you decide to hike the many available trails, check in at the Visitors Center for the information. Here you can view a short film about the history of the volcano. Across from the Visitors Center is Volcano House, a charming old hotel and restaurant, long a favorite with tourists and residents alike. This is an excellent spot from which to view the main caldera. Perhaps you will be lucky and Madam Pele will decide to favor you with a display far beyond man's ability to duplicate. So far Madam Pele has been somewhat predictable, and even at her wildest presents no real danger to life. But as we know with the gods, one can never be too sure.

Along the Chain of Craters Road there are many scenic views, and visitors are able to walk out and stand right on the edge of the main caldera, an experience like no other we have had. There are other drives to take, such as the eleven mile drive up Mauna Loa. Even if you don't take this drive, be sure to take the short drive to the Tree Molds, which gives one a graphic idea of how deep lava flows can be.

One word of caution, under no circumstances should you pick up any of the lava to take home for a souvenir. It is not that the lava is in short supply. All of the lava is sacred to the goddess Pele and dire things will happen to you if you take the lava off the Island, or so we are told. At the Visitors Center you can read many letters from people who made that mistake and were forced to mail the lava back to stop the bad luck. We can attest to people sending back the lava having received several at our office from the Mainland. In our cases not once did the people identify themselves, so we were not able to follow up on what happened. Of course, being at Volcano National Park and just looking at the lava is about as good luck as you can possible have.

**HOST**

### H-24
Located in Volcano Village, Kilauea Crater, immediately adjacent to Hawaii's Volcano National Park. This home is one of the oldest in Volcano, built around 1886. Accommodations consist of three bedrooms. One can accommodate a family as it has two double beds and two roll aways. The other two bedrooms are for single or doubles as each has twin beds. Each room has a private bath. Guests are welcome to use the entire home except for the kitchen. The home is located on eight acres, three of which have been landscaped into a botanical garden.
  Gordon, born in Hawaii, is a travel expert and historian. Joann is a transplanted Bostonian, an artist, and famed for her specialty, Hawaiian pies and candy.
RATE: $25 single, $40 double, $5 extra per child under six, $10 under sixteen.

## RESTAURANTS

**VOLCANO HOUSE**
The setting here is hard to beat and the food is good while the prices are what one would expect at this location. During the day there is a little snack shop for a sandwich or a sweet roll.

**VOLCANO COUNTRY INN**
In Volcano village. Open for breakfast, lunch, and dinner, this is a small cafe. We had breakfast there and were very pleased. The prices are modest as is the setting. Every day they have different specials for lunch and dinner. The pies and cakes are homemade.

**VOLCANO GOLF AND COUNTRY CLUB RESTAURANT**
This opened in October of 1985 and we hear from our hosts and guests that it is good. The cuisine is American and Japanese. They are open daily for breakfast, lunch from 7 a.m. to 5 p.m. Their prices are moderate.

**VOLCANO STORE AND DINER**
Also in Volcano Village. This is a little hamburger stand with window service and a room provided for eating. We were told that the hamburgers were great, but the bun was unheated.

## NIGHT LIFE

The Volcano House offers a dance band three times a week along with vocal entertainment in the bar during weekends. Square dancing happens every Monday night at the Kilauea Military Rest Camp. There are bridge groups on Tuesday (day) and Wednesday nights. The Kilauea Art Center publishes their activities a month in advance. Visiting scientists give free lectures (usually illustrated) almost every Friday or Saturday evening at the National Park auditorium. Of course, if Madam Pele favors you with a display, that should be enough night life for anyone.

## SPORTS

Volcano Golf and Country Club, located on the mauka side of the highway just west of Volcano national Park. The course is short but tricky and cannot always be played without long pants and a sweater. The green fee is $14.50 with a cart $8 on a share basis. A couple then could play for $45. for more information call 967-7331.

## SOUTH OF HILO

### KEAAU

Where have all the flower children gone? Gone to Keaau everyone, and all the rest down the road a piece to Pahoa. About ten miles south of Hilo, where Highway 130 heads down to Black Sand Beach, is the little town of Keaau. There are a few shops here that are worth visiting. The Christmas Store is no more but has been replaced by the Hawaiian Island Candle Company. While their specialty is candles, one resembling a volcano, there are all sorts of gift items available. The little mall across the street didn't seem to make it and most of the shops mentioned in our first edition are no more. Whether this spot will be revived in the future is anyone's guess. Where the Poi Bowl used to be, ie. across from the Candle Company, there is a little Filipino store that sells papaya very cheap, around seven for a buck. Also, there are a couple of restaurants which are mentioned below.

### HOSTS

**H-4**
Located exactly 20 miles south of the Hilo Airport, four miles from Pahoa, and fourteen miles from Keaau at the Hawaiian Beaches development, this newly constructed dome home, furnished mostly with antiques, offers two rooms to B & B guests. The master bedroom, which is used for guests, has a double bed, plus a large private bath with a huge shower. The sliding glass doors lead to a covered deck where guests can relax. There is also another bedroom available which has a single bed and a guest would share the bath with the host.
  Margo, the host, is a self employed family health consultant for the Neo-Life Health Company of America and her main interest is people.
RATE:   $35 for master bedroom, $25 for single room.

## RESTAURANTS

**LOCAL STYLE**

### KEAAU STEAK HOUSE
On the same side of the street as the Poi Bowl just a little makai. We have heard of it, we saw it, but alas that is all we can say at this point. We were able to contact the former owner who informed us they have closed at this location and plan on reopening in Hilo.

-------------------------------------------------------------

**local/Tourist**

### MAMA LANI'S MEXICAN
In the main shopping center in Keaau. If you like Mexican food, this is absolutely worth the drive down from Hilo. Open Monday through Saturday from 11 a.m. until 9 p.m. and on Sundays from 4:30 to 8:30 p.m. Whether for lunch or dinner, the prices here are moderate to low. Dinner entrees are in the $5.00 to $6.00 range, while full lunches are under $5.00 with ala carte enchilada only $1.95 Liquor is served and Master Charge and Visa accepted.

## <u>PAHOA</u>

In our opinion this is the funkiest little town in all Hawaii, a curious mixture of local folk and late '60 hippies who somehow or other found enough capital to open that business they had always dreamed of. While we were there we eavesdropped on a conversation of several Pahoa entrepreneurs discussing the approaching opening of a new restaurant. "Serve good breakfasts, " he urged the prospective restaurateur. "Serve good breakfasts and you can't miss." This conversation went on for some minutes until the budding businessman shot back. "Well, I know the whole thing will be a great success. Unless I go broke before I get the damn thing opened." From the looks of things in Pahoa, a really good restaurant just can't miss. As with Keaau, this is a fun place to just walk around. You probably won't find any great buys, but you might enjoy looking at the boomerang store, and, if you decide to buy one, you will get it for half the price you would pay anywhere else, or so we were told.

As we explored here this year one of the shop keepers asked to read what we said about Pahoa. We were a little worried that she might be offended, but when she finished she smiled and said, "Well, you folks really got a fix on Pahoa." Neither Pahoa or our opinion of it has changed much over the year.

## RESTAURANTS

**LOCAL STYLE**

**CHOP SUEY HOUSE**
On the mauka side of the road as you enter Pahoa from Hilo. If you like local food you will like this. We tried it and found it palatable and cheap.

**local/Tourist**

**LUGUIN'S**
In the center of town on the mauka side of the main road. Mexican cuisine with prices a little higher than at Mama Lani's and not as nice an atmosphere. But the people in town said it was very good. Open for breakfast, lunch, and dinner, closed Tuesday.

**RIB CAGE**
We heard about this before we got to Pahoa. "Finger licking good!" is what we heard. Prices are moderate, $9.75 and lower and naturally chicken and ribs are the specialty.

**PAHOA INN**
Well, the breakfast place has been opened and is doing very well, thank you. It is now open for breakfast and lunch from 7a.m until 2p.m. with breakfast served all day. They are planning to open for dinner soon.

**NOT JUST JUICE**
We had just eaten so did not sample their wares but the aroma had us thinking this might be the best spot in town. It is small and nothing fancy, but everything is home made, fresh, and we think pretty tasty, besides being very reasonable.

## POINTS OF INTEREST/BEACHES

**LAVA TREE STATE PARK**
From Pahoa take Highway 132 toward Pohoki or Kapoho for a couple of miles and you will see the park on your left. The most amazing thing to us about this park is how few people visit it. Not only is it a beautiful tropical setting but the aspect of the lava sweeping through here and burning out what was once a lovely grove of ohia trees, leaving behind a fossil forest of lava, inspires us with awe. Wandering among these bizarre formations causes one to appreciate why the ancient Hawaiians created the myths and legends of the fiery goddess Pele.

**KAPOHO**
Just past Lava Trees take the turn to the left and follow the road to the sea and you will be at the eastern most point of Hawaii. Until 1960 Kapoho was a thriving little village, but, for whatever sins, Madam Pele did her in and now she is no more. We suggest you

take this route because the drive from here down Highway 137 to Black Sand Beach is very scenic, going through mango groves, verdant jungle, a grove of iron wood that slightly resembles the pines of the Sierra Nevada Mountains, sparsely vegetated stark lava formations and often skirting the bluest water in the Islands.

## ISAAC HALE BEACH PARK & MACKENZIE STATE PARK
You will see these as you drive down 137. There are camping and picnic facilities at both. A permit is required for camping.

## KALANI HONUA
As we drove down this isolated stretch of road toward Black Sand Beach, we were just a little surprised to come upon a sign "Kalani Honua Center" and could not resist driving in to see what it was all about. To our surprise we discovered a rather large retreat lodge which has the capacity to house over 50 couples. No one was staying there at that time, but they were actively getting ready for a church group arriving in a few days. The rates are modest, $25.00 a night with a shared bath, $35.00 with a private bath. There are lower rates for weekly or monthly stays. For more information write to Kalani Honua Cultural Center, P.O. Box 4500, Kalapana, Hawaii 96778.
(We tried to get in touch by phone this year and found the number was not in service. We are not sure if they are still operating.)

## BLACK SANDS BEACH
While this is by no means the only black sand beach on Hawaii, it is the most famous. No matter how calm the ocean looks, swimming here is not advised since, as the drive guide says "dangerous currents and sharks make swimming out of the question." Since a swim at this point would be refreshing, move on down 137 to Queen's Bath, where you can swim in a rock pool once used by Hawaiian Royalty.

*Bed & Breakfast Guide*

# NORTH OF HILO

**HONOKAA**
    Forty miles north of Hilo, on what the locals call the belt road, you will come to the little town of Honokaa. You must, however, pull off the main highway or you will pass right by and go on to Waimea. Since doing that would cause you to miss Waipio Valley and the lookout above plus the other things Honokaa has to offer, look carefully for Highway 240, the Honokaa turnoff. Once considered the macadamia capitol of the world, Honokaa probably cannot even claim that distinction any longer, and as the highway has passed it by, its future is not bright. One can even get to Waipio Valley without journeying through Honokaa, but what's the hurry? Take a little time and wander around town. Believe us, the town folk will be glad to see you. One new thing we learned about this year is Honokaa Town Western Week held the weekend preceding Memorial Day Week End. This gets started with a Portuguese Bean Soup contest, and is followed by a fashion show, steak fry, all with a two day Rodeo.

## RESTAURANTS

**LOCAL STYLE**

CC JON'S
  On the makai side of the main street as you come into town, you are not likely to miss it. We ate breakfast here on our first trip to the Big Island in 1980 and were pleased with our meal and the price. If you do eat here, you will probably be the only tourist, but have no fear, they will treat you nice. Lunch will run you somewhere around $3.50 or so, and it is cleaner than it looks at first glance. It is just a little family run restaurant, those places that are getting more and more scarce as "Where's the Beef" gets more and more common.

------------------------------------------------------------------

local Style
HONOKAA HOTEL
  A Honokaa resident told us he liked this better than CC Jon's since the prices were no higher and they had a salad bar with no restrictions on helpings. The food is a mix of Japanese and American with a little Hawaiian thrown in. Lunch here will run in the $4.00-$5.00 range with dinners just a little higher.

HONOKAA PIZZA AND SUBS
  On the mauka side just past Hotel. Reasonable prices but we didn't get a chance to try it.

------------------------------------------------------------------

local/Tourist Style
TEX DRIVE INN
  On the main highway at the Honokaa School intersection. Open for breakfast, lunch, and dinner, Tex's is more popular than the three mentioned above if for no other reason that it is on the main drag. Stop by here even if it is not meal time and try some of Tex's malasadas, Portuguese doughnuts without the holes.

## POINTS OF INTEREST

### KAMAAINA WOODS
On the road to Hawaiian Holiday Macadamia Nut Factory. If you want to purchase products made of local woods, koa, milo, monkey pod, mango, and be assured that what you are getting is authentic and not high priced, this is the best place we have found. The work is done on the premises, unless it is done by one of the other local artists, in which case you will be informed. They are very willing to discuss the different woods with you and even though we made no purchase they were very helpful and friendly.

### HAWAIIAN HOLIDAY MACADAMIA NUT FACTORY
As you drive through Honokaa watch for the sign on your right. It is hard to miss. We guess one could say, "If you have seen one Mac Nut Factory you've seen them all," but still we liked the free sample, which was very generous.

### WAIPIO VALLEY
Located some six or seven miles north of Honokaa on Highway 24, you cannot miss it as the road stops here. We urge that you do not pass this by. Best of all, make some time and take the shuttle down into the valley. The history of the valley is long and varied so we will not go into it here. Suffice to say that just as one should not miss Haleakala on Maui or Waimea Canyon on Kauai, one should not miss Waipio Valley on Hawaii.

### KALOPA STATE PARK
Around three miles south of Honokaa a couple of miles mauka of Highway 19. This park has a picnic area, rest rooms, showers, and cabins which can be used only by groups (for information call 808/961-7200). This is a good place for hiking.

## BEACHES

### KOLEKOLE BEACH PARK
About sixteen miles north of Hilo watch for the sign on the makai side of the highway and it is a short ride down to the park. One can swim in the stream that comes in here but to swim in the surf would be foolhardy. There are picnic tables, rest rooms and showers, but no food sold.

### LAUPAHOEHOE BEACH PARK
When you reach the twenty-five (25) mile marker start watching for the sign on the makai side of the highway. From the highway it is about one mile drive down to the beach. This makes a good place to picnic; rest room and showers available, but by no means try swimming here.

*Bed & Breakfast Guide*

## SPORTS

**TENNIS**
There are two lighted courts at Honokaa Park in Honokaa.

**GOLF**
In Honokaa there is a nine hole course, Hamakua Country Club, which was built by the plantation personnel and is the site of the Macadamia Nut Masters Golf Tournament in August. The course is short, 2520 yards, but since the greens are small, the fairways narrow, and the course hilly, it is by no means easy. The fee is $5.00 and one can play all day if desired. Power carts are available for $12 but not mandatory. For more information call 935-7388.

# WAIMEA/KAMUELA

If some of the terrain you have just passed through looks a little like West Texas that is as it should be for now you are in cowboy, oops, paniolo country. Waimea is in the heart of the Parker Ranch, which is the largest privately owned ranch in the U.S. If you are ever going to need a sweater in Hawaii, this will be one of the places, for at night the temperature here can fall all the way into the fifties, and during the winter months even into the forties. But you will have little sense of being in the mountains since the climb from Hilo is so gradual. A stay in Waimea is a far different experience than a stay in most other parts of Hawaii. About the closest thing to it would be a stay in Kokee on Kauai. However, some of the most beautiful beaches in Hawaii are just a few minutes drive from Waimea. Our hosts tell us that it is great to be able to horse back ride in the mountains in the morning and then spend the afternoon relaxing at the sea shore. A vacation in the Kamuela/Waimea area settles the age old argument about which is better, the mountains or the seaside. Here one gets the best of both worlds.

# HOSTS

## H-17

This country guest house sits on over an acre at the 2500 ft. elevation at Kamuela, the heart of the Parker Ranch. To preserve the only building remaining on land that for generations was farmed by a Hawaiian family, the old wash house was kept intact by the farm's present owners, Charles and Barbara. A full kitchen, bath, and bed/living room were added. Horses graze along a stream that runs through the back of the property at the foot of the rolling green Kohala Mountains. This charming cottage is available to B & B members when not being used by the hosts' many visitors. The hosts are avid gardeners who enjoy using their garden produce and fresh eggs to feed their guests. Barbara works in the tourist industry and understands the importance of the Aloha spirit. Charles is a veterinarian. Since Barbara and Charles both leave early for work, breakfast fixings are provided.
RATE: $47 one rate, $286 week, $990 a month, plus 4% tax, 2 night minimum.

## H-18

This home is in the country, two and one half miles from Waimea, bordered by a stream lined with tree ferns and ohia lehua, surrounded by the pastures of the Parker Ranch and has an unsurpassed view of the mountains. The room for B & B has a double bed plus a double sofa bed so four people can be accommodated. The hosts, Joan and Bob, have a crib and other baby furniture for those traveling with children. The room is separate and private with its own bath. After twenty-five years on Oahu, Bob and Joan moved to Waimea in 1975. Formerly an outreach counselor for the West Hawaii Schools, Bob is now an elementary teacher in Waimea. Joan, who worked in the Hearing Impaired class at Waimea, now devotes her time to her sewing company, Fern Forest Fashions, and her many B & B guests. Both Joan and Bob are outdoor enthusiasts, swimming, skin diving, camping, and hiking, and are glad to share their knowledge of the natural beauty of the Big Island. No smoking in the house.
RATE: $27.50 single, $33 double, $7.50 for each extra person.

## H-18A

Lin and Harry's B & B home is situated on five acres three miles outside of Kamuela in ranch country, complete with horses, sheep, chickens, and a big super friendly dog named Sam. The accommodation offered is a spacious one bedroom apartment with a full kitchen. The apartment is the upstairs of a separate building designed like a Swiss barn and affords guests a great view of Mauna Kea. The unit has one bedroom with a queen sized bed and a double bed as well as a full size kitchen. There is also a first class gym with lots of exercise equipment and weights for anyone who wishes to work out, or maybe instead just a stroll down a nice country road.

Lin keeps busy with their four children and their activities and still manages to work part time in real estate. Harry is a home builder, and he has also built an experimental airplane that he keeps at the Waimea Airport. Continental breakfast fixing are provided in guests kitchen.
RATE: $45 single or double, $5 for child under 12, $7.50 over 12, $250 week double.

*Bed & Breakfast Guide*

### H-19
This home is located on Mamalehea Hwy., which is the old highway and now labeled the scenic route on the map. At about the 3000 ft. level, it is cool and peaceful, great for good sleeping in a king size bed. Guests share the bath with the host. Sitting on five acres, the home has an unobstructed view through the Parker Ranch of Mauna Kea. Beautiful eucalyptus and ginger lined roads make this a great place for jogging or walking. It is just fifteen minutes from the macadamia nut factory and the Hawaiian wood carving factory. It is also a good starting place to visit lush Waipio Valley with its large black sand beach.

Hostess Maryann enjoys sharing her home with guests. When she is not at her shop in Honokaa, she can be found paddling a canoe at the beach as she is a member of the canoe club.

RATE: $25 single, $30 double.

### H19A
This home is located just about a 15 minute walk from Waipio Valley Lookout. From there one can hike, ride the shuttle, or go horseback riding in the Valley of the Kings where once over 10,000 Hawaiians lived. Then come home to this little hideaway, a house just for guests, completely private and very quiet. Guests relax to the sound of the year round stream, and look out on a spectacular ocean view or mountain waterfalls. It is great for whale watching in the winter months. This spot could be a honeymooners dream or for those who want to get away from it all and just sit back and relax. The accommodation offered is quaint and rustic, very clean, and loaded with charm. Guests have a full kitchen for their use so that meals in are no problem. There is also a fireplace. Waimea is about a thirty or forty minute drive, while Hilo is some fifty miles south. There is access to horseback riding into Waipio Valley but a waiver must be signed. Charlie, a teacher at Honokaa, is building a new home. Kristan is a registered nurse. Since both hosts work and the accommodation has its own kitchen, a continental breakfast is provided but not served.

RATE: $35 single or double, $220 a week, $800 a month.

### H-27
Molly and Warren have been residents of Hawaii for over 25 years. Warren was the chief photographer at the Honolulu Star Bulletin and is now teaching photography at Parker School. Molly is a homemaker and teaching assistant. Both have traveled extensively and this is reflected in their home and their interests.

The guest accommodation is a ground floor bedroom with twin beds and is decorated in simple early American style. There is a bath across the hall for the exclusive use of the guests. The home has open-beamed ceiling, fireplace, and a 5 ft. x 4 ft. sun garden window and is located in Parker Ranch territory just 5 minutes from Kamuela and 20 minutes from the finest beach on Hawaii.

RATE: $25 single, $35 double.

### H-27A
Gale and Michael have just completed a 4000 square foot home and have used about 800 feet of it for a completely seperate apartment for B & B guests. Guest quarters include a bedroom, private full bathroom, a living room. The apartment also has a sink and a small frig. The home borders a stream and has a 360 degree view of the Kohala Mountains, Pacific Ocean, and the famous Mauna Kea and Mauna Loa.

RATE: $40 one rate, two night minimum.

RESTAURANTS

## LOCAL STYLE
-------------------------------------------------------------------

### HOMER'S RESTAURANT
Located on Highway 19 as you enter Waimea from Honokaa behind the Fukishima Store. Open from 10 a.m. to 4 p.m. every day but Sunday, this is the best spot in town for a good, low price lunch.

### KAMUELA OKAZUYA
In the same parking lot as the Cattleman's mentioned below. Takeout local food, perhaps a good spot to pick up a picnic lunch.

### WAREHOUSE CAFE
Just across the street from Cattleman's, set off the main road. Open only on weekdays. We have had some good reports of this place from several guests.
-------------------------------------------------------------------

## local/Tourist Style

### **EDELWEISS**
Dining out in Hawaii is not always a great experience and unlike the metropolitan centers of the Mainland such as San Francisco, New Orleans, and New York, interesting little restaurants at reasonable prices are rare. We stopped in for lunch here with no prior knowledge except that it had recently been taken over by a German fellow. One bite of just the potatoes so excited our taste buds that we had to know more of this "German fellow." Hans-Peter Hager was good enough to talk to us and when we exclaimed that he was a gourmet chef he modestly replied, "No, just a cook, but we enjoy what we do." Hans-Peter, we learned, had worked for twenty years at the famed Mauna Kea. Well, we hope Hans-Peter keeps up the good work in Waimea, unless he chooses to move to Kauai. Lunch prices are low ($4.50 for Edelweiss specialty, knockworst, sauerkraut, and potatoes) in spite of the elegant food and good service. Dinner entrees run a little higher, from $12.00 to $20.00. However, a light meal is much less, around $7.00 to $8.00. Since they do not take reservations and everyone we talked to on the Big Island considers this the best restaurant on the Island, you may have a little wait. Closed on Monday.

### PARKER RANCH BROILER
In the Parker Ranch Shopping Center. If you eat here you will discover "where the beef is" since the specialty of the house is Parker Ranch cattle. Long a favorite with residents and tourists alike as *the special occasion dining spot,* the atmosphere is a little more formal than most places in the Islands. Shorts not suitable attire here; slacks and casual shirt, however, acceptable. Open for lunch and for dinner with lunch around $10.00 and dinner $15.00 to $20.00. Liquor is served.

### CATTLEMAN'S
You will find this at the back of a small center on the right as you enter Kamuela from the Hilo side. This is a Mainland chain very well known for their large steaks and prime ribs.

### PANIOLO COUNTRY INN
This is fairly new, and seems to get plenty of action. The prices are reasonable.

### GREAT WALL CHOP SUI
Just across the street from Edelweiss. Next time we are in Kamuela we will try it, if we happen to be there on Monday.

### AUNTY ALICE'S
Hosts tell us that this little pie shop has the best pie in the Islands. It is near the museum at Parker Ranch Center.

## POINTS OF INTEREST

### PARKER RANCH MUSEUM
In the Parker Ranch Center, admission $2.50. Some people feel this is little more than a glorified history of the Parker family and not worth the price. Perhaps we are easy to please. While we agree that it is not one of the high points of a trip to Hawaii, it is interesting enough if you have the time.

### KAMUELA MUSEUM
At the junction of Highway 19 and 250. Not as slick, but in many ways far more interesting than the Parker Museum. It is open from 8 a.m. to 5 p.m. Founded by one of the Parker offspring, here you will find a potpourri of Hawaiiana, as well as other things from all over the world. We had a lengthy chat with Harriet Soloman who, as her card says, is the "Great-great granddaughter of John Palmer Parker, founder of world-famous Parker Ranch."

### NIKKO GALLERY
We came upon this by accident and enjoyed it very much. This building, called the Spencer Building, is the oldest building in Kamuela and once served as an Inn for those traveling between Hilo and Kona. They specialize in Japanese antiques but have many artists displayed also. Check out the inscription on the window pane on the front door.

## BEACHES

(SEE BEACHES UNDER NORTH KOHALA)

# NORTH KOHALA

Not a lot of tourists get up to the North Kohala district of the Big Island; we would encourage all to drive into this area via the high road, Highway 25 which goes north off 19 and to return down the coast via Highway 270. Called Kohala Mountain Road, it reaches an elevation of 3,500 feet. The vista of the plains and ocean below makes this one of the finest views in the Islands. A journey into this region gives one a good example of just how slow paced life in Hawaii must have been long ago. It was here that King Kamehameha, the great warrior who united the islands into one Kingdom, was born. At the little town of Kapaau you will see the original statue of Kamehameha. The statue in Honolulu is a replica, which was made when the original was lost at sea in 1880. It was subsequently found and returned to this spot.

If you take this drive, be sure to continue to the end of the road, past Kapaau, to Pololu Valley Lookout and, if time permits, hike the 1/2 mile into the valley. As you backtrack towards Kapaau, you will see a sign pointing makai for Keokea Beach Park.

As you travel south down Highway 270, watch for Lapahiki State Historical Park, an ancient Hawaiian Village. You get an idea of how the Hawaiians lived hundreds of years ago. The park closes at 4 p.m. From here on down to the town of Kailua, the scenery is stark and dry; the vegetation, mostly pili grass and kiawe trees and prickly pear cactus, fights for life among the jagged beds of lava.

When you reach Kawaihae you may be ready for food or drink. If it is budget time, stop by the Harbor Inn, which serves breakfast, lunch and dinner from 6 a.m. until 9 p.m. daily. *(Since our first book there has been a fire here and as of this writing the restaurant has not been reopened.)* The menu is extensive and prices are low. If, on the other hand, the sky is the limit, stop by the Mauna Kea Beach Hotel. Brunch there is more of an experience than a meal. Eating there every day might cause your spread to match Mauna Kea. Further down the road you could stop at the new Mauna Lani Hotel and enjoy their elegant surroundings. A little south of here is the fairly new Sheraton Waikoloa, nice but not as elegant as the other two.

*Bed & Breakfast Guide*

## BEACHES

### POLOLU
It takes about a half an hour to hike down to the beach from the lookout. There are no facilities so if you plan to be there long, pack in food and drinks. Swim with caution.

### KEOKEO BEACH PARK
You will see the sign on the makai side of the road between Kapaau and Pololu Valley. There are picnic facilities, rest rooms, and showers in this secluded little park. Swimming here is not advisable.

### KAPAA BEACH PARK
There are picnic tables and rest rooms but no drinking water here. No sand beach but on a wind-free day, this makes a nice spot to picnic and to try your luck at shore fishing.

### SPENCER BEACH PARK
If one is staying in the Waimea area, this is the spot for beaching. The swimming is excellent as is the snorkeling, even for the beginner. The facilities are good: picnic tables, rest rooms, showers, tennis courts, but no food sold there. Big white sand beach.

### HAPUNA BEACH STATE PARK
Access to this beach is just south of the Mauna Kea, in fact the Mauna Kea is at the north end of this beach. Because private beaches are not allowed in Hawaii, the Mauna Kea must give access through their property to the beach and several parking places are reserved for that purpose. We prefer this beach to any on the Big Island. Swimming is great as is snorkeling. There are picnic tables, rest rooms, and showers, but no food sold.

## SPORTS

### TENNIS
There are two lighted courts in Waimea at Waimea Park and two lighted courts in North Kohala at Kamehameha Park.

### GOLF
The North Kona Coast could be called the "Golf Capital" of Hawaii since there are four championship courses available and all of them are truly spectacular. However, all of them are privately owned and not inexpensive to play. The least expensive are the Waikoloa Village (883-9621) and the Waikoloa Beach (885-6060), located at the Waikoloa Sheraton. For Sheraton guests the green fee at the Village is $27, for non-guests it is $31. At the Beach the fee is $31 for guests and $34 for non-guests. The Mauna Kea (882-7222) is $48 for non-guests and 40 for guest. The Mauna Lani (885-6655) is $50 for non-guests and $40 for guests.

## KAILUA/KONA

We once saw a sign on a Caribbean Island that read "sunny today - and for the next 364". That sign could reside in Kailua and would not be much of an exaggeration. Up from Kailua, along the belt road, it is another matter. Here it rains almost every day at least a little, and in the evening the air moves down from Kualalai Mountain to keep things refreshingly cool.

Kailua starts at the north end with the King Kamehameha Hotel and ends some eight miles south at the Kona Surf. In between along Alii Drive there is a smattering of hotels (Uncle Billy's Kona Bay, the Kona Hilton) many condos and more little shops and restaurants than we care to count. Almost all of the tourist activity takes place here, at sea level along Alii Drive in Kailua Town, with most things geared to tourism. If Kailua had the huge white sand beaches that exist on Oahu, Maui, and Kauai, there is little doubt that a high percentage of tourists would head here. Nowhere in Hawaii is the ocean more beautiful and warm, the sea life more plentiful, and all this with a backdrop of Mt. Hualalai.

From the pier in the center of town, one can catch a fishing boat and try his luck at marlin fishing, for some consider Kona the marlin capitol of the world, and several tournaments with sizable purses are run each year. It is quite a sight to see fish of hundreds of pounds being hoisted from the boats and weighed in at the dock. But it is not only marlin they fish for, but ono, sail fish, ahi, and mahi mahi.

In October they hold the Iron Man Competition at Kona, and for weeks before triathletes train for the grueling event which starts with a two mile swim across Kailua Bay, a seventy five mile bike race, and ends with a marathon run, ending up in Kailua Town where thousands await the outcome.

While Kailua seems to be striving to be like Lahaina and Waikiki, with an abundance of malls and shops, it is still more low key and laid back and, for visitors who shun crowds a much nicer pace.

*Bed & Breakfast Guide*

## HOSTS

### H-7A
We have a little difficulty in knowing just where to list this since it is not really in Kailua nor Waimea, but about five miles from Waimea on the ocean; however, the location can only be described as super, at Puako Beach in a quiet residential community right on the water. This completely separate apartment, fully furnished and very roomy is newly built, in fact as of this writing it was not quite finished. Puako Beach is just south on the famed Mauna Kea resort and just north of the new and getting famous Mauni Lani. So as you can see, this moves in pretty fancy company. Snorkeling just in front of the home is excellent and one of the largest petroglyph fields in Hawaii is just across the street. There are excellent white sand beaches within a few minutes drive, and it is, of course, close to several excellent golf courses.

Pat was born and grew up in Honolulu while his wife, Pattie, came to the Islands in 1949. They have lived at Puako for the last ten years, but since their property has been in the family since 1955, they know the Island well. Pat is retired, while Pattie is employed by a local airline.

RATE: $60 single or double, $400 a week, two night minimum, two week maximum.

### H-8A
You will find everything at your door step when you come to stay with Bob and Ginger in Keahou Bay, just five miles south of Kailua Town. Their lovely, open beamed ceiling home is located on the 11th fairway of the Keahou Golf course and is less that a mile from the new Keahou Shopping Center and several of Kona's finest restaurants. From their home you can walk to the ocean. There are also several water activities you can take advantage of at the Bay, including snorkeling cruises and jet skiing. Bob and Ginger's large and airy home offers you a private bedroom with a double bed, private bath, color TV, and a small private lanai. Their home is tastefully decorated in antiques and collectibles and has a warm and homey atmosphere.

Bob and Ginger were in the deli business in California, and now that they have moved to Kona, Bob in now employed at one of Kona's restaurants. Ginger is a full time homemaker with a four year old and a new baby. (the nursery is out of earshot.)

RATE: $40 one rate.

### H-10
This contemporary home is located in the hills above Kailua less than a mile up from the ocean and the center of town. The accommodation offered is a charming garden bedroom, separate from the main house with a private entrance and a private bath. The bedroom has a queen sized bed. There are no cooking facilities provided. Breakfast is a special treat served on the large deck overlooking the blue Pacific and Kailua.

Eleanor, the hostess, has lived in Hawaii for over seventeen years and hails originally from Chicago. She likes to spend her time playing bridge and golf and is active with the Kona Outdoor Circle. Fishing enthusiasts will be especially pleased to hear that Eleanor will gladly make arrangements for a chartered fishing boat.

RATE: $35, two night minimum

### H-10A
Relax and enjoy the tranquility in the middle of 27 acres of a macadamia and coffee orchard just 15 minutes from Kailua-Kona, yet a world away from heat and the noise of people. Enjoy a beakfast of papaya, pinapple, banana, and fresh Kona coffee from the farm, as well as home-made fruit and berry preserves, all the while enjoying a panoramic view of the blue Pacific.

Lydia, the hostess, was born and raised in the Islands so is a good source of information on where to go and what to see. The accommodation for B & B guests has a private entrance, a private bath with shower, one double and one single bed.

RATE: $40 double, $5 for extra person.

### H-11
Upon leaving Keahole Airport at Kona it is just a short three minute drive to the home of Sue and her son David. The twins, Kristin and Karen, are away at college in Indiana, but if you are lucky the *Dynamic Duo* might be home to help greet you. As you can see, this is a people oriented family dedicated to the comforts of their guests. Sue and her family are originally from Chicago, which they left to find a better life. They are convinced they found Paradise.

A palm fringed driveway leads up to this comfortable home that has both an ocean and a mountain view. Lush tropical foliage, exotic flowers, and a wide variety of fruit trees surround this home. Two rooms are available to B & B guests. There is a bath between these two rooms which is for guests use only. Smoking O.K. but not in bedrooms, please.

RATE: $40 single or double. Family of four or two couples traveling together, $70. 4% State Excise Tax added.

### H-16
Strictly speaking, this is not B & B since no host lives here. This condo is located at Kona Bali Kai and is available to B & B members. When we first started B & B we had no hosts on the Kona side so we took several no-host condos to accommodate our guests who wanted to do the whole Island. There is, however, a contact person, Enid, who is very efficient and helpful. This one bedroom condo could accommodate four since there is a sofa bed in the living room.

RATE: $45.50 a day, $260 a week, $906 a month.

### H-22
This home is located in Sunset View Estates, three miles from town. The view of Kailua Town and the Kona Coast is spectacular. The hosts have a five bedroom home, each with a private bath and a private entrance. The Blue Room has two twin beds: the Green and Yellow Rooms have queen sized beds: the Rose room has a double bed and bunk beds if children are included in your travel plans.

The hosts, George and Pat, are from Alaska, where George is a commercial fisherman. They winter in Hawaii and that is when their home is available to guests. George is an outdoor person who likes also to hunt in the fall in Alaska. He loves taking his three children and their families fishing when they are visiting from the Mainland. Pat is a Christian homemaker who has a variety of interests. She enjoys church and her new interest is taking water aerobic classes.

RATE: $30 single, $40 double, weekly rates available.

### H-23
For spectacular sunrises, sunsets, and star-watching, enjoy the quiet elegance of this hillside home overlooking Kialua town just one mile below. Mary, your hostess, offers her home which is tastefully furnished with a combination of antiques and Island decor. Breakfast is served on the spacious garden lanai which affords a lovely ocean view. There are two bedrooms available to B & B guests, one for a couple and one for a single so a small family or three adults could be accommodated. The bath the guests use is private. Nearby there are tennis courts available for the guests to use.

Mary, a former resident of Alaska, Colorado, and Arizona, is enthusiastic about sharing her knowledge of the Big Island and would be happy to assist you in making suggestions for sightseeing and/or reservations for tours and activities.

RATE: $30, single, $35 double, two night minimum preferred but not required.

### H-26
Escape to the peaceful hillside of Hualalai Mountain, overlooking the beautiful Kona coast, to the lovely 2500 sq. ft. custom home of Tracy and Peter. The interior is meticulously furnished and quite spacious in its design. The B & B guest quarters are on the first level and have two bedrooms with one bath and a complete kitchen and living area. There is a large deck and a wonderful hot tub for all to use. The view here is magnificent. Tracy provides her guests with breakfast fixings since she and Peter leave for work early in the morning. They do, however, have plenty of time for getting acquainted and love to answer questions you might have about the Big Island. Both Peter and Tracy have lived in Hawaii for many years and are there to share their aloha spirit with you.

RATE: $55 double, $60 for three, $65 for two couples, two night minimum.


## HOSTS SOUTH OF KAILUA


### H-25
A Kona style open home located on the slopes above the Place of Refuge in Honaunau with a panoramic view of the ocean. The hosts have just completed a king sized bedroom and bath in separate guest quarters on the garden level, also with an outstanding view. The home is located just eighteen (18) miles volcano side south of Kailua and is surrounded by 1/2 acre of gardens. It is cool, quiet, and private. Breakfast is served upstairs on the 50 ft. lanai. There is a small refrigerator in the room.

The hosts, Peggy and Curt, are avid fishermen and scuba divers. A fully equipped 18 ft. Mako boat is kept at the home for private trips: fishing, diving, or exploring the calm Kona coast line. Rates are very reasonable with food and beverages included.

RATES: $40 single or double.

## H-28

Located in the cool coffee and macadamia nut region of the Kona Coast, eight miles south of Kailua, in the tiny town of Kealakakua, in a quiet neighborhood of the village at 1300 ft. elevation is the home of Marge and Howard. Their home is perfect for two couples traveling together as it has a complete one bedroom apartment on the garden level of their two story home. The second couple can be accommodated on the hide-a-bed in the living room. The apartment has a private entrance and lanai, bath with shower, and full kitchen. Meals can be prepared and it is a short drive to excellent restaurants.

Howard and Marge came to Hawaii in 1980. Howard built their home and continues to do custom furniture and cabinet work. Marge is a retired R.N., trying hard to become a gardener. They both love Hawaii and are anxious to acquaint visitors with its many attractions. Having lived in England, the Philippines and Micronesia, where they served in the Peace Corps, they feel Hawaii is paradise. Smoking on the lanai only.

RATE: $35 double, $45 for three, $60 for four, $200 weekly for two, $350 for four.

## H-28A

This B & B home is located about 30 minutes from the airport at the 1300 foot elevation. It overlooks the blue Pacific, Kailua-Kona, Kailua Bay, and the western slopes of Hualalai. The garden level accommodations include two bedrooms, each with a queen sized bed, a livingroom with cable TV, and a refrigerator. There is a bathroom with a shower/tub and a large dressing table. These rooms are located on a lower level than the main quarters and are very quiet. The unit has a separate entrance and a lanai for relaxing or sunbathing. Breakfast is served on the upper lanai, which is also available for guests who wish to enjoy the gorgeous view or sunsets with the aid of binoculars or telescope. The garden always is colorful with tropical flowers as well as many of the tropical fruits.

The hosts, Pearl (a retired educator from Albuquerque), and Myrtle (a nurse from Dallas), have lived in Hawaii for five years. They enjoy tropical gardening, hiking to beautiful isolated areas not available by car, Island hopping, and helping visitors plan an unforgettable vacation to beautiful Hawaii.

RATE: $35 double, $45 for 3, $60 for 4, $200 per week double, $350 week for 4.

## H-30

For a truly unique experience and absolute privacy Karen and Richard's beautiful custom home is available. Located on over seven acres of orchids and pasture with spectacular views of both ocean and mountains, they are 25 minutes south of Kailua in the heart of one of the most historical and verdant valleys on the Big Island. The accommodations are more than just a bed. The hosts offer you over 1700 sq. ft. of their home, including spacious koa wood kitchen, screened in breakfast area, large deck area, and lots of privacy. They will be close at hand, staying in the separate quarters of their shop and studio. Of course, breakfast is a treat with all the farm fresh fruits. Both being artists (Karen specializing in stained glass and hula, Richard in woodworking) their home is full of evidence of their craft. With over a thousand miles of experience cruising under sail, they sailed to Kona on their small sail boat, fell in love with the place, and stayed.

RATE: $65 double, $10 per additional double futon, two night minimum.

*Bed & Breakfast Guide*

## RESTAURANTS

Because Kailua is so geared to tourists, much like Lahaina on Maui and Waikiki on Oahu, we will dispense with our usual method of classification. All restaurants in Kailua depend primarily on tourists and we cannot remember seeing one place that served Loco Moco, our litmus test for LOCAL classification. Most of the <u>locals</u> on the Kona Coast are from the Mainland. We will group restaurants into two categories: 1.) lunch and snack places, 2.) dinner houses. In category 2 we will list them somewhat as they ascend in price.

## **LUNCH AND SNACK PLACES**

### BETTY'S CHINESE
In the Kona Coast Shopping Center which you pass as you drive into Kailua from the north. Fast food, cafeteria style, Oriental/Hawaiian fare at very low prices, little or no atmosphere.

### MONSTER BURGERS
In the same center as Betty's. However big these burgers are, they are not inexpensive, around $5.00. One might do better right in town.

### AMY'S CAFE
This is a little tricky to find but well worth the effort. Just as you pass the Kona Coast Shopping Center, at the stop light, turn right, then turn right again into the shopping center and Amy's is at the top of the hill. The emphasis here is on health food, but meat dishes, chicken and hamburgers, are served also. Everything is very fresh, home made, and the prices are very reasonable. Lots of home made baked goods.

### SIBU CAFE
At the back of Kona Banyon Court on the mauka side of Alii. A very small, sort of take out, Indonesian food, not expensive and we found it very tasty. It was started by Indonesian people who have since sold out but not before teaching the new owner how to prepare the food.

### *STUMBLE INN*
At the back of one of the first shopping malls as you enter Kailua and open for breakfast, lunch, and dinner. Good food and low prices. They had a breakfast special of eggs, ham, and toast for $1.99. For lunch they specialize in submarine sandwiches which go up to $5.50 but look big enough to feed two people, while dinners such as pork cutlets or chicken run between $3.75-$5.00. We absolutely recommend this unless you are looking for atmosphere.

### STAN'S
A nearby spot from the Ocean View, mentioned below. The signs outside indicate low prices. Very "tourist" oriented spot and very competitively priced.

### MCGURKS FISH AND CHIPS
New since last year, this will probably be here awhile. Very clean and spiffy with fish at good prices. Counter service with a few tables provided.

### THE WORLD'S GREATEST SANDWICH SHOP
A little take out stand on the mauka side across from Kailua Bay. The specialty here is Mac Nut Burger, made of macadamia nuts and cheddar cheese. Many other kind of sub sandwiches available, too.

### BILLY BOY'S CAFE
This is a little almost take out place but a few tables are provided. The menu is limited, hamburgers and hot dogs, but also a fish or shrimp plate for $4.25 and $4.75 respectively. The style is local, run by Uncle Billy's son.

### DOUG'S DINER
This is a terrific little place located in the Kam Center just before you get to Kailua town. To find turn right at the stop light just before Kailua town and you will see the Center on your left. Not only are breakfast, lunch, and dinner prices reasonable, but they have a great juke box with songs from the '40 and '50. There is a small dance floor and we were told that patrons were welcome to dance. They do not serve liquor but have no objection to diners bringing their own. They are open 24 hours a day.

## DINNER HOUSES

### OCEAN VIEW INN
At the north end of Alii Drive on the mauka side. The Ocean View is the ultimate chowdown, two scoop rice restaurants in Hawaii, with a menu schizophrenic enough to be committed. The only place to go if you are looking for lots to eat at low cost. They must be doing something right because at times the action here is so fast that some patrons finally get discouraged with the wait and wander off to one of the nearby spots.

### JOSE'S MEXICAN
This is an excellent spot for reasonably priced Mexican food. They are open for lunch and dinner.

### REUBAN'S
Behind Crazy Shirts and run by the same family who runs Reuban's in Hilo. We ate here and found the food acceptable and prices not high. One thing we did notice is that the people working there seemed to be of Mexican ancestry, which we can assure you is rare in the so called Mexican restaurants in Hawaii. Liquor is served.

### UKULELE LADY
A new restaurant in Kona, located in the Keauhou Shopping Center. Prices here are very reasonable with several dinners under $10. It is open for lunch also and again prices are not too high.

### DRYSDALE'S
On the makai side of Alii Drive in the Kona Inn Shopping Village. This is a good place for lunch if you want a little more atmosphere than the previously mentioned spots. Prices here are moderate, not as low as the ones above. They have a comfortable cocktail lounge with reasonable prices.

### DRYSDALE'S TWO
Located in the new Keahau Shopping Center just before you get to the Kona Surf. Beautiful view and stylish surroundings.

### MARTY'S STEAK AND SEAFOOD
This was once Buzz's and the fare hasn't changed that much, ie. steak and seafood. Good view of Kailua Bay in a fairly nice atmosphere with prices on the high side.

### KONA RANCH HOUSE
On the mauka side of Kuakini Highway, the one that brought you to Kailua from the north, just past Palani Road. There is a casual family section and a more formal *special occasion* section. The food is good, the service is excellent, and prices are in the $12.00 to $20.00 range.

### SPINDRIFTER
On the makai side of Alii Drive a little south of all the restaurants mentioned above. The best thing about this is the setting, right on the ocean. Our hosts tell us that this is a great place for early evening pupus. The food is typical Spindrifter/Chart House/Anybody's Broiler type, ie., broiled steak, fish, or lobster with the ubiquitous salad bar, with bronzed surfer type waiters who insist on telling you their name. The food is O.K. and prices run from $10.00 to $20.00. Liquor is served and all plastic accepted.

### KONA INN
This is located in the Kona Inn and is one of the oldest restaurants in Kailua with the Inn going back to 1928. It is right on the water and has a very nice atmosphere. It is open for lunch and dinner.

### THE POTTERY STEAKHOUSE
Located on Kuakini Highway just south of Kailua Town. Prices range here from $9 to $18.50 and the specialty is steak. Another specialty they are famous for is the cornish game hen cooked in a clay pot, and you keep the pot, $14.50. We talked to the owner and he told us that they were going to vary the menu in the future to include more fish and pasta dishes, playing down the beef.

### ECLIPSE
On the mauka side just a few doors south of the Kona Ranch House. Open only for dinner from 5-9 p.m. This is one of Kona's night spots with dancing from 9 'til closing.

### FISHERMAN'S LANDING
This is the newest elegant restaurant in Kailua and it is owned and operated by Uncle Billy. It is in the Kona Inn Center on the south side. The menu is extensive with chicken being the lowest priced item ($10.95) The setting is about the best on the Island. Lunch and dinner are served.

### HUGGO'S
On the Makai side of Alii Dr. just before the Hilton. We have tried to eat here several times but we have never been able to. Our hosts say it is good but only if you are satisfied with either steak or lobster.

## DORIANS

As you drive south on Alii Dr. you will see this on the right at the far end of one of the condo complexes. The cuisine is French international and very good. Our hosts tell us that the best thing here is the Sunday brunch.

## KANA ZAWA TEI

On the mauka side of Alii Dr. across from the Hilton. This is authentic Japanese cuisine, not at all inexpensive, but very good if this is what you are looking for. You can get a seven course dinner for $35 or if you like Funamori, a wide variety of sashimi for $100.

## LA BOURGOINE

This may be the highest priced restaurant in Kailua and it may be the best, at least that is the opinion of several of our hosts. We don't imagine you will be displeased with either the food or the service.

## POINTS OF INTEREST

You will not have to search out the interesting things to visit in Kailua since they are right there on Alii Drive. To us the most interesting place in town is the Kailua Wharf, where the action seems to go on all day, culminating in the middle afternoon with the return of the fishing boats, which fly different flags to herald their catch, either ono, ahi, or biggest of all, if not the best, the marlin.

One place of interest we might mention is Hilo Hatties which is located across from the Kona Coast Shopping Center just before you enter Kailua Town. This is the closest thing to a department store on the Kona Coast. While the main emphasis is on Hilo Hattie products, there are several concessions in the store, such as Hill and Hill Kona Coffee, and one of the Mac Nut companies. Soon they hope to add seamstresses so patrons can see the garments being made.

For those captivated by the historical aspect of Hawaii there is the Hulihee Palace or the Mokuaikaua Church, the oldest in the Islands. There is a small fee to visit the Palace, now a show place for Hawaiiana. Also, there is the Kamakahono Beach and the Ahuena Heiau, located behind the King Kamehameha Hotel, which is on the site of King Kamehameha's last residence.

As you drive down Alii Drive toward Keauhou Bay you will pass all the beaches that Kailua has to offer, including Disappearing Sands, which tends to wash away during the winter months.

## BEACHES

**HONOKOHAU BEACH**
 To get to this beach take Highway 19 north of Kailua for about two miles until you see the sign for the Honokohau Harbor. From the north side of the harbor, walk about a quarter of a mile north to the beach. There are no facilities here at all. Swimming is safe. The rest of the beaches in this area are along Alii Drive and quite obvious.

## NIGHT LIFE

Most of the night life in Kona takes place at the various hotels, which often have entertainment and dancing. The *This Week* magazine, free at all tourist locations, lists the various entertainers appearing. There is a Hula Show on Tuesday and Thursday nights at the Kona Inn. Duplicate Bridge is played on Tuesday and Thursday night at Hale Halawai on Alii Dr. We hear that the hottest spot for dancing is at the Eclipse. Doug's Diner is open all night and since they have a juke box maybe there is dancing there. At the Kona Surf there is a free Polynesian show daily at 7:45-8:30 p.m. The Spindrifter has live entertainment Monday through Saturday, starting at 8:30 p.m. First run movies are shown at the World Square Theater, 329-4070, and there is a theater at Captain Cook, 328-8111.

## SPORTS

**TENNIS**
 Many of the hotels in Kailua have courts that are open to the public. There are four locations where public courts are available. At Kailua Park there are four lighted courts. There is one unlighted court at Keauhou Park. Kailua Playground and Greenwell Park each have one lighted court.

**GOLF**
 The Keauhou Golf Course, located at the south end of Alii Drive is available to the public. Unless one is a guest of the Kona Surf the fee is $27.00, cart $10.00 on a share basis. It is an excellent course, where the wind is not as much a factor as on the North Kona courses. For more information call 322-2595.

## THE BELT ROAD

If you take Palani Road mauka from Kailua for about four miles up the hill, you will come to the Belt Road which runs above Kailua. Take this road south and you will join Highway 11, which continues on to South Kona and the Volcano area. Since this area is very different from Kailua, far older and less tourist oriented, we urge you to try this road. The scenery is spectacular, whether you are looking at the vegetation along the road or the awesome views of Kailua and the blue Pacific below. When we first took this drive, the growth of ginger, bougainvillea, royal poinciana and wild orchids was so overpowering that we failed to see the many coffee trees along the way. Should you be lucky enough to be there when the coffee trees are in bloom, you are in for a treat. Coffee trees are in the gardenia family and the blossom is as beautiful and as fragrant, but, alas, much more transitory, lasting only a few days.

As you drive this road you will pass through several old towns, still very busy little centers which serve the folks who live in this area. Before Kailua was developed mainly for tourists, all the action was in the higher elevation, which, when you think of it, makes much more sense for living due to the cooler climate. On the Mainland we are more used to having our towns right on the water's edge on both coasts. In Hawaii, this is not always the case.

*Bed & Breakfast Guide*

## RESTAURANTS

**LOCAL STYLE**

MANAGO HOTEL
We would urge you to stop by and pay a visit here, for such old hotels are becoming rare. We spent some time looking through the guest register and noted that few Mainland people use this facility. While we think B & B is the best deal around, we would think anyone on a budget or with just a spirit of adventure would enjoy staying here. Rooms start at $13.00 for a single with a shared bath up to $27.00 for a private bath on the third floor accommodating three people. Meals are served: breakfast from 7-9, cost around $3.50, lunch from 11-2, from $4.00-$7.50, dinner from 5-7, priced from $5.75-$7.50. We imagine that after dinner one and all adjourn to the lobby where easy chairs are neatly lined for T.V. viewing.

------------------------------------------------------------

local Style

TESHIMA'S
Just past where Highway 180 joins 11 on the mauka side of the road. Even if you are staying down in Kailua Town, it is not much of a drive up here, and if you want Japanese food this is a good place. Not many tourists stop here, but plenty of residents do since the food is good and the prices are low. The menu is a curious mixture of Japanese and American, so you can choose hamburger steak for $3.50, pork chops for $5.75, or Nabe Yaki Udon for $2.50. They also fix a box lunch from $3.00-$3.50 in case you would like to picnic somewhere along the way.

------------------------------------------------------------

local/Tourist Style

CANAAN DELI
South of Teshima's on the makai side of the road. You can get a pretty good sandwich here for a modest price.

GARDEN CAFE
If all you want is a cup of coffee and perhaps a torte or fresh croissant, stop by here and sit at one of the side-walk tables, and perhaps you can imagine you are in Paris. Since last year this has changed hands and is now run by two ladies whom we were not able to meet since we passed by on Monday when they were closed. Open from 7 a.m. to 5 p.m.

ALOHA CAFE
Located on the makai side of the road as you enter Keallakekua. Open from 8 a.m. to 2 p.m. Monday through Friday, from 8 a.m. to noon on Saturday and closed Sunday. Moderately priced and features homemade soup and bread.

KONA THEATER CAFE
In Captain Cook on the makai side of the road. Last year we starred this as we felt it was the best restaurant on the Belt Road. It has changed hands several times in the last year. At the present time they are serving German style food. We did not get a chance to try it as it was closed when we went by in spite of the fact that the sign said open and we were there during their posted hours. They are open for lunch and dinner and our hosts say it is very good.

## POINTS OF INTEREST

### SUNSET COFFEE MILL
Located on Route 16, which goes to Kealakekua Bay and the Captain Cook Monument. This is not a coffee mill but simply a coffee roasting station. They buy their beans from the co-op located next door, and it is here where the coffee cherries are processed. Believe us when we say that the whole process is complicated. We have several coffee trees on Kauai and have gone through the process of picking, pealing, drying, shucking, and roasting, and never will we complain about the price of coffee again. At the Mill you will read about this process and if you like you can buy some fine Kona coffee.

### CAPTAIN COOK'S MONUMENT
At the end of Route 16 you will come to Kealakekua Bay, where Captain Cook was done in by the Hawaiian Chiefs. Also, there is a heiau that was very important to the ancient Hawaiians.

### PU'UHONUA O HONAUNAU or PLACE OF REFUGE
You can get to this by going on the small road which runs south from Kealakekua for about four miles. If you are traveling south toward Volcano, take Route 16 from here back to Route 11. There are other Places of Refuge in Hawaii, but none as large or elaborate as this one. At the Visitor Center you can pick up a self-guiding leaflet which will explain what it is you are seeing. Once called "the City of Refuge," the name was changed by an act of Congress at the request of the Native Hawaiians to *PU'UHONUA O HONAUNAU*. The Visitors Center will also provide you with a short history of the area. If you like, you can have a picnic lunch here. We spent quite a while exploring the ceremonial areas and looking for the petroglyphs.

## FROM CAPTAIN COOK SOUTH

Once you leave Captain Cook, you will not see much civilization until the little town of Waiohinu some sixty miles south of Kailua. The stark, natural beauty of this area is unsurpassed anywhere we have travelled. Huge lava flows have in years past cascaded down the slopes of Mauna Loa to the ocean thousands of feet below. Unlike the slopes just behind Kailua Town, which are rich and verdant, here arid conditions keep some spots so bleak that at times one can imagine being on the moon. And yet in the middle of this seeming desert of lava, land developers ply their trade. Do people really look forward to building on these jagged lava stones? Already some homes have been built. As one wonders about homes built on earthquake faults, or along flooding river beds, one must wonder if Mauna Loa and goddess Pele are just dozing and will someday awaken to show man the folly of his ways.

As the road goes south along this coast line it passes through one of the largest macadamia nut plantations in Hawaii. Whatever this area looked like before the mac trees were planted, it is now a lush forest.

Just before the town of Waiohinu there is a sign on the right pointing the way to South Point, and if you want to be able to say you have travelled to the southern most part of the U.S., take this eleven mile drive that ends at sheer cliffs above the Pacific. This is a favorite fishing spot for the locals, so you are bound to see someone trying his luck. Just remember fishing is fishing and catching is catching. You may not see any fish.

In the town of Waiohinu you can sit under the Mark Twain Monkey Pod Tree, which he planted in 1866. This original tree, unfortunately, fell in high winds several years ago, and now a new "original" was planted; original, of course, because existentially it occupies the same space.

From Waiohinu to Volcano you pass through the southern edge of the Ka'u desert. Vegetation is sparse, with a sprinkling of sugar cane along the way. Unless you take the turnoff going mauka, you will pass the town of Pahala, a plantation colony where few tourists stop. We did stop here as we had heard of a Tibetan Monastery located somewhere in the area in a place called Wood Valley. Unfortunately, we were incorrectly informed that we needed a permit to drive that road. Evidently to get to the Monastery, you take the road that goes through Pahala to the right for about five miles. Beyond Pahala you will rise slowly to around 4,000 feet at Kilauea Volcano.

## RESTAURANTS

### LOCAL STYLE

#### GREEN SANDS
In the Shopping Center in Pahala. Eating here would give you a good excuse to drive into town. You will most likely be the only tourists, but don't let that stop you since the locals are friendly, prices are low, and the food is good local fare.

---

### local/Tourist Style

#### OCEAN VIEW RESTAURANT
Somewhere near the seventy-five (75) mile marker on the mauka side of the road, you will come to this restaurant and a real estate office, so stop by and have lunch or buy a lot. They are open for breakfast, lunch, and dinner. It is the kind of place one might expect, at least on the Mainland, to see huge semis parked helter skelter along the side of the road. We have heard that the food is not bad, and the prices are not high.

#### NAALEHU COFFEE SHOP
When you reach Naalehu, the southern most town in the U.S., drive into the shopping center and you cannot miss seeing the Coffee Shop. We were told by the owner that the place has been there for forty years. If you are starved and can wait no longer, feast on the papaya fruit salad and banana bread. The prices are low.

#### SEA MOUNTAIN GOLF COURSE DINING ROOM
At Sea Mt. Golf Course, this little restaurant is open for lunch and dinner and makes a nice place to stop when driving the southern route from Hilo to Kona.

## PLACES OF INTEREST

### MILOLII
Around thirty-three miles south of Kailua there is a road going makai to a fishing village that is well worth the five mile detour it takes to get there.

### MANUKA STATE PARK
This botanical park has great ocean views and makes an excellent picnic spot on the way to Volcano. It is located about forty-one miles south of Kailua.

### SOUTH POINT
(see above)

## NIGHT LIFE

Movies are shown at the Southern Star Theater in the little town of Naalehu. For more information, call 929-9011.

## SPORTS

### TENNIS
On the extreme south end of the Big Island there are two public tennis court sites, both lighted; 1) Naalehu Park, 2) Pahala School Grounds.

### GOLF
Sea Mountain Golf Course is located at the southern tip of Hawaii, near Pahala. The fee is $22, and $9 for the cart on a share basis. The setting is beautiful and the wind is a very big factor here. During the off season they run some very good specials. For more information call 928-6222. If you want to play golf in the southern most point in the United States, play Discovery Harbor, located five miles from Naalehu. This is a development that looks as if it went sour. There are a few homes in the area, plenty of streets and cul-de-sacs, but not much else. Oh yes, there is a golf course and even a club house. The club house was closed when we were there and except for a fellow hitting balls from what used to be a driving range, we saw little evidence of golf. The green fee is $5, $10 for a cart. We would suggest that you call first. For more information call 929-7353. Going here reminded us of the time we followed a guide book to a course in Canada just outside of Hope, B.C. When we got there all we found was a cow pasture. All of those we talked to along the way for directions must have thought us foolish indeed.

*Chapter VI.................................................................OAHU*

# OAHU.....THE GATHERING PLACE

.....DRIVING TIMES.....

From Honolulu airport to: (approximate)

```
Downtown Honolulu...................  5 miles, 15 minutes
University of Hawaii................ 10 miles, 30 minutes
Waikiki............................. 11 miles, 30 minutes
Aloha Stadium.......................  3 miles, 10 minutes
Hanauma Bay......................... 20 miles, 45 minutes
Sea Life Park....................... 24 miles, 50 minutes
Pearl City.......................... 10 miles, 30 minutes
Kailua.............................. 20 miles, 40 minutes
Kaneohe............................. 18 miles, 36 minutes
```

*Bed & Breakfast Guide*

# OAHU

To many people, both those who have been to the Islands and those who have not, Oahu is synonymous with Hawaii. In fact, Oahu is thought of as Honolulu and to narrow it down even further, many people equate Waikiki with Honolulu. In reality Honolulu is much more than Waikiki and Oahu is much more than Honolulu, and the State of Hawaii is more than these put together. Yet, around 80 percent of Hawaii's population live and work in Honolulu. Also, Waikiki gets more visitors by far than any other place in Hawaii. The effect is that many people who have vacationed at Waikiki think they have seen Hawaii and nothing could be further from the truth.

The real meaning of *oahu* has been lost to antiquity. Tourist industry people like to say it means the *Gathering Place*, and for a long time that appellation has been used. Residents of Hawaii refer to it as the *Main Island* since everything and most everyone passes through Honolulu. It is also called the *Capitol Island* since it is the seat of all State Government.

Oahu, the third largest island in the chain behind Hawaii and Maui, is made up of two fair sized mountain ranges: the Koolau Mountains in the east, and the Waianae Mountains in the west. In between is a broad expanse of flatland devoted either to the military or to farmland. Honolulu, the dominant city in Hawaii, sits just in the lee of the Koolau Range.

Unfortunately, when most people think of Oahu they think only of Honolulu and Waikiki and fail to realize that Oahu has as much natural beauty as any of the neighbor Islands. Few drives in Hawaii are more scenic than the drive east of Honolulu, past Hanauma Bay, around the point past Sandy Beach and then a few short miles on to Waimanalo. Nor can the north shore of Oahu be rivaled for its expansive beaches, where in the winter waves twenty feet and bigger crash with unimaginable fury. When this surf is at its highest, even the greatest surfers back off.

By no means do we intend to suggest that Honolulu and Waikiki are places for tourists to bypass. While we have heard the claim that Honolulu is just like any city except warmer, there are enough differences to make a visit here unique. We simply want to urge people who have heard the bad rap (that Oahu is too crowded, just a big city, a tourist rip off) to realize that there is much to do and see besides the Honolulu/Waikiki scene. Do yourself a favor and explore the rest of the Island and we feel sure you will be pleasantly surprised.

## HONOLULU

Located on the south shore of the Island of Oahu, protected by one of the Island's two mountain ranges, the Koolaus, with the Waianaes far to the west, the city of Honolulu contains more people, stores, restaurants and whatever else is needed to make a city than all of the rest of Hawaii combined. If the population of the state nears one million, seventy to eighty percent reside in Honolulu. It is a large city and has the attendant problems that all large cities have: overcrowding, heavy traffic, crime, and even some smog, but not much. Even with these detractions Honolulu is a pleasant place, easy to get around either by car or public transportation, a city that is unique in many ways.

For anyone with an interest in the history of Hawaii, time spent visiting historical sites in Honolulu is invaluable. Then, Honolulu's Chinatown is small but certainly worth seeing. Even in this bustling city, however, nature's beauty is close by. Just a few short blocks from Chinatown is the Foster Botanical Garden (see Points of Interest below) where tourists can see most of the flora of Hawaii and other tropical climes.

For our purposes we have divided the city into four areas: 1) downtown, 2) Waikiki, 3) Kaimuki/Kapahulu, 4) east of Honolulu. For each area as for other areas throughout the Islands, we will list first our host homes, then restaurants, points of interest, beaches, night life, and sports activities. We do not cover all restaurants in Honolulu by any means but have chosen some that both we and our hosts have enjoyed. Since we intend updating this guide every year, we invite your comments and suggestions.

## DOWNTOWN

Finding downtown Honolulu can be confusing since the Ala Moana Shopping Center is where you will find most of the major stores, and Waikiki is where you will see most of the tall buildings. The downtown area is just a few blocks from Chinatown with the main streets being King and Beretania. It is in this area that one will find the Iolani Palace, the Court House, the King Kamehameha statue, the State Capitol, the Mission Houses Museum, the Academy of Arts, and most of the financial institutions of Hawaii. This area is small and it is best to park in one of the garages and tour the area on foot. Parking can be found at Alakea and Hotel Street, right in the center of things, for $1.00 a day.

As stated above, most of the department stores and shops are in Ala Moana Center but one good place to shop is in the Liberty Penthouse at the corner of King Street and Bishop. While there are lots of bargains, you need to look to find them. There is also a Liberty Penthouse discount department on the top floor of Liberty House in Kailua. If you are looking specifically for a muu muu, watch for Muu Muu Factory and Especially For You, as these stores present some attractive prices.

*Bed & Breakfast Guide*

## HOSTS

### O-6A
This home, located half way up Pacific Heights Drive with a great view of Honolulu and the south coast of Oahu, offers several possibilities for the B & B traveler. First, there is downstairs full apartment complete with kitchen, three bedrooms, one with queen sized bed and a private bath, one with one twin bed, and one with a sofa bed. There is a bath between these two bedrooms. This downstairs apartment could be rented by a family or by several couples traveling together and then guests would have the use of the kitchen facilities. Or any one of the three rooms could be used. There is also a room available in the main home upstairs with twin beds and a private bath. This home is close enough to downtown Honolulu to make exploring this area easy. One of the things that Lorraine, the hostess, wants to point out is that there are quite a few stairs to climb to get to the home. Breakfast is served in the main house.
RATE: $45 queen bed and bath, $35 twin and bath.

### O-10A
This is a perfect location for anyone visiting the University Of Hawaii, Manoa Campus, since this is in the Manoa area, about one mile from the University. Of course, that also makes it a perfect location for anyone who wants to be fairly close to the Honolulu area. The bus stops just at the bottom of the driveway so guests who did not wish to rent a car, could get around fairly easily from this location. The accommodation offered is a room with a double bed with a private bath adjoining. The home is surrounded by a beautiful tropical garden that guests are encouraged to enjoy.
  Maggie, the hostess, who is an artist and designer, is a long time resident of Honolulu and can be very helpful in pointing out the spots that should not be missed.
RATE: $35 one rate.

### O-21
Above Honolulu, in the Tantalus area, about five miles from the center of town, we call this our *In Town Hideaway*. This lovely home has much to offer: stone fireplace with plenty of wood to keep it going, a beautiful lanai with comfortable outdoor furniture, a carefully planned botanical garden, with hiking trails nearby. The accommodations here could handle a party of three traveling together since there is a small bedroom with a single bed and a loft area that has a queen sized bed. One of our guests made the comment that this was the most beautiful spot he had ever experienced.
  Joline, the hostess, has lived in Hawaii for almost twenty years and has lived before in the Philippines, Germany, and Scotland. Her main interest is her art, working extensively with stained glass and wood sculpture in her studio which is attached to her home. She also loves traveling and hiking anywhere, including Hawaii. She loves animals and has both a dog and a cat.
RATE: $46 double or single, $10 for extra person, $286 a week, two night minimum.

## O-27

Armanita's B & B is located in beautiful Manoa Valley, a quiet, old residential area about one mile from the University of Hawaii. Their two story, four bedroom home is about sixty years old and has a panoramic view of the mountains, Diamond Head, the Waikiki skyline, and the ocean. Two rooms are offered. One, formerly daughter Lisa's room, has a queen sized bed, with the bath just across the hall. The other, formerly son David's, has twin beds. Breakfast is usually served on the deck so that guests can enjoy the view. Arman is a structural engineer whose hobbies include photography and cooking. He speaks fluent French, Spanish, Armenian, and Turkish. Anita is a clinical social worker in private practice, a lecturer at the University of Hawaii, and an avid folk dancer and accordionist. They are both non-smokers and ask that smoking be done outside on the porch or deck. They hope you are not allergic to cats since they have two, Mitzie and Morris.

RATE: $33 single, $44 double, $264 a week. Children over 6.

## O-30

This large family home, located in Manoa Valley just behind the University of Hawaii, could accommodate a party of three since the accommodation offered is one room with a double bed and one room with a single bed with bathroom between the rooms for the guests use. The home has a large living room, and a family room with T.V. which the guests are welcome to watch. The home has a good view of Manoa Valley and Honolulu. Breakfast is served on the front patio in a quiet area.

Karen and John, the hosts, are very well informed about what is happening on Oahu and love sharing that knowledge with their guests. Karen plays cello in the Hawaiian Symphony Orchestra and also teaches violin and cello. John is the news editor for the *Honolulu Advertiser*. Both are interested in civic and cultural events.

RATE: $27.50 single, $38.50 double.

## DOWNTOWN RESTAURANTS

**LOCAL STYLE**

**MABUHAY CAFE**
186 North Hotel Street. We suggest you do not judge from the outside and give this a try. Inside it is very cute, and the food is delicious and very inexpensive. If you have ever wanted to try Filipino food, this is the place.

**PIER 8 CHINESE**
Located at Pier 8 under the Aloha Tower. This is LOCAL food to da max. Eat here if you like this style, want to save money, and do not mind getting a few quizzical looks.

---
**local Style**

**WO FAT LTD.**
Located in the heart of Chinatown at 115 North Hotel Street. Be sure to visit here even if you choose to eat elsewhere. No Chinese restaurant outside of Hong Kong offers a wider variety to choose from. They must be doing something right since they have been serving meals for close to a century. Prices are moderate and the food is good, 537-6260.

**SEA FORTUNE**
Located in Chinatown at 111 North King Street. We had lunch here and feel we could not have picked a better spot. The food is Cantonese style and, at least on the day we were there, the patrons were all Oriental. If you like Dim Sum, the little stuffed buns, this is the place to go. The waitress passes through with trays and you take what you like. Each serving cost $1.20 and you are charged by how many steamer trays are on your table. They also have an extensive menu. Be careful with the Dim Sum as it is easy not only to over eat but to over spend, 536-3822.

**KING TSIN**
Even though this is one of our favorite Chinese restaurants in Honolulu, in our first edition we somehow managed to get the address wrong. No matter, for this year they are at a new location, on Mc Cully, one block mauka of King St. They are open for dinner only and close at 9:30 or a bit before. If you are not familiar with how hot this food can be, ask for dishes that are not so spicy. Try, for example, the Moo Shu Pork, 946-3273.

**MEKONG**
There are two of these, the original at 1295 South Beretania, and a second one at 1726 South King Street. Either one serves excellent Thai food at reasonable prices, 521-2025 or 941-6184.

---

**local/Tourist Style**

### SEPARATE TABLES
Located on the west side of Nuuanu St. between King and Hotel St. They could not show us a menu since there is a different lunch special every day. The prices are not low but we have been told that the food is excellent. This seems to be a big favorite with the local business people.

### JAKES
Located at 1126 Bishop Street. This is another favorite with those who work in the area and the food is just like you would find in any Mainland city. They are open from 6 a.m. until 9 p.m. Lunch prices are around $5.00 while dinner prices range between $6.00 and $9.00, 524-4616.

### AUNTIE PASTO'S
Located at 1099 So. Beretania. They are open for lunch and dinner, Italian cuisine and, at least for lunch, the prices are not high (Breast of Chicken Cacciatore $5.50), and several specials from $4.50 to $5.50. When Frank Sinatra brought his band over for the show that A.T. & T. put on at Aloha Stadium, Auntie Pasto's catered their dinner. They all seemed to like it. 523-8855.

### GREEK ISLAND TAVERNA
Located at 2570 South Beretania St. and open for dinner from 5:30 to 11 nightly. Dinners are in the $8 to $12 range and feature such things as Kotopoulo Krasato (chicken sauteed in wine sauce-$10.25) and Kolokithakia Yemista (baby zucchini stuffed with ground beef, rice and topped with a egg and lemon sauce. This can really be a fun place to go as there is also belly dancing, 943-0052.

### CASTIGNOLA'S
This is not really downtown but actually in the Manoa area and is not often found by tourists. Some of our hosts felt we should leave it that way since it is often hard to get in here. To find, take University Ave. mauka and go until you come to Manoa, turn right and go about 1/2 mile to the shopping center. Turn right into the shopping center, past the market, turn right again and you will drive straight ahead to the restaurant. We had a very good dinner here, but we did have to wait about 1/2 hour even though we had a reservation,988-2969.

### WAIOLI TEA HOUSE
To find this continue up University Ave. past Manoa and you will see it on the left. We have not yet tried this but we have heard good things about it. We will try it the next time we are in Honolulu, 988-2131.

### JAMESON'S
This is the original Jameson's but it is now in different hands. At the present time it is open for lunch only and seems to be one of the favorites of the people who work in that area. it is located on Merchant St. which is one block makai of King. Lunch runs around $6 to $8, 531-0422.

### ROYAL HAWAIIAN TAVERN
You can get a Luau meal here but it will cost twice as much as the Ono Cafe on Kapahulu St. Of course the atmosphere is a bit fancier and you may have an easier time understanding the waiter. You can also get other dishes more familiar, Crab Louie $8.50, Ham and Cheese sandwich $5.95. They are open for lunch only. Located at 2 Merchant St.

### CAFE BON BON
Located at 200 Merchant St. This seems to have taken the place of the defunct Downtown Deli. There are lots of local dishes to choose from, counter style.

### CROISSANTERIE
At 210 Merchant St. This is a large deli that has an excellent selection of sandwiches and pastries at reasonable prices where you eat in a nice setting.

### CUNHA'S SHOPPING ARCADE
This arcade runs between King and Merchant St. in the 100 block. There are several little places to eat. The one that looked and smelled the best to us was Heidi's, located on the Merchant St. end.

### WARD WAREHOUSE
This is located one block mauka of the Nimitz Freeway just east of Ward Ave. There are several places to eat in this center, all fairly modest in price. Our favorite is the Upstart Crow, a bookstore/restaurant combination. There is also the Old Spaghetti Factory, the Chowder House, and Orsons, where prices range from $8 to $20. While this is patronized very much by local residents, the restaurants and shops are geared to tourists.

### WARD CENTER
This is located just a few blocks east of Ward Warehouse and is a much more luxurious Center. Both the shops and the restaurants bring higher prices. We would recommend any restaurant in this center as a good splurge spot, but not the place to get an inexpensive light meal.

## POINTS OF INTEREST

### CHINATOWN
This is one of the oldest sections of Honolulu and one of the most interesting. Located at the start of South King Street, it only goes for about three short blocks. One block mauka is Hotel Street, which has several Chinese stores and restaurants but is much more famous for its night life, for this is where the Ladies of the Evening ply their trade, at least when they are not working the Waikiki area. Chinatown has long been an area for those struggling to achieve the American Dream, and lately there seem to be many Vietnamese setting up shop. The huge market located in the first block of King, where many independent butchers and greengrocers sell their wares is by no means all Chinese.

At least half the shops are owned by Japanese. While many Mainland cities have larger Chinatowns, few are more interesting, for Honolulu's Chinatown is not geared for the tourist but simply an area where people live and work and where people from all over the Island come to shop and dine.

## ALOHA TOWER
Located at the Port of Honolulu, at the foot of Fort Street across the Nimitz Highway. You can see the tower from most of the downtown area. Take the elevator located at the rear of the Port Reception area to the tenth floor viewing platform and get an excellent view of Honolulu, Pearl Harbor, and the entire south coast of Oahu. On Saturday, you will get a good view of the cruise ships that travel inter-island. There is a small maritime museum located on the eighth floor of the tower.

## FALLS OF CLYDE
Located at Pier 5 just east of the Aloha Tower, this Museum Ship was damaged by Iwa, the 1982 hurricane, but has been repaired and is now open to the public. The fee is $3.00 for adults, $1.00 for children.

## IOLANI PALACE
Open Wednesday, Thursday, Friday, and Saturday. The admission charge is $4.00 for adults and $1.00 for children.

## ACADEMY OF ARTS
Located at 900 Beretania Street. This Art Museum need not take a back seat to many museums in the world. There is no admission charge but donations are accepted and a receptacle is provided. If one has an interest in Asian Art, stopping here is a must. Since the gallery has a small restaurant, which features home made soup and sandwiches with seating at 11:30 a.m. and 1:30 p.m., it is possible to spend all day here. On Thursday evenings, except during the summer, a light supper is served. It is best to make reservations for either lunch or dinner. Call 531-8865.

## MISSION HOUSE MUSEUM
Open every day from 9 a.m. until 4 p.m. $3.00 for adults and $1.00 for children.

## FARMERS MARKET
Selling occurs here only once a week, on Mondays from 10:00 a.m. until 11:15 a.m. Most of the fruits and vegetables sold here are much lower priced than in the stores. It is an interesting sight with lots of local color.

## BISHOP MUSEUM
Located at 1525 Bernice Street. To get there, take the Likelike Highway off H-1 and immediately watch for Bernice on your right. Turn right and go about 1/2 block and you will come to the entrance on your right. The fee is $4.75 for adults and $2.00 for children. We feel that it is well worth the price; it tells an interesting story of Polynesian culture.

## FOSTER BOTANICAL GARDEN
Located at 180 North Vineyard Boulevard. This is a perfect downtown location for a picnic. The admission fee is $1.00 and that also admits you to the zoo. You will see trees here that as far as we know exist nowhere else in Hawaii. The strangest to us was the Cannon Ball Tree with the Sausage Tree a close runner up.

## PUNCHBOWL
This National Memorial Cemetery of the Pacific is open from 8 a.m. to 5 p.m. In this extinct volcano, called by the ancient Hawaiians *the Hill of Sacrifice*, over 20,000 servicemen are buried. To get there take Punchbowl Avenue where it crosses King in the downtown area and go mauka. After you go under the freeway, watch for the signs to Punchbowl Memorial. When you see Puowaina Street, take that right into the crater. From the lookout at the top of the crater there is a magnificent view of the greater Honolulu area.

## PUU UALAKAA PARK
Located about half way up Round Hill Drive, the first part of Tantalas. This is a good spot to picnic and to get a great view of the south side of Oahu. The day we visited, they were filming *Magnum P.I.* so our view was obstructed by Tom Selleck.

## TANTALAS
This drive, starting and ending in the heart of Honolulu, is dramatic, as it goes through what is essentially a tropical rain forest. Just a few miles beyond the noise and traffic of town, one reaches an area as peaceful as can be found in the Islands. This is an excellent drive to beat the heat on a hot summer day as it is always cooler on Tantalas. If you are interested in hiking, there are some good trails in this area.

## QUEEN EMMA'S SUMMER PALACE
Open Monday through Friday from 9 a.m. until 4 p.m. and on Saturday from 9 a.m. until noon.

## SPORTS

### GOLF

There are around fifteen courses on Oahu that are open to the public, and for retired military persons, there are another nine courses. There are five private country clubs where one can play as a guest of a member. Many people who stay at the Kahala Hilton are surprised and disappointed when they learn that the Waialae Country Club, home of the Hawaiian Open, which is played every February, is private and unavailable to tourists. In the Honolulu area courses are crowded, and it is a good idea to call ahead for a starting time. The best bet for play is in the rural areas, Makaha Valley Country Club, for example. Do not listen to those who tell you that one must plan to spend close to $50 to play golf in Hawaii. Even the semi-private courses are often somewhere between $18.00 and $30.00 including a cart. For more information on specific courses, check under sports in the section desired. For complete information on courses in Hawaii we refer you to *Hawaii's Golf Guide*, which sells for around $4.00. To obtain a copy write to Golf Association, 575 Cooke Street, Honolulu, Hawaii 96813.

### TENNIS

Oahu has many public tennis courts, both in Honolulu and around the Island, in fact there are about forty different locations with a total of 154 courts, half of these are lighted for night play. For a complete list of these courts, send a stamped self addressed envelope to the Department of Parks and Recreation, 650 South King Street, Honolulu, Hawaii 96813. We will include most locations under the specific areas.

In Honolulu there is Ala Moana Park, 1201 Ala Moana Boulevard. They have ten courts, lighted. For more information call Max Neves, 521-7664. Also, there is Keehi Lagoon Courts, located at 465 Lagoon Drive, which is makai of the Nimitz Highway, west of Downtown. Here there are twelve courts, but none lighted. Call 521-7664.

*Bed & Breakfast Guide*

## WAIKIKI

It is only an area of a few square miles between the blue Pacific and the Ala Wai Canal, but it has a world wide reputation, and while sometimes a tarnished one, people come from all over to be there, summer, winter, spring, and fall. You rarely hear anyone say he likes Waikiki, as if to admit it somehow makes one suspect. And yet, no place in Hawaii packs them in like Waikiki. At the peak of the tourist season, January through March, one must arrive early to insure a good spot on the beach, which is not large by any means. All day and half the night, people parade up and down Kalakaua Avenue, some dressed in outfits that defy description.

As one might expect in a tourist spot like this, just about any kind of action can be found. During the day card and chess players dominate the scene at the tables along Waikiki Beach. Just at dusk, people line the beach and the street to catch a last glimpse of the sun as it drops into the sea. Later, people walk along Kalakaua Avenue shopping, looking for that special place to eat, or watching and being watched.

There are pluses and minuses to all this activity. To some it is exciting and colorful, not quite like anything they have ever seen. To others it stands for blight and they talk about it with scorn. Perhaps because our life on Kauai is so peaceful, we kind of like Waikiki, for the brief time we are there. Everybody should see it, if only once. What is unfortunate in our view is that too many people think Waikiki, and for that matter Lahaina and Kaanapali on Maui, is Hawaii.

The beautiful thing about Hawaii is that it is like its people, variegated and multicolored, and all of it has its own special quality. Many people think Waikiki is nothing more than a tourist trap, but, because of the fierce competition of the place, great buys can be found if you know what to look for. In that way it is a bit like Mexico; some great buys, but, boy can you get taken. Even the restaurants run the gamut. One of the most expensive, and in our minds one of the best, is the Third Floor of the Hawaii Regent Hotel, coat and tie required. Then there is the Salad Bowl at 421 Nahua Street, which has plate lunches for as high as $2.50, and a plain hamburger for $.50, or their special breakfast for $.99, which consists of two eggs, two sausages, and two pieces of toast or rice. There are so many restaurants that we could not cover them all in our book, nor, as far as we know, does anyone else.

## HOSTS

### O-3B
It is just one and a half blocks to Waikiki beach from this studio condominium located on the 16th floor, where guests enjoy views of Diamond head and Kapiolani Park as well as the blue Pacific. Since the owner of this condo lives east of Honolulu where she does B & B, this is actually a "no host" B & B, ie., no breakfast is served. We offer it to B & B members at a rate far lower than the established rate of the other units in this project. While the studio is not spacious, it could accommodate a small family, since there is a queen sized sofa bed and a corner unit of twin beds. The unit is air-conditioned and guests have the use of the pool and spa as well as a viewing deck located on the top floor.
RATE: $50 a night, $10 for third person (children 12 and over only), $1000 a month.

### O-22
This sprawling two story family residence houses Joanne, the hostess, her two dogs, and sometimes her five adult children who come and go but no longer live there. Even when some of them are "at home", there is still room for B & B guests, since there are three bedrooms, each with a private bath, in the main house, and a spacious bedroom just off the garden with a sitting area and a private bath. All of the rooms have their own lanai with either a garden view or a view of Diamond Head. Each bedroom is decorated with elegant antiques.
Joanne, a practicing artist, is a long time Honolulu resident who is active in what is happening in the arts. Presently she is a Commissioner for the State Foundation on Culture and the Arts, and she is also a trustee for the Academy of Arts. Her home is an expression of these interests. Joanne was raised in Oregon, but she has been in Hawaii so long she is Kamaaina. Keeping up with a large home while staying as active as she does is not an easy task, and, Joanne assures us, it would be more difficult if she did not have faith in the Lord.
RATE: $75 one rate.

### O-35
This friendly, airy home is near Diamond Head and everything in the Waikiki area since is as at the foot of Kapahulu St. The accommodation offered is a bedroom with a queen sized bed and T.V., and a bath that is for quests use only. There is a washer and dryer available for guests use and also a VCR and movies.
Caroline, the hostess, is a travel agent, an importer from Europe and Asia, a designer, specializing in masks created out of a variety of substances. She also designs costumes, clothing and other items. Also part of the household is her white part Persian cat, Bianca. Caroline loves sailing, diving, snorkeling, and gourmet food. She would be happy to arrange tours or gourmet meals if guests so desire.
RATE: $40 single or double, $50 Dec. 15 through April 15.

## RESTAURANTS

As we say above, there are too many restaurants in Waikiki to mention them all. For example, the Royal Hawaiian Shopping Center on the makai side of Kalakaua Avenue has over ten restaurants and about ten other places where you can get a snack. The International Market Place has many little restaurants and fast food stands. Kalakaua Avenue is lined with places to eat. This intense competition, especially during the "off season" drives down prices. We recently saw a special at Don The Beachcomber for an all you could eat spaghetti buffet for $3.95. Considering that this is some of the highest priced real estate in the world, such prices are rather surprising. What we have attempted to do is pick out a few that either we or our hosts have tried and liked.

### LOCAL STYLE

#### MONGOLIAN BAR-B-Q
At the rear of the International Market Place, it can best be found by entering from Kuhio Street and going to the right. This is the same as the one in Chinatown at the Cultural Center. We tried it and must admit that you get filled up for a low price but some people would find the taste a little strange. Try it if you feel adventurous.

-------------------------------------------------------------------

### local/Tourist Style

#### THE SALAD BOWL
At 421 Nahua Street and open 24 hours a day. Since nothing in the place is over $2.50, it would be hard to beat the prices.

#### MINUTE CHEF
On Kalakaua Avenue just west of the Hyatt Regency. Prices are reasonable and they give a 20 percent discount to senior citizens.

#### DON THE BEACHCOMBER
In the center of Waikiki on Kalakua Ave. As well as what we mention above, they have an early bird special of prime rib for $7.95.

#### MAIKO/JAPANESE STEAKHOUSE
On Koa Avenue right behind the Hyatt. You can get Japanese food here but you can also get food for western tastes. The setting is very nice and the prices are reasonable.

#### THE PATISSERIE
On the mauka side of Kuhio Street just behind the International Marketplace. If all you want is a sandwich or the makings of a sandwich for a picnic on the beach, this is a pretty good spot. We purchased some roast beef which was as good as any we have ever had, well seasoned and nice and rare.

#### TOP OF WAIKIKI
On Kalakaua Avenue, this revolving restaurant is good value for lunch for around $6.00 - $7.00. Dinner prices are in the $10.00 to $20.00 range.

#### FISH MARKET RESTAURANT
On the corner of Kuhio and Seaside, reasonable prices for fresh fish and other seafood.

**\*RUDY'S\***
On Kuhio at Nohonani. This is a very good Italian restaurant where you will get more than you can eat and the prices are not too high. They have an early bird special of a lasagna dinner for two for $11.95. There regular dinners run between $10 & $14.

**WAILANA COFFEE HOUSE**
On Kuhio at Lewis St. This is always open and the food is very low priced.

------------------------------------------------------------------

**SPECIAL OCCASION**

**THIRD FLOOR**
On the third floor of the Hawaiian Regent Hotel, located on the corner of Kalakaua and Oahu Street. We had one of the best meals here that we have had in Hawaii. It is expensive, and there is a dress code, ie., jacket at least, and they like it if a tie is worn, but that may not be insisted upon.

## POINTS OF INTEREST

**KAPIOLANI PARK**
This park at the east end of Waikiki offers much to visitors and residents alike. Not only does it contain excellent picnic areas, jogging trails, tennis courts, but also a Rose Garden, the Waikiki Aquarium, and the Honolulu Zoo, for which there is a small charge.

**ALAWAI CANAL**
There are often canoe races along the Alawai Canal that are fun to watch, but if not actual races, there is much practice that goes on here.

**DIAMOND HEAD**
When the first Caucasian sailors saw this crater, they mistook the volcanic crystals for diamonds, hence the name. To get into the crater, take Diamond Head Road and proceed through the tunnel to the parking area. From here you can hike to the rim of the crater, which is over 700 feet above sea level and affords some great views.

## BEACHES

**WAIKIKI**
Directions are not needed. Somehow we think you will find this. If you intend to have a spot to sit, get there early for after a while it is hard to put a towel down. The swimming is great, and people watching the best.

**KAPIOLANI BEACH PARK**
Right on Kapiolani Boulevard at the east end of Waikiki. This beach has all the facilities including a defunct Natatorium, the world's largest salt water swimming pool.

### ALA MOANA BEACH PARK
All the facilities are here and this park gets much use from locals and visitors. It is located at the west end of Waikiki, across from the Ala Moana Shopping Center.

## NIGHT LIFE

There is so much going on in this area that there is no need for us to point out any specifics. There are several different theaters, and at the hotels entertainers of world wide reputation appear. We find it interesting to just stroll through the various shopping malls, where one can often see local performers for free.

## SPORTS

### GOLF
### ALA WAI GOLF COURSE
The entrance to this course is on Kapahulu Avenue. This public course, as you can well imagine, gets an intense amount of play. The fee is $8.00 weekdays, $12.00 weekends. Carts are available for $10.00 but they are not required. Since the course is flat, a hand cart should suffice unless the temperature is up. For more information call 732-7741.

### TENNIS
Diamond Head Tennis Center at 3908 Paki Avenue has ten courts, not lighted. To find simply walk to the Diamond Head Side of Kapiolani Regional Park. Call Don Andrews, 923-7927.

*OAHU*

## KAIMUKI/KAPAHULU

    This area is mauka and east of Waikiki Beach and for our purposes Kaimuki is along Waialae Avenue between where Waialae starts at the end of King Street and then east to 15th Avenue. Kapahulu runs from King St. all the way down to the east side of Waikiki. Unlike most of Oahu, which seems to be an endless string of shopping centers, from big, bigger, and biggest to new, newer, and newest, these are more neighborhood areas of little shops and restaurants, beauty salons, neighborhood bars, and service stations. For those of us who grew up before the days of the shopping center, areas such as this are refreshing. Without a doubt, the mammoth centers are more practical but just a little short on personality. If you agree, explore Waialae Ave. and Kapahulu St. as we did and we know you will not be disappointed. One little shop to be sure to check out is the Varsity Club Thrift Shop located on the corner of 12th and Waialae. All of the proceeds from this shop go to the Varsity School for the learning disabled. Not only can one make a good buy, the money goes for a good cause.

    Also, we realize that the restaurants mentioned are not all of the restaurants in this area. Perhaps you will try one of the ones we fail to mention and will want to tell us about it for our next edition. If so, we will mention it on your recommendation and will try it the next time we are in Honolulu.

*Bed & Breakfast Guide*

## HOSTS

### O-2
This one bedroom apartment is completely separate from the main house, affording the guests plenty of privacy. The location is ideal for those who want to be close to most things in Honolulu, and it is a convenient location for starting a drive east of Honolulu. Plate glass windows allow the guests to enjoy the view of the Waikiki skyline and the ocean beyond. The unit has its own patio and barbecue for guests. Since it has minimal kitchen appliances, cooking light meals is possible. It is right on the bus line yet enough off the main drag to afford quiet. The unit can accommodate four as there is a king sized bed and a double sofa bed. Kurt and Margaret came to Hawaii from Switzerland about thirteen years ago, and now Kurt works for a world class hotel as a Master Chef. He is often called upon to be present when a new hotel is opened to make sure everything is perfect. In the meantime Margaret devotes herself to making sure her guests needs are met.
RATE: $35 one rate, two night minimum, no children.

### O-2A
Also hosted by Kurt and Margaret, this accommodation is a room in the main home with a separate entrance, a private bath, and twin beds. Breakfast is served on the lanai. The room is equipped with T.V., coffee maker, refrigerator, and a few utensils.
RATE: $30 one rate, two night minimum, no children.

### O-14
This charming older home is located in Wilhelmina Rise, almost to the top of the mountain in a well established residential area and has an unobstructed view of Diamond Head and the Waikiki skyline. The home has been newly redecorated. The accommodation offered is located on the lower level of the home, affording much privacy. The guest room has twin beds and a private bath. Breakfast is served in the dining alcove surrounded by large bay windows.
George and Paula, the hosts, are from Boston and New York and have been in Hawaii for over twenty years. Now they are semi-retired, but the great love of their life, folk dancing, keeps them busy. Not only do they teach folk dancing at the University part time, they choreograph new folk dance performances. Their home is on the bus line and the bus goes by once an hour but no later than 10 p.m.
RATE: $33.00 single, $38.50 double, two night minimum.

## WAIALAE RESTAURANTS

### LOCAL STYLE

**KAL BI**
Located on a little alley makai of Waialae Avenue off 12th Avenue. Low prices and the food is tasty if you like the style.

---

### local style

**DUK KEE**
On 12th Avenue makai of Waialae. Szechuan style, very reasonably priced, with a nice decor.

**CAFE SIAM**
At 3365 Waialae Ave. For the most part this is Thai food with a few of the spicier Chinese dishes also available. They are open for lunch from 11-2 and for dinner from 5:30-10. The food can be very hot but if you ask them they will tone it down and then the food is nothing but very tasty. There are places with a lot more reputation but we doubt if the food is any better or as low priced. They do not serve liquor so we assume you are welcome to bring beer or wine.

**AZTECA**
Just a few doors from Cafe Siam, the standard Mexican fare priced in the $6 to $9 range as well as some interesting house specialties in about the same range. A La carte is much less, $3 to $5.

**THAI HUT**
At 3196 Waialae Avenue on the mauka side of the street. Small but very cute, good Thai food in a casual atmosphere and the prices are low, 732-2978.

**KING'S GARDEN RESTAURANT**
Located on the makai side of Waialae at about 10th. Cantonese style, the prices are not as low as they might be, but the decor is nice and our hosts tell us the food is very good, 732-0724.

**KAIMUKI CHOP SUEY**
At 3454 Waialae Avenue. Cantonese style and not much to look at from the outside but clean on the inside and inexpensive.

**KAIMUKI INN**
At 3575 Waialae Avenue. All kinds of food here-American, Oriental, or a combination of both. This is a good chow-down place for the budget minded. They have a very funky little salad bar and sometimes they have a buffet lunch with a limited selection and a low low price, 737-5785.

---

### local/Tourist Style

**POTTERY STEAK HOUSE**
At 3574 Waialae Avenue. Open daily from 5:30 p.m. until 10:00 p.m., they specialize in beef, lobster and cornish game hens. Most entrees, which are cooked in a clay pot the diner can keep, run slightly over $10.00, 735-5594.

**CHE PASTA**
This is a very chic restaurant for the neighborhood, very big city in concept and execution. The prices are not low, nor are they out of line. The only thing that makes it a bit expensive is that everything is a la carte. For salad, pasta, and an entree, the bill would run well over $20.00 a person. One could get by, however, on the pasta for under $10.00. We have heard nothing but raves about it. Unfortunately we were on a diet the last time we were in Honolulu and could only enjoy the aroma. Almost all of our hosts give this a big boost and this place is building its reputation, 735-1777.

**INDIA HOUSE**
Not right in Kaimuki but close at 2632 South King Street just east of University Avenue on the mauka side of the street. We love Indian food, hence this is one of our favorite restaurants in Honolulu. We include it only for those who are of like mind. It is not inexpensive; dinners run around $15.00. One good thing is that you are welcome to bring your own wine; corkage is not charged. You can specify how you like your food, ie., mild, hot, or very hot. Unless you really like it hot, better say mild. The last time we were there we had Chicken Vindaloo, the hottest thing we have ever eaten, 955-7552.

**PHIL PAOLIS**
This is not exactly in the Kaimuki district either, but close, located at 2312 So. Beretania where Sherrie's White Flower Inn used to be. We visited here and checked the menu because we were told by several hosts that it was excellent. The decor is nice and the menu is interesting, Italian for the most part. Most of the entrees were over $10.

## KAPAHULU RESTAURANTS

This street is building a reputation as a restaurant center and in fact has several places that are a big favorite with the local folks. The nice thing is that they are not all fancy and expensive. On the contrary, the funkiest little places on Oahu are on this street. If all you have is a sweet tooth, try Candy Land at 750 Kapahulu.

### LOCAL STYLE

**ONO HAWAIIAN**
If you want to sample Hawaiian food try this place, but you better get there early as the place can get packed and they close when the food runs out. It is located on the west side of the street about half way down.

**PAKE CHINESE**
At 820 Kapahulu St. This is new and very low priced.

-------------------------------------------------------------------

local style

*IRIFUNE'S*
This is small little place with a big reputation on the east side of Kapahulu just past Keo's (mentioned below). The food is Japanese style and the prices are very low. We have been told by many people that this is one that should not be missed, 737-1141.

---

local/Tourist

**KEO'S**
This is getting to be one of the most popular places in Honolulu, noted for the number of celebrities who dine here. We have eaten here several times and do agree that the food, ambience, and service is hard to beat. The prices are a little higher than some of the other Thai restaurants we mention but the setting that is created makes it worth it for most people, 737-8240.

ANTHONY'S ITALIAN
At 802 Kapahulu and open for lunch and dinner every day but Sunday when they are open only for dinner. The prices here are modest, almost all dinner entrees under $10, while lunch runs around $6.

RAMI'S THAI
Located across the Street and up from Anthony's. We did not get to try this but we will before the next edition. We mention it because it looked clean and bright and the prices are not high. They are open for lunch on Monday through Saturday from 11:30 to 2 p.m. and for dinner every day from 5:30 to 10, 735-2789.

## POINTS OF INTEREST

PARADISE PARK
This is a little hard to find and we are not sure it is worth the effort. But if all the ads you see tempt you beyond control, take University Avenue in a mauka direction. When you pass the University this will become Oahu Street. Go about three miles and you will come to Manoa, which you follow to the end where the park is located. Mainly it is a haven for tropical birds, not necessarily ones from Hawaii. Perhaps the most important thing you will learn about Hawaii is that it has many mosquitoes, so bring your repellent.

*Bed & Breakfast Guide*

## SPORTS

**TENNIS**
There are at least three spots in this neighborhood: 1) Kaimuki Recreation Center at 3521 Waialae Avenue, two lighted courts, 734-2629, 2) Maunalani Playground, 4525 Sierra Drive, one lighted court, 737-4141, 3) Petrie Playground, 1039 12th Avenue, two lighted courts, 737-9433.

# EAST HONOLULU

At one time the area east of Diamond Head was farm land and there were fairly large dairy ranches out this way. As the city of Honolulu expanded, the farms were subdivided and homes were built, and the farmers moved to other places on Oahu, the Waianae area for example. Today, between Diamond Head and Koko Head there are a series of subdivisions, each one supported by a shopping center. Just east of Diamond Head is the Kahala area, where the Kahala Hilton and the Waialae Country Club are located. Further east is Aina Haina, Niu Valley, Portlock, and Hawaii Kai, which is the newest development in this area.

This is a residential area and visitors often simply pass through as they drive from Honolulu to Hanauma Bay. However, since we have some excellent host homes here, we want to point out the restaurants and points of interest. But even if you are not staying in this area, keep in mind the fine restaurants out this way.

## HOSTS

**O-4**
This home is located just three blocks from the ocean in a quiet residential neighborhood just beyond Kahala. The home is handy to stores, the bus line, a beach park, restaurants, and tennis courts. The hosts, Don and Joanne, are happy to provide rackets. The room offered has a separate entrance and a private bath, sometimes shared by their college-aged daughter. It has twin beds, and a small refrigerator for the guests use. For added enjoyment there is a small lanai as well. Both Don and Joanne are originally from Kentucky where they finished college. They have been in Hawaii for over twenty years and both work full time as librarians. Both have traveled through England and Don has traveled all over Europe. One of their main interests now is genealogy and how computers can be applied to that field. Since they are long time residents of Hawaii and well informed on Hawaiiana, guests could learn much by conversing with either host.
RATE: $27.50 single, $32.00 double, two night minimum.

### O-10

Discover the quiet tranquility of Aina Haina Valley, a small community nestled between the mountains and the sea. This location is ideal for the traveler who wants to be in touch with the pulse of the city but appreciates a cool retreat at the end of the day. Situated on the southeast corner of Oahu, this home is just 15 minutes from Waikiki, and in the other direction are great beaches for snorkeling and surfing. A small shopping center and restaurants are nearby, and the Oahu bus system serves the area. The home is spacious and very comfortable, surrounded by a large garden with numerous fruit and flowering trees. In a quiet wing are two charming bedrooms reserved for guests. One has a queen sized bed and the exclusive use of the adjacent bathroom. The other smaller room has twin beds. The entire suite could be rented and then the bathroom is shared. In another area of the home is a third guest room with twin beds and an adjoining bathroom. The comfortable living room with a large color T.V. is a favorite place for guests to unwind at the end of the day. Refrigerator space provided.

Shirley, the hostess, came to the Islands from England so she is no stranger to B & B hospitality. She is involved with the Sierra Club and has hiked throughout the Islands. She plays tennis and bridge and takes advantage of the numerous cultural events which abound in Honolulu. She is a good source of information about happenings on Oahu.

RATE: $28 single, $35 double, suite $55.

### O-12

The small separate guest room with twin beds off the garden area is nice, but "nice" does not do justice to the lanai and pool area which the guests are encouraged to use. Since this patio area is covered, guests can be out of the sun if so desired and there is ample outdoor furniture for their use. Bud and Marilyn provide a fan in the cottage for the guests to use, and one can cool off in the pool at any time. There is a small refrigerator for cool drinks or snacks. The home is in the Kahala area.

The hosts have been in Hawaii since 1958 so can be helpful to guests on the best spots to go. Bud owns his own business specializing in taxes, and financial planning and investments. Marilyn teaches violin and piano, mostly to small children, using the Suzuki method. Their hobbies are music, travel, swimming, and Bud is the Choir Director of their Congregational Church.

RATE: $38.50 one rate, monthly rates available.

### O-13

Peggy's home is a charming, older two bedroom home located in the exclusive Kahala district, a residential area of Honolulu. The location is ideal as it is within walking distance of the ocean, the world class Kahala Hilton Hotel, and the very modern Kahala Shopping Mall. The bus stops one half block from the home (it does not run after 9 p.m. but there is one several blocks away that runs later). The bedroom is large, light and cheerful, has twin beds that can be pushed together to make king size, and a lanai facing lush gardens where a breakfast consisting of rolls, fresh fruit, juice, butter and jam, and all the coffee you want is served. Guests may use a small section of the refrigerator for snack food and cold drinks, but no large meals. Guests have the use of the whole house except the kitchen, which is small, a "one person" kitchen. There is a shared bath, but Peggy makes sure that guests are not inconvenienced. There have been no complaints and the arrangement seems to work nicely. Peggy, who took an early retirement from the Federal Government, has had a love affair with Hawaii ever since the day, twenty five years ago when she walked down the gang plank from the Lurline and was greeted by bright sunshine, gentle breezes, and the fragrance of plumeria and ginger blossoms.

RATE: $27 single, $33 double, two night minimum.

### O-19
"Oh to be in England" which some say is where all this bed and breakfast started in the first place. Well here the guests can imagine they are since our hosts, mother and daughter are from England, and really have learned to combine that old world charm with new world Aloha to make sure that their guests have a good time. In this home there is a spacious bedroom with a queen sized bed and an adjoining bathroom. Breakfast is served in the dining room or on the lanai where guests have a spectacular sweeping view of the ocean and the Honolulu area.

Barbara, the daughter, came to Oahu around fifteen years ago and wrote home such glowing reports about Paradise that her mother, Joan, joined her. Barbara occupies herself with a small business she owns, marketing about twenty items she imports from England and sells to small shops and also promoting her Hawaiiana playing cards. Also, they have a little gift shop where guests can purchase at discount prices. Since they have many guests, Joan spends plenty of time seeing to their needs, but still manages to play a little bridge and majong.

RATE: $49.50 one rate, two night minimum.

### O-19A
With the same hosts as O-19, this garden level bedroom with an outside entrance and lanai, has a sweeping view of Hawaii Kai and Diamond Head. The room has a private bath, a queen sized bed, and a small refrigerator. Breakfast is served upstairs.

RATE: $49.50 one rate, two night minimum.

### O-25
This home, located in a quiet residential neighborhood of Hawaii Kai, is about 15 minutes to Waikiki and about five minutes to Hanauma Bay. The Hosts, Hellmut and Linda, have completely renovated the home. It is a large, airy home with big rooms and cathedral ceilings. The accommodation offered to B & B guests is the master bedroom, queen sized bed and its own private bath. Since the owners living quarters are quite separate, guests have a feeling of privacy. The view from the bedroom is through the valley toward the ocean.

Hellmut and Linda are experienced in receiving guests since that is a way of life in Hawaii. They are also very experienced in home renovation and interior decorating, which is what Hellmut specializes in. Their home is an excellent example of this. Linda, who is Hellmut's right hand person and partner in home renovation, is by profession a gemologist and works on appraisals and jewelry design when she is not working with Hellmut.

RATE: $40 single, $45 double.

### O-29
Kathy and Lee have been doing B & B for some time in their Hawaii Kai home and have just moved to a new and larger home in the same basic area. The accommodation offered in this home is two bedrooms, one with a queen sized bed and the other with two twin beds, with a private bath between the two rooms. Both rooms would be available for a family or for two couples traveling together, but they are not both used to accommodate separate travelers, so guests always are assured of a private bath. The home has large decks which guests are welcome to use to enjoy the ocean and sunset views.

Lee was born and raised in Hawaii, a true Kamaaina. When he gets the chance, which is never often enough, he loves to play a game of golf. Kathy, an almost kamaaina, loves hiking and is a guide for Lyon Arboretum. Each morning Kathy serves a breakfast of home made treats. Lee and Kathy have been in the travel business and are very knowledgeable about the Islands.

RATE:   $40 single or double, $80 for both rooms.

## O-33

One of Ruth and Ed's favorite activities is whale watching from the large lanai of their Kahala home, which is also where they serve breakfast to their B & B guests. From this vantage point one can also see Molokai if it is not shrouded in clouds. Originally Ed and Ruth are from Iowa, but they have been in Hawaii long enough now to be considered Kamaaina. One of Ruth's interest is bridge, and she looks forward to her weekly game.

The accommodation offered is a suite on the garden level of their two story home. There are two large bedrooms, one with a queen bed and one with twin beds, a private bath, a large living area with TV. Just outside the door are the swimming pool and garden area just right for relaxing after a busy day of sightseeing. The accommodations can handle two couples traveling together or a small family. Other than that the suite is used for only only one couple so there is a maximum of privacy.

RATE:   $50 double, $15 extra for third person, $80 for two couples.

## RESTAURANTS

### KAHALA

local/Tourist

#### YUM YUM TREE

There are a number of these on Oahu and we have found them to be very nice. The food is very middle America as is the service and the decor, 737-7938.

#### TONY ROMA'S

This is located across the highway from the Shopping Center. As far as we know the original Tony Roma's is in Waikiki. The house special is ribs and they must do a bang up job because in Waikiki they are usually packed with a line outside, 732-5505.

#### YEN KING

Open for lunch from 11-2:30 and for dinner from 5-9:30. The decor is nice and the prices are a little higher than some of the restaurants in China Town.

#### THE PATISSIRIE

This is an excellent spot for a sandwich in the $3 to $4 range.

-----------------------------------------------------------------

*Bed & Breakfast Guide*

## NIU VALLEY

**local/Tourist Style**

**\*\* SWISS INN\*\***
Open for dinner only from 6:00-10:00 closed Monday. Be sure to call for a reservation as this is one of the busiest restaurants in Honolulu and for very good reason: the food is excellent and the prices are not outrageous. We did not expect it to be so good in spite of the fact that several people urged us not to miss it. The cuisine is continental. If one is not too hungry, they have a light dinner for around $6.00 which is a really excellent buy, 377-5447.

**DI MARTINO**
As the name suggests, Italian cuisine. We had a very nice dinner here and while we prefer the Swiss Inn this is an excellent second choice.

**LUNG FUNG**
Either Cantonese or Szechuan, open daily from 10 a.m. until 9 p.m. Prices moderate.

---

## AINA HAINA

**local Style**

**DUCK YUN**
The food here is Cantonese style with prices not too high. The decor is nice.

**JACK'S**
Open Monday through Sunday from 7 a.m. until 2 p.m. for breakfast and lunch, and at 5 p.m. for dinner every day but Sunday. Last year we had this in the local/Tourist category; that was before we ate here. It really is pretty heavy local and we mean that in the best sense of the term. Dinners range from $6 to $13 for a big steak. Lunch is in the $4 to $5 range, plate lunch special style.

---

**local/Tourist Style**

**RANCH HOUSE**
For some reason we failed to include this in our first edition in spite of the fact it was in our notes. Since this is almost a tradition on Oahu, we apologize. This is an excellent family style restaurant that has prices B & B guests will appreciate, 373-2177.

**RADA'S PIROSCKI**
Unfortunately, this is strictly take-out. We tried one of the piroscki stuffed with chicken, cheese, and mushrooms. It was excellent but very rich.

**OTOMI RESTAURANT**
The grand opening for this was in July, 1986. The cuisine is pretty authentic Japanese. The decor is very nice and the prices are not too high, unless you get carried away at the sushi bar.

---

## HAWAII KAI

### local/Tourist Style

**STROMBOLLI'S**
This is a fairly new place which is doing pretty well. We tried it for lunch and really enjoyed a meatball sandwich and a fresh vegetable salad. They are open for lunch and dinner. The setting is nice and the food is good but not cheap.

**SIZZLERS**
Just the same as the Mainland chain.

**JAKE'S**
This is owned by the same people who own Jake's Hidaway in downtown Honolulu. They are open for lunch and dinner and if they are just like downtown we would have to recommend them.

## BEACHES

**KAHALA HILTON**
Even though the Hilton "built" this beach, that is, they brought in the sand to create a white sand beach where none previously existed, public access and use of the beach is not denied. We have used the beach many times and have never stayed at the Hilton. In fact, we have used the pool side bar with no problem. Watching the dolphins swim in their pool is almost a tourist attraction.

## SPORTS

**TENNIS**
There are at least four spots in this area: 1) Aina Haina Playground, 827 Hind Drive, two lighted courts, 373-2722, 2) Kahala Field, 4495 Pahoa Avenue, two unlighted courts, 3) Koko Head District Park, Kalaianiole Highway, six lighted courts, 395-5189, 4) Niu Valley, 5510 Kanau Street, two unlighted courts, 373-2722.

*Bed & Breakfast Guide*

## EAST OF HAWAII KAI TO MAKAPU

For scenic beauty it is hard to beat the drive east of Hawaii Kai to Waimanalo. Many get no further than Hanauma Bay and some, unfortunately, not even that far. Until one reaches Waimanalo, there are no stores or restaurants, although there are a few Snack Vans parked along the road if you decide to spend some time in this area. Below is a list of the points of interest along the way.

### HANAUMA BAY
Just after you pass Hawaii Kai, you climb the hill to Koko Head where you find the access road to Hanauma Bay. This is a must stop for any Oahu visitor. Most people think of it for snorkeling, but one need not snorkel to see fish. Simply walk a little way into the water and you will see plenty of fish. Should you have food for them, you will see even more. No fishing is allowed here so the fish are quite tame. If you want to snorkel, the best time to do it is early in the morning as things get a little crowded after 10 a.m.

### HALONA POINT
About three miles past Hanauma Bay you may get a chance to see one of Hawaii's Blow Holes. This one is not as consistent as Spouting Horn on Kauai but it is nice to stop here anyway. If it is at all clear, you will see Molokai in the distance.

### SANDY BEACH
A mile or so further on you will come to Sandy Beach, a huge stretch of sand where surfers and body surfers come to frolic. This beach is always crowded but if body surfing is your thing, don't pass this one by. Further on the waves are either too rough or once past Makapu, too gentle.

### HAWAII KAI GOLF COURSE
This is a private course, open to the public. The fee is $25.00 on weekdays, cart included and mandatory, and $28.00 on weekends. There is also an executive course of mostly par threes with fees of $7.75 and $9.25, no cart required. This is a nice course to play to sharpen up your wind game.

### MAKAPU BEACH
Two or three miles past Hawaii Kai Golf course, this is another favorite surfing area.

### SEA LIFE PARK
One of Oahu's major tourist attractions. People who live on Oahu say, "Why go to Sea Life when we can watch to dolphins for free at the Kahala Hilton." There is much more to see, however, at Sea Life Park. Admission is $7.00 adults, $5.25 juniors, $2.25 children from four to six years.

## PEARL CITY/AIEA

As the plane approaches the Honolulu Airport, the first sight is Pearl Harbor. Anyone old enough to remember December 7, 1941, no doubt remembers exactly where he was and what he was doing on that fateful Sunday morning. Whether one had much of a consciousness of Hawaii before then, from that point on Hawaii assumed an importance in the world that has done nothing but grow.

Since Honolulu Airport is in the Pearl City/Aiea area, most people conclude that this is a part of greater Honolulu, and most guide books treat it that way. In fact, Pearl City and Aiea are as separate from Honolulu as Kaneohe or Kailua.

One of the main supports for this area, as well as others on Oahu, is the military. Except for the Arizona Memorial, a veritable tourist mecca, there is not much for tourists in this area. Restaurants and stores rely on residents for their success. The net effect of this is that prices in both restaurants and shops tend to be lower than in some of the tourist areas.

There are no beaches here, but there is a very nice park, the Neil Blaisdale Park, which is a good place to picnic or lie in the sun if one does not wish to bother going to the beach.

Our host homes in this area are close to the airport, just a few minutes drive, and it is just a short drive to the center of Honolulu or Waikiki. Pearl City is also a good place to start a trip to the north shore, up through the center of the Island.

*Bed & Breakfast Guide*

## HOSTS

### O-1

This beautiful four bedroom, three and a half bath home has all the comforts one could ask for. Located in the hills of Aiea, away from the noise and the bustle of the city, it is just a short drive to Honolulu and Waikiki and an excellent place to start exploring the north shore of Oahu. It is near the bus line, making a trip to town both inexpensive and convenient. The home has a lovely pool, garden and lanai, and an exquisite view of Pearl Harbor, downtown Honolulu, and the south coast of Oahu. Three of the four bedrooms are sometimes used for B & B, but Fely, the hostess, would prefer only one or two guests at a time as she likes to give guests plenty of attention. Two of the rooms have double beds and one has twin beds. There is also a ping pong table which the guests are welcome to use, and Herwig, the host, might take you on in a game, but watch out, he is pretty good. Guests are often delighted when some of Fely's family stop by and the children treat them to a hula demonstration. One of Fely and Herwig's main hobbies is deep sea fishing, which Fely says she enjoys most when the ocean is dead flat calm. When the surf is up, getting back is her favorite sport.
RATE: $38.50 single or double: two night minimum.

### O-5

Helga and Cory were our first hosts on Oahu and much of our growth is due to them. They have enjoyed B & B guests so much they have convinced many of their friends to join us. Their home is in the Pacific Palisades, a residential area above Pearl City at the foot of the Koolau Mountains. Two bedrooms in the main house are used for B & B. One room has a half bath, while there is a hall bath for guests and family to use. Both rooms have T.V. For book lovers there is a Victorian library which the guests are welcome to use. Both Helga and Cory are collectors of antiques and curios and their home is loaded with many fascinating items, many in a Bavarian flavor so that one can almost imagine a home in the Alps. One of the rooms has twin beds, while the other has a king sized bed. Cory, a marine electrical engineer, hails from the heartland of America, but when he joined the navy to see the world, he discovered Hawaii, and now he considers himself a native. Helga sojourned to the U.S. from Germany in the early '50's, and did not get to Hawaii until the '60's. Ever since they bought their home in the Palisades, they have been working to enlarge and improve it, and we accuse them of constructing the Winchester Mystery House. One of Helga's great loves is animals, cats and dogs, and she breeds and raises Maltese dogs, and should a stray cat appear at her door, she could never turn it away. Since the home is a two story residence, guests are not exposed to the animals.
RATE: $33 single or double, $5 extra for one night.

### O-5A

This is also hosted by Helga and Cory and is a separate bedroom at the rear of the home with a separate entrance, private bath, and a color T.V. Breakfast is served in the Tyrolian room in the main home.
RATE: $33 one rate. $5 extra for one night stay.

# RESTAURANTS

## LOCAL STYLE

### TOPPER
Located in the Pearl City Shopping Center on Kamehameha Highway. Lots to eat at low price, good if you like this type of food.

### YAKINIKU BI WON
Located underneath the Pearl City Business Plaza, which is on the makai side of Kam. Hwy. If you like Korean or Japanese food this is a good spot, very reasonably priced. They are open from 10 a.m. to 10 p.m. Lunch runs from $3.95 to $4.95 while dinners go from $6.50 to $7.95.

### PEARL CITY CHINESE
In the Pearl City Business Plaza. Cantonese style. The prices are not high but we did not eat a full meal here.

### NAONORI RESTAURANT
Located in Newtown Square, which in on Kaahumanu St. in Aiea, at the back of the Center. Lunch goes from $4.60, where you have a choice of any two of a dozen Japanese dishes, up to $10 for Steak Taishoku. If you like authentic Japanese, you will probably like it here.

### ORIENTAL HOUSE
In the Aikahi Shopping Center next to Safeway. Open Monday -Saturday from 10 a.m. to 8 p.m. If they did not offer chili, hamburgers, french fries, and a Super Canadian Hot Dog we could understand the name since the rest of the menu consists of Shoyu butterfish ($5.10), Kal Bee ($5.40), Man Doo Kook Soo ($3.90). Oh well, living in Hawaii we should be used to this sort of thing.

---

## local Style

### FLAMINGO
On the makai side of Kamehameha in the Pearl City Business Plaza. The most expensive thing on the menu is lobster at $13.95. Many of the dinner entrees are in the $6.00-$7.00 range, with spaghetti at $5.15. Their lunch prices are lower: hot roast beef sandwich for $3.50. They are open from 6:00 am. until 11:00 p.m., 456-5945.

### *PEARL CITY TAVERN & SUSHI BAR*
On the makai side on Kamehameha Highway at Waimano Home Road. In some ways we would put this in the do not miss category. Not only is the food good, with a large variety of dishes offered, from sushi to corn beef sandwich, but there is more of interest here. For example, behind the bar is a monkey cage. Patrons can have a drink and watch the monkeys cavort. On the roof is a bonzai garden. Each tree is labeled, giving not only the name but also the age. The restaurant is huge, so in spite of the fact they do a large business you are sure to be accommodated, but if you have to wait you should not be bored, 455-1045.

*Bed & Breakfast Guide*

**\*BEACON\***
At 98-108 Lipoa Place which runs makai off Kamehameha Highway. This is what the local crowd considers the best value in the Pearl City/Aiea area. We whole heartily agree. The food is excellent and the prices are very reasonable. The menu is extensive, not especially geared to local tastes, and fresh fish of several varieties is always available, 488-1881.

------------------------------------------------------------------

**local/Tourist Style**

ELEPHANT & CASTLE
Located in Newtown Square. Named after a very famous English Pub and also styled along those lines. Where else in Hawaii can you play a game of darts? Open every day from 8:00 a.m. until 2:00 a.m. The food is good and moderately priced, 487-5591.

COLUMBIA INN
Located across the street from Elephant and Castle. This is a good place to get lots of food for a decent price. Dinner comes with a choice of soup, salad, or fruit cup with prices ranging from $5.95 (Spaghetti) to $11.95 (U.S. Choice Rib Steak). A la carte ranges from $3.95 to $9.95. There is a wide selection of entrees, 487-0091.

BUZZ'S ORIGINAL STEAKHOUSE
Located at 98-751 Kuahao Place, Pearl City. This is owned and operated by the same people who run Buzz's out in Lanikai. They are open for lunch and dinner. Most dinner entrees go from $10 to $15, while lunch is in the $6 to $8 range. 487-6465.

MONTEREY CANNERY
Located in the Pearl Ridge Center. Open every day for breakfast, lunch, and dinner. The food is not high priced, the menu is extensive, and the atmosphere is nice. Below and in front of the entrance to the restaurant is a small farm totally devoted to water cress, 487-0048.

STUART ANDERSON'S
This is strictly western fare, ie., lots of beef, chicken, shrimp. Prices, especially for lunch, are very reasonable and the food is good, 487-0054.

UNCLE JOHN'S
Located at the Pearlridge Shopping Center and open every day from 7 a.m. to 10 p.m. Very Mainland like food at reasonable prices, French Dip sandwich for lunch $5.35, broiled half a chicken for dinner for $7.65, a four egg omelette $3.45, 488-8402.

## POINTS OF INTEREST

U.S.S. ARIZONA
The Visitor Center is located off Kamehameha Highway at Pearl Harbor Naval Station, about a twenty minute drive from central Honolulu. From this Center a boat ride out to the Memorial is free as is the twenty minute movie that precedes it. There is also a museum that tells the story of the attack on Pearl Harbor and some of the story of the war in the Pacific. The Visitor Center is open from 8:00 a.m. until 3:00 p.m. Tuesday through Sunday.

## NIGHT LIFE

There is often entertainment offered in some of the local bistros or restaurants. Other than that there is a movie theater at the Pearl Ridge Shopping Center.

## SPORTS

### GOLF

**PEARL COUNTRY CLUB**
This is a private club, open to the public. To find, take the H-1 Freeway to the Aiea exit. Take Moanalua Road to Kaonohi Street and turn mauka for about a mile or so and you will see the entrance to the course on your right. On weekdays the fee is $21 cart included and mandatory. On weekends the fee is $29. After 3 p.m. the rate drops to $18 on weekdays and $22 on weekends. Club rental is $10.00. For more information call 487-2460.

**TED MAKALENA GOLF COURSE**
This public course, located in Waipahu, is a challenge because of all the water holes in spite of the fact that it is short and flat. The fee is $6 weekdays, $8 weekends, 1/2 price for nine holes. Either power carts or hand carts are available for $10.40 or $1 respectively. For more information call 296-7888.

**MOANALUA GOLF COURSE**
To find, take Moanalua Road to Ala Aolani Street. The course is located west of Tripler Army Medical Center, a huge pink building that is hard to miss. The course is public, nine holes, with a fee of $10 weekdays and $15 weekends. After 3 p.m. on weekdays the fee drops to $5 and on weekends $7. Carts rent for $9 and clubs for $3. For more information call 939-2411.

### TENNIS
There are five locations in the Pearl/Aiea area: 1) Aiea Recreation Center, 99-350 Aiea Heights Drive, two lighted courts, 488-0411, 2) Pacific Palisades Playground, 2292 Auhuhu Street, two unlighted courts, 455-9911, 3) Pearl City Kai, 1962 Lehua Avenue, eight lighted courts, 456-2444, 4) Pearl City Recreation Center, 485 Moomaemae Street, two lighted courts, 455-2936, 5) Pearl Ridge Community Park, 99-940 Moanalua Road, six unlighted courts, 488-5406.

*Bed & Breakfast Guide*

# AROUND OAHU

## FROM MILILANI TO WAIMEA BAY

When one leaves the Honolulu/Pearl City area to get to the north shore of Oahu, there are several different routes possible. One way is to take either H-2 or Highway 99 west of Pearl City through the center of the Island, through Mililani Town and Wahiawa out to the coastal town of Haleiwa.

This great flatland, which lies between the two mountain ranges, the Koolaus and the Waianaes, is for the most part Oahu's farmland. Land that is not growing sugar or pineapple is probably controlled by the military. The first stop along Route 99 is Mililani Town, which is as much like a Mainland city as you will find in Hawaii. As one looks at all the tract homes, one gets the feeling that Los Angeles cannot be far away. The only "center" to the town is the shopping center, which had all the restaurants we could find other than the golf course. In July of 1986 Mililani won the *All American City* award, which is something no other city in Hawaii has been able to do.

One thing that interested us was the cooperative farm located on the right hand side of Highway 99 just past Mililani Town. We could see that the land seemed to be separated into many small plots of land with many different crops planted. This land was set aside years ago by Mayor Fasi so that people who did not own enough land to grow their own gardens could raise vegetables and fruit. What makes it most interesting for visitors is that one gets a chance to see some local foods growing that one would hardly get a chance to see on the Mainland.

A few miles beyond Mililani Town is Wahiawa, which like Waimanalo on the east side of Oahu is cowboy country. We walked from one end of Wahiawa to the other and could find nothing that would cause us to stop again other than the Botanical Gardens mentioned below.

Just beyond Wahiawa on the right hand side of the road you will see a sign for Dole Pineapple. This is a good place to get a refreshing bite of pineapple and a chance to see pineapple growing, but the pineapple is not processed here and basically this is a gift shop.

Next door to Dole, however, is a most interesting place, Halemano Plantation, a number of small shops including a restaurant, set in a little mall. The purpose of this project is to train retarded people and to give them the job skills to make it on their own. Anthony La Peria, who manages the restaurant, told us they have been quite successful in their venture.

## HOSTS

At the present time we have no hosts in the Mililani or Waiiawa area. We do have a host at Sunset Beach which you will see under Haleiwa.

## MILILANI RESTAURANTS

All of the restaurants mentioned in this section with the exception of Mililani Golf Course and Halemano Plantation are in the Mililani Shopping Center. If you have any trouble finding it, ask anyone in town for directions.

**LOCAL STYLE**

HALEMANO PLANTATION
As stated above, this is actually past Wahiawa and before Haleiwa, but this seems to us the best place to put it. It is open every day from 8:30 to 4:30. You can get a buffet lunch for $6.35 and if you like local style food, you can't beat the value and it's for a good cause.

INN & OUT
Take out only, box lunches. We did not try it, but from the amount of food they were preparing, it was obvious that this spot is popular with the local folks. This might be a good spot to pick up a picnic lunch to take to the beach a few miles beyond. Everything was priced under $4.00.

SUN'S B-B-Q
Korean style food at moderate prices.

MILILANI RESTAURANT
Open from 10:30 a.m. until 8:30 p.m., counter style. The food is a mixture of Oriental and American and the prices are quite low.

----------------------------------------------------------------

local Style

MAILE CHINESE
Cantonese style food at reasonable prices. They are open daily from 11:00 a.m. until 9 p.m. The atmosphere is plain and the place is clean.

MILILANI GOLF COURSE
Open for breakfast, lunch, and dinner, but closes fairly early in the evening, around 7 p.m., unless they are very busy. The food is a mixture of Oriental and American. The prices are low.

----------------------------------------------------------------

local/Tourist Style

ARBY'S
You will see this chain all over Oahu. We don't always mention them since they are in the fast food category. However, should you be in Mililani and starving, this offers a very safe place to eat.

## CHUCKS
Open for lunch and dinner, this is the fancy dining out spot in Mililani. Most of the dinner entrees are between $12.00 and $15.00, salad bar style. Lunch is a much better deal.

## WAHIAWA RESTAURANTS

### PEARL GARDEN
This is a Chinese restaurant located in Wahiawa behind Macdonald's. Both hosts and guests have told us this is a good place to get a good meal for a low price. We did not get a chance to try it but will before the next publication.

## POINTS OF INTEREST

### WAHIAWA BOTANICAL GARDENS
Located at 1396 California Avenue, which is right of the highway as you come into Wahiawa from Mililani. The admission is free for this four acres of tropical gardens. This makes a nice stop on the way to the north shore.

## SPORTS

### MILILANI GOLF COURSE
This is one of Oahu's nicer courses and the price is not bad; weekdays are $19 with a cart, $12 without. On weekends it is $23 with a cart mandatory. The best deal is the twilight special, after 4 p.m., when the price drops to $8 with a cart on weekdays and $10.50 on weekends. For more information call 623-2222

### HAWAII COUNTRY CLUB
To find this take Kunia Road west from the center of Wahiawa. This is an eighteen hole, rather short course, and since it is far out, it is not too difficult to get on. The fee is $16 on weekdays and $21 on weekends cart included and mandatory. For more information call 621-5654.

### TENNIS
There are two spots in Mililani and one in Wahiawa. The two in Mililani are: 1) Mililani Neighborhood Park, 95-245 Kaloapau Street, two unlighted courts, 623-5258, 2) Mililani Waena Park, 95-590 Naholoholo Street, two lighted courts, 623-5258. In Wahiawa at the Wahiawa Recreation Center, 1139-A Kilani Avenue, four lighted courts, 622-4751.

## HALEIWA

When you reach the north coast of Oahu, a right turn will take you to Haleiwa and then east around the north side and eventually back to Honolulu. If you go on, past Thompson corner, a short drive will take you to the north west corner of Oahu, where there are beautiful expansive beaches that the surfers just love, the glider planes at Dillingham Airfield, and polo grounds at Mokuleia. Polo season opens in March, and matches are held at 2:30 p.m. each Sunday all spring and summer.

Haleiwa is surfer territory and the place resembles areas south of Los Angeles. Little shops and new restaurants open and close with a frequency reminiscent of the tides. Some of the places we write about will no doubt be closed by the time this book is finished, and they will be replaced by those convinced they have found Paradise. Then there are the few spots that have been there forever. (When we wrote this in our first addition we had in mind the Seaview Inn but now even that is gone.)

If you happen to be a fudge freak you will think you have died and gone to heaven if you visit the Fudge Factory located next to and in the same building as Jameson's restaurant.

### HOSTS

**O-18**
Some visitors to Hawaii avoid Oahu because they are under the false impression that it is all city, ie. Honolulu and Waikiki. Those of us who know the Islands know better. This home is a perfect place for anyone who wants to get away from it all and enjoy the beach. Bob and Val, the hosts, purchased this five bedroom, five bath home with accommodating guests in mind. Three different accommodations are offered; the largest has the privacy of a condo with a complete kitchen, one bedroom with twin beds, private bath, and a double sofa bed in the living area and also TV. The other two units have private entrances and private bath, a TV, and a small frig. One bedroom has a king sized bed and the other has twin beds. Each T.V. is hooked by cable to a V.C.R. in the main quarters so that quests can watch a movie at night. One of the bedrooms can be connected to the studio unit making it perfect for a small family or a group traveling together.
The home is located on a quiet cul-de-sac about two hundred yards from a beautiful stretch of Sunset Beach in an uncrowded area. A six foot deck provides guests with both an ocean and mountain view. It is one block from the bus line for those who would prefer not driving and is close to shopping, restaurants, golf, tennis, sand buggies, glider rides, and much more.
RATE: $50 for the studio, $40 for bedroom, $15 for each additional person over two.

*Bed & Breakfast Guide*

## RESTAURANTS

### LOCAL STYLE

**BONZAI BOWL**
On the mauka side of the main highway in about the center of Haleiwa. This is as close to LOCAL STYLE as you can get in a town that is dominated by haoles. Prices are very low. For example, steak and shrimp are offered for $6.50. The food seems to be a blend of Korean and American.

**COUNTRY DRIVE IN**
This is located next to the Bonzai Bowl and is the action spot of Haleiwa- lots of food for low price, two scoop rice style.

-----------------------------------------------------------------

### local Style

**SEAVIEW INN\*\***
This was almost an institution on the North Shore, but alas all good things come to an end. When we were there in July, 1986, the sign said "Open soon under new management."

-----------------------------------------------------------------

### local/Tourist Style

**CAFE HALEIWA**
On the mauka side of the highway just as you enter Haleiwa. Mostly this is a breakfast place but they have recently started dinner service with a limited menu. They have an early bird breakfast special between 6:00-7:00 a.m. for $1.29 which consists of two eggs and three hot cakes.

**STORTO'S**
This is a new sandwich shop across the street from Cafe Haleiwa, 66-215 Kam. Hwy. They are open every day from 10 a.m. to 5:30 p.m. Here you can order any of twenty different sandwiches with "cutsey names" as *Ike and Tina Tuna* or *Joan Livers*. The names may make you sick but the food and prices won't.

**KUH AINA SANDWICH**
This small place on the mauka side of the main highway boasts of having the "world's best hamburger." It is open from 11:00 a.m. until 9 p.m. We had a hamburger there several years ago and while we are not sure it was the best in the world, it was pretty good.

**SASSY SPROUTS SANDWICHES**
We found the name here more appealing than the place. It is tucked behind, as we remember, Country Drive In. They are open every day from 10 to 4.

**ROSIE'S CANTINA**
This Mexican restaurant is located in the same Shopping Center as Steamer's which is mentioned below. Hosts tell us it is good.

### THE PELICAN
This may not be in existence by the time you read this. It is not that the food is not good or that it is too expensive. Our hosts like it very much and found the food good value; it is just that nothing seems to make it at this location, a little shopping center on the mauka side of King Kam. Hwy. in about the center of Haleiwa, 637-3514.

### STEAMER'S
This and Jameson's by the Sea are the "hot" spots of the north shore. The food is good but not cheap. The garden like atmosphere is attractive. They are open for dinner every day. There is dancing until 2:00 a.m. if you decide to make a night of it, 637-5071.

### *JAMESON'S BY THE SEA*
Across the street and just east of the Seaview. Owned by the same people who started Jameson's in Honolulu, this place has much appeal. During the day a light lunch is served on the porch just outside the bar, or, if you don't care to wait, at a table inside. Dinner is served upstairs where the view is the best in Haleiwa. The prices for dinner are not low, but this is the place we would recommend for that special occasion, 637-4336.

### D' AMICOS
This is located beyond Haleiwa at Sunset Beach. The specialty here is pizza, but there are plenty of other dishes available, mostly Italian, or sandwiches in the $3 to $4 range.


## POINTS OF INTEREST


### CONGREGATIONAL CHURCH
Be sure to stop and see this small church which is most famous for its clock which was made in England for Queen Liliuokalani. Not only does it tell time but the day of the week, the year, the phase of the moon, and something else we have forgotten. When the clock was made it was mechanical, but it has since been made electric. Behind the Church there is a thrift store operated by the Church.

### WAIMEA FALLS PARK
This privately owned park, encompassing over eighteen hundred acres, and the Polynesian Cultural Center get most of the tourist attention on the north and windward side of Oahu. The cost is around $6.00 for adults and $4.00 for children. If you do not mind crowds, a stop here is worthwhile, and to fully enjoy it, several hours should be allotted. You can either hike or take a free tram ride to the falls and then swim in the pool at the base of the falls.

## BEACHES

Except for a few spots, swimming on the north shore of Oahu is never perfectly safe, and during the winter months just playing in the waves is foolhardy. One has to see to believe the size of some of these waves. Keep in mind, too, that the waves are not constant. You can manage them one minute and get knocked around like a cork the next. This huge surf brings surfers from all over the world to try the Bonzai Pipeline, and even they back off when the winter surf is at its highest. At times the main highway is closed as huge waves cascade across the road. Most of this area is *look but don't touch* country.

### HALEIWA BEACH PARK
Here is the exception that proves the rule as far as swimming conditions are concerned. It is almost always safe to swim here since this beach is set in Waialua Bay. It is right at Haleiwa so it is easy to find. There are picnic facilities, rest rooms, showers, and a playground for children.

### KAIKAKA STATE RECREATION AREA
This spot is better for picnicking than swimming since the shoreline here is rocky. There are picnic and rest room facilities.

### WAIMEA BAY BEACH PARK
Swimming during the summer months can be safe here since again there is some protection. The main problem with this beach is that it attracts huge crowds and unless one gets there early, finding a parking spot could be a problem.

### SUNSET BEACH
Except for Waikiki this is surely the most famous beach in Hawaii, and around the world Sunset Beach means surfing. There is no time of the year that we would swim here unless the water were too calm for surfing. Yet this is a beautiful spot for sunbathing or beach combing.

## SPORTS

### AIRPLANE RIDE
Plane rides are available at Dillingham Field for various lengths of time; there is a ten/fifteen minute ride for $.10 a pound. The best time for this ride is just before lunch. The thirty minute ride up to Waimea Falls Park cost $29.00. For $39.00 one can fly to Waikiki, a ride of forty-five minutes. The Island tour ride takes one hour at a cost of $49.00. No reservation is needed.

### GLIDER RIDES
Also at Dillingham one can take a glider ride, one person for $29.00 or two for $49.00. It looks like an outstanding trip and the people who take it rave about it. Just watching them soar through the air is an experience worth having, so whether you go for a ride or not, stop by for a look.

*OAHU*

## FROM WAIMEA BAY TO KANEOHE

After one passes Waimea Bay going around the east side of Oahu, there is not much civilization with the exception of the Turtle Bay Hilton and the Polynesian Cultural Center. As stated above, the Polynesian Cultural Center, which is owned and operated by the Mormon Church, is a major destination point for tourists. Visitors arrive by the bus loads. Comments from travel writers vary from glowing to insulting. We have spoken to many people who have visited and find that most people enjoy it. The admission is not cheap, around $15.00, and this does not include the Polynesian show in the evening. Since good shows can be seen for free elsewhere in the Islands, some choose to skip this.

The Cultural Center attempts to bring to life seven primitive Polynesian cultures: Hawaii, Fiji, Samoa, Tonga, Tahiti, Marquesas, and Maori (New Zealand). One can either walk among these seven villages, or take the open air train and listen to the guide's talk. At different times of the day, the people from each village get together for a performance, such as the Pageant of the Long Canoes held every afternoon. The Center is closed on Sundays.

## HOSTS

### O-11

Nestled between the mountains and the sea in the little town of Kaaawa, this three bedroom, two bath home offers one room and a private bath to B & B travelers. The room has twin beds, color TV, and a private entrance off the lanai. The home is just across from the ocean, and sandy beaches are just minutes away. Kaaawa is just 20 minutes south of the Polynesian Cultural Center, and 10 minutes away from the new Kualoa Ranch Activities, which include horseback riding, dune buggy rides, and other ocean activities. There are restaurants in the area so dining would be no problem.

Wilf and Frances, who hail from Ontario and Boston, have been on Oahu for over seven years.
RATE: $25 single, $30 double.

## RESTAURANTS

**local Style**

LOTUS INN CHOP SUEY
   Located in the Hauula Shopping Center, Cantonese style, clean, and the prices are modest. They are open for dinner only.

## LAIE CHOP SUEY
Open from 10:00 a.m. until 9 p.m. The food is Cantonese with a liberal sprinkling of other dishes. Prices are low; for example, a lunch plate goes for $3.50 and dinner for $4.25.

------

**local/Tourist Style**

### HUEVOUS
This is located in the little town of Kahuku, across from the High School, several blocks off the highway. They are open for breakfast, lunch, and dinner. The food is good and plentiful, the prices are low, and the service is friendly. We put it in this category, but not many tourists will find it.

### COUNTRY HEALTH FOOD SANDWICH
Strictly vegetarian with low, low prices. All of the sandwiches were under $3.00 and a fruit salad goes for $2.75. Located in the Laie Center.

### PAT'S SEABREEZE
Located a few miles south of the Cultural Center at Punaluu, they are open for breakfast, lunch, and dinner. The food is Mainland style, prices modest for lunch, but higher for dinner. For example, lunch runs between $3.50 and $6.00, while dinner goes from $10.00 to $15.00. What you get here, however, is a very nice atmosphere, right on the waterfront. Tour buses also stop here for lunch, 293-8502.

### PANIOLO CAFE*
Paniolo in Hawaiian is cowboy, so restaurants that use that name suggests western fare, ie., thick char broiled steaks and lots of fried potatoes. Here you can get that and more; Mexican food, for example, or if you care to you can get some nice fried rattlesnake meat. Prices are moderate with entrees going from $6.00 to $12.00.

### CROUCHING LION INN
Open for lunch and dinner, the Crouching Lion, named for the huge rock off the coast that some say resembles a lion, is popular with locals and tourists alike. Its strong point is the setting, on a bluff overlooking the ocean. Lunch prices are moderate, but dinner prices go up fast, to $20.00 a person. Since tour buses stop here, it can be crowded, 237-8511.

## POINTS OF INTEREST

### LAIE POINT
From the Laie Shopping Center, take the road that goes makai into the residential area. At the top of this hill, turn right and drive to the end of the road. You are bound to see some local fisherman trying their luck. This is such a scenic spot that we suggest it for a picnic or just a good place to rest for a while.

## SACRED FALLS

This is one of the most popular hikes on the east side. It is two miles to the falls and hikers are advised to read the sign at the start of the trail. We stress not trying to cross the stream if it is raining in the mountains or it is obvious the stream is raging. Also, do not start this hike without insect repellent as there are many mosquitoes here. But with all this in mind, it is a wonderful hike.

## BEACHES

### KAHUKU BEACH

To get to this beach you must cut across the Kahuku Golf Course. This is a secluded spot, very beautiful, white sand beach. There are no facilities. If the ocean is not too rough, swimming here is safe.

### MALAEKAHANA STATE RECREATION AREA

You will come to this just after you go through Kahuku arriving from the north or just after you go through Laie coming from the south. This is one of the good swimming spots on the windward or north side of Oahu. All of the facilities are here: picnic tables, rest rooms, showers.

### HAUULA BEACH PARK

Since this is right on Kam. Highway, just south of Laie, you are not likely to miss it. All of the facilities are here, it is easy to get to, and swimming is usually safe. It is not as beautiful as some of the others.

## SPORTS

### GOLF

#### TURTLE BAY COUNTRY CLUB

Located at the northeast tip of Oahu and part of the Hilton Hotel but open to the public. For guests of the Hotel the fee is $27 cart included and mandatory. For non-guests the fee is $29 on weekdays and $33 on weekends. For more information or starting time, call 293-8811.

#### KAHUKU GOLF COURSE

This short, nine hole course on Oahu's east shore does not get much play in spite of the fact that it is only $4 on weekdays and $6 on weekends, 1/2 price for nine holes. For more information call 293-5842.

*Bed & Breakfast Guide*

# KANEOHE

Kaneohe is located on the windward side of the Koolau Mountain range, about a twenty minute drive from Honolulu. Most of the people who live in Kaneohe work in Honolulu, and in the morning and late afternoon cars pour over the Pali and Likelike Highway in a seemingly endless line. Like many places on Oahu, there is a military influence here. Kaneohe Marine Base is located along Kaneohe Bay.

Neither Kaneohe nor Kailua are thought of as tourist areas. One indication of this is that there are no hotels, motels, or overnight accommodations of any kind other than Bed & Breakfast homes and many little vacation cottages along the east and north coast. Restaurants and shops in the Kaneohe/Kailua area depend on local trade for their survival, which is a major factor in keeping prices lower than in resort spots. Kaneohe boasts the largest shopping center outside of Honolulu, the Windward Mall. Once inside this mall, it is easy to forget you are in Hawaii. Some of the restaurants in this area resemble Mainland places, but there are plenty of ethnic restaurants also, and in both prices tend to be lower than in the typical tourist areas.

At first glance this area may not seem to offer much, but we urge visitors to take a closer look. Beaches from Kailua to Waimanalo are as beautiful as any in Hawaii. Stores which are not geared to tourists sometimes offer bargain prices. At any rate, those who wish to avoid the *typical tourist* locations can do it here.

## HOSTS

### O-23
This stunning round house, a home of stylish simplicity in a select community, is set in almost two acres of rich tropical flora. High on the slopes of the Koolaus, the range that lies between Honolulu and the windward coast, this home has a spectacular view of both Kaneohe Bay and the palis. The room offered has a double bed, private bath, its own entrance, and there is a garage for the guests' use. Facilities for tennis, swimming, bowling, shopping, and dining are available in the immediate neighborhood.
 The hostess is a former Californian, who is now retired from the University of Hawaii. She has travelled extensively and is interested in writing and story telling with emphasis on Hawaiiana. She is happy to share her enthusiasm for Hawaiian myths and legends and historic places with her guests.
RATE:   $30 single, $40 double.

### O-24
There is lots of room in this separate studio overlooking the town of Kaneohe. Guests are welcome to cool off in the pool and lounge on the deck right outside the door. Since this unit sleeps four comfortably, five if needed, it is ideal for a family. There is a hot plate, a sink, and a small refrigerator if guests wish to cook a meal. The home is in a residential area of Kaneohe.

Leroy was born and raised on Kauai and attended college in Illinois. Adele, who works for the Hawaiian Telephone Co., was born and raised in Kaneohe and is a graduate of the University of Hawaii. Pottery making is Leroy's vocation and his advocation, and he does much of his work in his studio near his home. Leroy's main hobby is potted plants with the raising of bonsai his particular interest.

RATE: $35 one rate. $5 for extra person.

## RESTAURANTS

**LOCAL STYLE**

CHUN'S B.B.Q.
In the industrial Park area. To find, turn mauka off Kam Highway on Kahuhipa St. and go about two or three blocks to Alaloa St., turn right and it is right there. Prices are low and food is cooked to local tastes.

KIN-SUN
A small place in the Foodland Shopping Center, just next to Flakie Jakes which is mentioned below. If you like local plate lunch style food, you will like this spot.

---

local Style

GOLDEN CROWN CHOP SUEY
At 46-018 Kam Highway on the mauka side of Kaneohe, they are open from 10:30 a.m. until 9:00 p.m. Cantonese style food, with low prices if one selects the plate lunch or dinner, which goes for $3.50 and $4.00.

MUI KWAI
At 45-1052 Kam. Hwy. and open daily from 10:30 to 9 p.m. The fare is strictly Hong Kong Cantonese. The dishes are mostly in the $3 to $5 range. The atmosphere is not fancy.

SMITTY'S*
At 46-077 Kam. Highway, across the street from the Windward Mall. Open from 7 a.m. until 10 p.m. daily. The great deal here is the early bird special between 3-6 p.m. One can get a good meal for as low as $4.45, and there are several selections. Another good deal is the all you can eat soup and salad bar.

KOA HOUSE
Just off Kam. Highway on the mauka side of Kahuhipa St. On weekends only breakfasts are served. During the week their menu for lunch and dinner is extensive and the prices are not high, many entrees under $10, 234-5772.

---

**local tourist Style**

**\*\*HAIKU GARDENS\*\***
We are embarrassed to admit that we missed this in our first edition. We had been told about it, but when looking for it we failed to drive far enough up Haiku Rd. We would urge anyone who is looking for a restaurant in a beautiful setting to be sure to try this. They are open for lunch and for dinner. The food is moderately priced. They are closed on Monday, 247-6671.

**KIN WAH**
This is a place that both hosts and guests love. We missed it first time around but any of our guests who stayed in Kaneohe or Kailua probably were told. The food is basically Cantonese, servings are generous, and the prices are not high, mostly in the $4 to $5 range, with many even less. They are located at 45-588 Kam. Hwy. which is on the mauka side. They are open daily from 10 a.m. to 9 p.m. 247-4812.

**ROSEY'S BOAT HOUSE**
Owned and operated by the same people who have Rosey's in Hilo, where they constitute one of the hot spots. The food is identical; ie., steak, fish, chicken. Prices are moderate to high. Usually there is dancing and they are open until 2 a.m., 247-0039.

**FLAKIE JAKES**
This is located in the Foodland Shopping Center at the Corner of King Kam Hwy and Kaneohe Bay Road. Maybe this is part of a chain from the Mainland that everyone knows about but us. The big deal here is hamburgers, not inexpensively priced, 1/2 pounder with cheese, $4.25. However, their dinners are not bad at $6.45 to $7.95.

## KAILUA/LANIKAI

The windward coast of Oahu has a population of around eighty thousand, which is around ten percent of the population of the Island. Most of these people live in the Kailua/Kaneohe area while most work in Honolulu. As stated above, this is not a tourist area as far as Mainland tourists are concerned, and yet this is one of the places that those who live in Honolulu come to get away from it all.

Kailua has become a special spot for windsurfers since conditions here are ideal: almost always a steady trade wind, a fairly calm ocean, and enough surf for it to be exciting. Good windsurfers make it look easy, but all one need do to see how difficult this sport is to master is to watch a beginner take fall after fall.

One of the surprising things to us about Kailua is the number of restaurants. Perhaps those living on the military base get tired of their chow line and eat out often. Whatever the reason, the benefit is that there is a wide choice of really good places to eat and the competition keeps prices in line.

It seems to us that the Kailua area is a perfect compromise for those who want to be close to lots of action (Honolulu is around 1/2 hour away) and those who want to get away from it all (either at the beaches of this area or the North Shore, also just a short drive away.) You can take our word for it that nowhere in Hawaii is the ocean any more beautiful than it is on this east shore of Oahu.

## HOSTS

**O-7**
Mary offers B & B guests a small comfortable one bedroom cottage separate from the main home. It is located right on the canal that runs through Kailua, and it also just a short walk to the ocean. The accommodation has a bedroom with a double bed and a private bath. The livingroom/kitchen area has a foldout sofa bed making this ideal for a family of three. Mary is an avid tennis player and both she and her husband enjoy golf. She is also a member of the Garden Club and her home reflects this. The outstanding feature of the yard is a huge monkey pod tree.
RATE: $45 single or double, $300 a week, $1200 a month.

**O-8**
Guests can enjoy breakfast on the lanai as they watch small sail boats, kyacks, windsurfers, and rowers go up and down the canal to and from the ocean. The accommodation offered is a garden bedroom, attached but separate from the rest of the home, with a private bath, T.V., double bed. There is also a roll away bed available so that a family of three could be accommodated. However, since roll is a large pool, Ron and Gay, the hosts, do not accept non-swimming children. Across the canal is the Mid-Pacific Country Club, nice to look at, but alas, very private and for members and their guests only. Even though Ron is an avid golfer, this sight does not bother him much as there are plenty of courses available in the area.
Ron, an executive with an international insurance brokerage, also likes a good game of paddle tennis and hiking. Gay enjoys the same activities, and as she says, anything else to keep in shape. However, when we stayed there, we noticed that their very bright, adorable little son Scott, now almost five, keeps them on the hop. In addition to the usual amenities, the hosts provide snorkeling equipment and boogie boards and a cooler for cold drinks.
RATE: $38.50, $5 extra for extra person.

**O-9**
There are two units offered for B & B guests in this home located in the Lanikai area of Kailua. One unit is called *Ocean View* the other *Sundeck*. Each unit is fully private, both with their own entrance and bath, and both are very well furnished, complete with TV's and radios. *Ocean_View* has a complete kitchen, so that long stays need not eat all meals out. *Sundeck* has a small frig and a toaster oven so that light snacks could be prepared. What is outstanding here is that the beach is just two houses away with beach access provided. *Ocean_View* has two twin beds that can be put together to make a king sized bed or kept apart as guests choose. *Sundeck* has a king sized bed and also a sofa bed. Since these two units can be joined together by the use of an adjoining hallway, they would be ideal for a family or two families traveling together. The hosts, a retired engineer and a homemaker, love traveling, golf, and sailing.
RATE: $100 for both units, $60 *Ocean View*, $45 *Sundeck*, $10 key deposit refundable, 4% State Excise Tax added.

## O-16

A gracious home in Kailua on a private access road one half block from a safe swimming beach. There are two large comfortable bedrooms with adjoining bath. There is a choice of twin or double beds. This is ideal for couples traveling together. Two covered lanais surrounded by tropical foliage are for the guests to enjoy. A separate refrigerator is provided for them. A shopping center is within walking distance and the bus line is also very handy to this home.

Ron and Donna, the hosts, have lived in Hawaii since 1960. Before that Nebraska was their home. Donna is a violinist with the Honolulu Symphony and Ron is an interior designer. Their four children are grown and now they have four grand children. Since Donna is with the Honolulu Symphony she can usually obtain tickets for guests who might be interested in such cultural events.

RATE:   $35 single, $40 double.

## O-17

This contemporary home, a short five minutes drive from the beach, offers guests one bedroom with two twin beds and one bedroom with a single bed. The two guest rooms share a bath. The home is open and airy and breakfast is usually served on the lush and secluded lanai. Lou Ann, the warm and friendly hostess, was raised on Oahu and is full of information for her guests. An administrator at the Kamehameha Schools, a private school for Hawaiian students, Lou Annis is also a counselor who conducts workshops for women and mediates for the Neighborhood Justice Center. Snorkeling is her favorite activity, and her son gives advice on Oahu surfing locations. Lou Ann usually attends music performances of all kinds, opera, baroque, and symphony and can assist visitors in obtaining tickets.

RATE:   $25 single, $35 double, a rollaway bed is available for a child, $7 extra.

## O-26

This home is located in the Enchanted Lakes area of Kailua, right on the golf course. The accommodation offered to B & B guests is a large bedroom/sitting room area with a private bath, with a sliding glass door which leads to a patio area where breakfast would be served. The room has a queen sized bed plus a day bed making this ideal for a family of three. Also, since there is no pool, small children would be safe playing in the yard.

RATE:   $40 one rate.

## O-28

This home is located in a residential area of Kailua very handy to everything in town and not far from the beach. The accommodation offered is a room with its own entrance and private bath. Not only does the room have TV but also a small frig, toaster, coffee maker, a microwave, and a few utensils. Guests could fix small snacks if desired. They also have use of the bar-b-que outside. The bedroom has two twin beds that could be put together as guests choose. Guests are also welcome to use the lovely pool to take a refreshing dip after a day of sightseeing, or just relax around the pool during the day.

Arnold and Marianne have been doing B & B for quite a while now and know how to make guests feel at home. Since they have a jewelry business, they are gone most of the day.

RATE:   $35 single or double, $215 weekly.

# RESTAURANTS

## LOCAL STYLE

### KIM CHEE #5 ONLY
That's the name, folks. It is located at 16 Kainehe St. in the same parking lot as Florence's (mentioned below). They are open every day for lunch and dinner and if you like Korean food you will not be disappointed here. You can get a good lunch for around $5.

### KOLOHE HAWAIIAN
Located at 415F Uluniu St. Unfortunately they are closed on Mondays, which was the day we were there, so we did not get a chance to sample the food. One of our guests liked it so much they ate there several days in a row.

### KAILUA OKAZU-YA
At 440 Uluniu St. just makai of Oneawa St. Very small, open for breakfast and lunch only. In this counter style restaurant, each item is priced and you select as much or as little as you want. Mostly the food is Japanese but there is a sprinkling of other Oriental dishes, also. Very low prices make this a good place to experiment if you have never tried this type of fare.

### IN SAM
Next door to Okaza-Ya. Korean food at low prices.

---

## local Style

### BAR-B-CUE-EAST
There are two of these in Kailua, one in the Kailua Shopping Center on Kailua Ave. and the other in the Industrial area on Hamakua Dr. You can get very ethnic food, but if you prefer you can get food that is more western. The prices are low and the atmosphere is O.K.

### CHINESE GARDENS
At 426 Uluniu St. Not much to look at from the outside but our hosts assure us that the food is good and prices are low. Cantonese style. For lunch they have plate lunches that are hard to beat.

### DRAGON PALACE
As you enter Kailua on Kailua road, take Hamakua to Keola, turn left and drive about one mile and you will come to the Enchanted Lakes Shopping Center on your right. It is located at the far left corner of the Center. This looked like a good place for a Chinese dinner as it was very clean and the prices were low, 262-2218.

---

## local/Tourist Style

### WALDO'S PIZZA
In the Aikahi Shopping Center which is at the north end of N. Kalaheo Ave. We have not included many pizza places, but our hosts assure us this the best pizza in the world.

*Bed & Breakfast Guide*

Next time over we will try it so we can be more informative.

**\*HARRY'S CAFE & DELI\***
Also in the Aikahi Center, closed Monday. This is a great place for a super sandwich, salad, or even an Italian dinner of lasagne or spaghetti for from $3-$5. Homemade soup. More than one host and guest has told us not to miss Harry's.

**THE SOURCE**
On the makai side of Kainehe St. a few doors down from Florence's. This is a very clean little health food store that serves vegetarian sandwiches, soup, and salad. We were told that the cook is a gourmet.

**SYLVESTER'S**
On Kekili St. a few doors down from L'Auberge (mentioned below). Open for lunch and dinner, kind of a pub like atmosphere. The sandwiches were fairly low priced, ie., steak sandwich for $5.95.

**CISCO'S CANTINA**
Also on Kekili St. We were told that this is really good Mexican food at low prices.

**\*CINNAMON'S FAMILY RESTAURANT\***
This is a little hard to find. It is located in the Kailua Center which is on Ulunui St. off Maluniu. They are open for breakfast, lunch, and dinner. We found the food good and the prices modest. Each day they feature a special from a different Nation.

**PLUSH PIPPIN**
This is located in a new Mall at the corner of Kekili and Hamakua. They are open every day for breakfast, lunch, and dinner. The specialty of the house is pies, all the way from apple to peanut butter. Their prices are in the modest range and they are much like many Mainland chains.

**GEE A DELI**
Somehow we forgot to put this in our last edition, unintentionally for sure. It is hard to find, but if you are looking for a good sandwich or a nice salad it is worth the hunt. It faces the parking lot behind Mac Donald's, which is not hard to find.

**ROB ROY'S**
Across from Los Arcos (mentioned above). Plenty of parking, open every day for breakfast, lunch and dinner, prices moderate, big naugahide booths.

**PAPAGALLO'S**
At Ululiu and Aulike. We did not get a chance to try this but we were told it was good Mexican fare and the prices are not high. It is a cute little place.

**\*LOS ARCOS\***
At 19 Hoolai St. This is a real sleeper. They specialize in Mexican food, but not the border style of enchiladas, tacos, and tamales, but such things as Bistec Pecado, cut up steak with onions, herbs, and peppers, or pork chops in a red sauce. From the outside the place does not show much, but do not be put off by appearances. They are open only for dinner. Prices run between $8.50 and $12.50, 262-8196.

### FLORENCE'S
At 20 Kainehe St. This is an old standby in Kailua, Italian food more or less. They are open for lunch and dinner with lunch being the better value by far. Dinner prices run a little over $10.00 except for a pasta dinner which runs $4.75, 261-1078.

### SOMEPLACE ELSE
This is located at 33 Aulike St. which used to be Buzz's Fish House. It was not yet open when we were there in July, 1986, but the sign said open soon. The place has been completely remodeled but we will have to wait to see what goes in there.

### BUZZ'S ORIGINAL STEAK HOUSE
On the mauka side of Kawailoa Rd. as you drive into Lanikai. We were glad to see that this was still in business since we have always enjoyed the ambience as well as the food, 261-4661.

### YUM YUM TREE
To find, take Kalaheo Ave. north from the center of Kailua and go around two miles and you will see it on your right. If you have tried the Yum Yum in Honolulu, you will know what to expect. There is a wide selection of entrees, most at moderate prices, in a very nice setting. We had lunch there and were pleased with the food and the cost. They are open daily for breakfast, lunch, and dinner.

### BUENO NALO
This is owned and operated and newly opened by the folks who have Bueno Nalo in Waimanalo mentioned below. It is located on Keola St., one of the main streets of Kailua.

### ORSON'S BOURBON
At the corner of Hoolai and Puniu just off Kailua Rd. This is another old stand by in Kailua, open for lunch and dinner. Lunch is not too high, but dinner prices run well over $10 and unfortunately not consistent in quality. They strive for elegance, 262-2306.

### **L'AUBERGE**
At 117 Kekili St. To find take Hahani St. mauka off Kailua, go one block and turn right. This is Kailua's special occasion restaurant, open for dinner only. This restaurant won an award for being one of the ten best restaurants on Oahu. That certainly indicates that it might be one of the best in Kailua, 263-4663.

### CELLA'S CAFE
At 324 Kalei Rd. We did not get a chance to try this new, small, attractive place, but we intend on doing so the next time we are in Kailua, if it is still in business.

## POINTS OF INTEREST

### HEEIA KEA BOAT HARBOR
Located on Kam. Highway just before you reach Kaneohe from the north. Fishing boats launch from this little harbor. There are no party fishing boats, but there is a glass bottom boat which would make a nice excursion. The boat leaves at 10 a.m., 11 a.m., 12:30, 1:30, 2:30, 3:30 p.m. The cost is $7 for adults and $3 for children.

## HEEIA STATE PARK
As you continue along Kam. Highway toward Kaneohe you will come to the Park on your left. This is a good place to picnic. The facilities are used mostly by the local folks for parties.

## BEACHES

### KAILUA BEACH PARK
To find take Kalaheo Ave. south from the middle of Kailua which will run into Kawailoa Rd. At Alala Rd., turn makai and go two blocks to the beach. There are full facilities here, picnic tables, rest rooms, showers, and the swimming is very safe. This is a good place to start a beach walk.

### LANIKAI BEACH
There is beach access all along Mokulua Dr. in Lanikai. This along with Kailua Beach is one of the nicest on Oahu and rivals any beach on the Islands.

## NIGHT LIFE

One of the hottest spots on Oahu is the 23rd Step, a disco located on Kalei St. in Kailua.

## SPORTS

### GOLF
#### PALI GOLF COURSE
A Public Course between Kaneohe and Kailua on the mauka side of Kam. Highway. Since this course gets lots of play, it is best to call ahead for a starting time. The fee is $8 on weekdays, $12 on weekends, carts $10.40 but not mandatory. Hand carts $1. For more information call 261-9784.

#### OLOMANA GOLF LINKS
This is a private course but open to the public. It is located just south of Kailua on the way to Waimanalo. The fee is $16 on weekdays, cart included, and $27 on weekends, cart included. After 12:30 the rate drops to $12 and $16. For more information call 259-7926.

#### BAY VIEW GOLF CENTER
Located makai of the Kam. Highway on Kaneohe bay Rd. This is an eighteen hole par three course right in Kaneohe. The fee is $5 on weekdays and $6.50 on weekends. Hand carts are available for a $1. For more information call 247-0451.

## TENNIS

In the Kaneohe/Kailua area there are three public courts: 1.) Kaneohe District Park, 45-660 Keaahaila Rd., six unlighted courts, 235-4731, 2.) Kailua Recreation Center, 21 S. Kaihalu Dr., eight courts, four lighted, 261-0686, 3.) Maunawili Neighborhood Park, Maunawili Valley Rd. one lighted court, 261-0686.

## WAIMANALO

This little town, squeezed between the sea and the mountains, gets a bad rap from most of the people in the tourist industry. While we have never had a problem there, we have spoken with others who have. Do not leave anything unattended either in your car or on the beach. Of course, that is the sensible thing anywhere, but we have been told that here things are sure to disappear. We would say just don't bother with the place except that Waimanalo has one of the most beautiful beaches in all Hawaii. Most of the problems occur at the public park where camping is permitted. Some of the people camping there are almost permanent residents.

The above was our last years comment, and, while we would still advise caution as far as leaving valuables in the car or on the beach when you went off swimming, we must say that Waiamanelo looked much different this year than in years past. First of all, the campers were gone. Oh, we saw a tent or two, but nothing like before. Most of the people we saw on the beach were local families having a picnic. Waimanalo seems to be on the upswing; if that is an accurate assumption, we strongly recommend a stop here as this is a really beautiful beach area that is in many ways unspoiled.

## HOSTS

### O-15A

Maria has a large property on the ocean in Waimanalo. Two separate accommodations are offered to B & B guests, each a little different. The Mauka Suite has a large bedroom with a queen sized bed done in Polynesian style. It has a small frig, TV, and a spacious bathroom with tub and shower. It has a private entrance that opens to a fenced secluded garden and lanai. The rapidly rising Koolau Mountain Range offers a breathtaking view. Also offered is the large and elegant Ocean Suite with sleeping/living room, private bath, and a separate entrance that opens to its on garden and lanai area. Large picture windows offer views over the wide expansive lawn area to the white sandy beach and ocean. Both of the units has a private access to a safe white sand swimming beach. Breakfast is served each morning and guests have use of the kitchen.

RATE: Mauka suite $55 one rate, five night minimum.
Ocean Suite $66 one rate, five night minimum.

## RESTAURANTS

**LOCAL STYLE**

KINGS CHOP SUEY
Just makai of the Kam. Highway on one of the side streets just past Waimanalo Beach Park. Not much to look at but the food is not bad and the prices are low. A mixture of Cantonese and local style food. They are open from 11 a.m. until 7 p.m., closed Tuesday.

DENNY BEE DRIVE INN
On Kam. Highway, take-out, plate lunch style, low prices. They have shave ice if all you want is something cool and refreshing.

---

local Style

*BUENO NALO*
On Kam. Highway, open Tuesday through Saturday from 11:45 a.m. until 9;15 p.m. As the name suggests Mexican cuisine. You cannot tell to look at the place, but this is a favorite with residents of Oahu. We were told that they drive out from Honolulu to eat here. The prices are fairly low.

CHER'S BUNKHOUSE
In a little shopping center at the north end of Waimanalo. They open around 9 a.m. and are open for breakfast, lunch, and dinner. They are attempting to be the night spot for Waimanalo. The prices are almost ridiculously low: fried chicken dinner for $5.95, BLT for $2.50.

## BEACHES

BELLOWS FIELD BEACH PARK
Because this is on a military base, access is given only on the weekends, starting at noon on Friday and going until 6 a.m. Monday. Many writers call this the most beautiful beach on the Island, and while it is nice, it is really no more beautiful than any beach from Waimanalo to Kailua. Camping with a permit is allowed and, in our opinion, that is what makes this a special place. Also, one feels very safe since access to the beach is controlled by the military. We have read that there is a lifeguard, but when we were there he was nowhere in sight. Swimming is safe and this is a good place for a beginner to learn to body surf as the waves are not too big.

WAIMANALO BAY STATE RECREATION AREA
Just north of Waimanalo. As mentioned above, this is an excellent spot, swimming is safe, and it has the added feature of lots of ironwood trees for shade should the sun prove too hot.

KAIONO BEACH PARK
At the south end of Waimanalo, this grass park makes a nice place to picnic, and it seems to get very little use

*Chapter VII*..................................................................MAUI

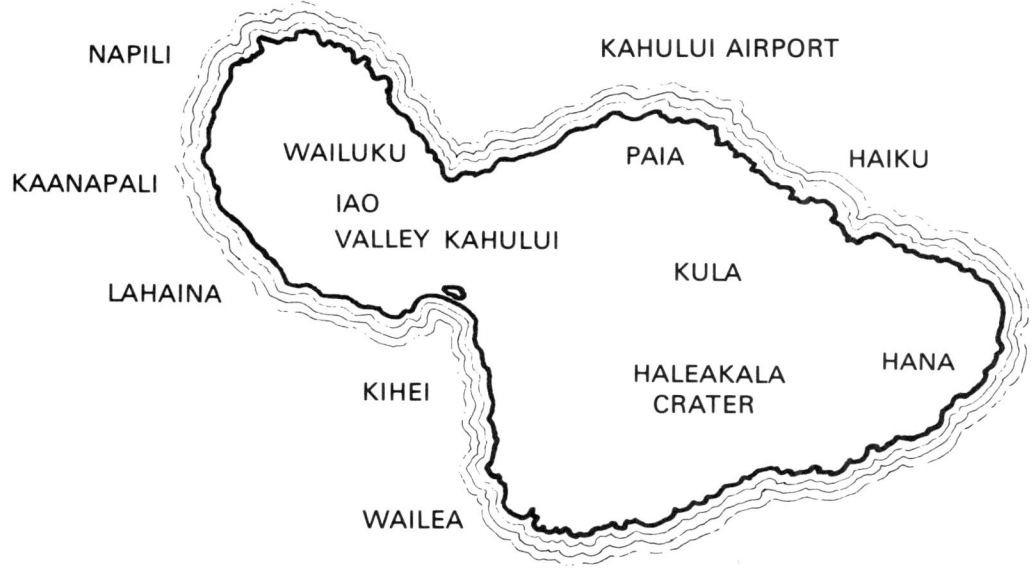

# MAUI.....THE VALLEY ISLE

.....DRIVING TIMES....

From Kahului airport to (approxmite)

Wailuku............................... 5 miles, 10 minutes
Iao Valley...........................10 miles, 20 minutes
Kihei....................................10 miles, 20 minutes
Wailea.................................15 miles, 25 minutes
Lahina.................................22 miles, 45 minutes
Kaanapali...........................27 miles, 55 minutes
Kapalua...............................37 miles, 65 minutes
Kula.....................................18 miles, 30 minutes
Haleakala............................36 miles, 90 minutes
Hana....................................52 miles, 2-3 hours

*Bed & Breakfast Guide*

# MAUI

When the average Mainlander thinks of Hawaii, it is probably Waikiki and Maui that come to mind; the numbers of visitors each receives attest to this. Indeed, the residents of Maui intone *Maui no ka oi,* which translates as *Maui is the best.* In fact, it is an old war chant which meant *Maui over all.* But Americans are used to regionalism, the attitude that makes Texans think they have it all when every Californian knows better, and New Yorkers put the Pacific several miles west of Manhattan and seem shocked they cannot get there by subway.

What is there about Maui that causes its partisans to shout its praises? Perhaps it all stems from the god whose name the Island bears, for it was this mighty god who pulled the islands from the sea, who later, to please his mother, caught the sun on a rope and forced him to slow his pace, and like Prometheus in another mythology, delivered to man the gift of fire.

On Maui is Haleakala, the world's largest dormant volcano and House of the Sun, where thousands trek annually at an ungodly early hour to glimpse the first rays of the sun. We rate this as one of the high points of a trip to the Islands.

While Mauians boast of the best of everything, we freely admit they have the best potato chips, the best onions, and incredibly beautiful scenery and beaches that rival the best. However, some would say that Maui along with Waikiki serves as the best example to the other Islands of what to watch out for, uncontrolled, poorly planned growth that has created more high rises than Hawaii ought to have.

Our view is that there is really no *best Island*. Each Island has its charm and its appeal. Too often neglected on any of the Islands are the non-tourist areas. So if Maui is your choice, be sure to experience Kahului, Wailuku, Paia, and the Upcountry of Makawao and Kula as well as all those white sand beaches.

# KAHULUI

When you land in Maui you will, no doubt, land at Kahului. Maui has three airports, Kahului, Hana, and Kaanapali, but only Kahului handles the larger planes. Most tourists' experience of the Kahului/Wailuku area consists of arriving and leaving Maui, places to drive through on the way to Kaanapali, Kihei, or Kapalua.

Kahului is the business and commercial center of Maui, with the only deep water harbor on the Island. The downtown area, all along Kaahumanu Street, consists mainly of three shopping centers: Maui Mall, Kahului Shopping Center, which is the oldest and funkiest of the three, and Kaahumanu Center, the newest, largest, and in many ways the nicest center on the outer Islands. Each Center has a number of restaurants, many of them in the fast food category. We have tried to point out those that in some way seem a little special. While this area is little frequented by tourists, there are good restaurants and several places of interest here.

### MAUI MALL
As you enter Kahului from the airport the first Center you come to is Maui Mall, which is newer than Kahului Center but older and smaller than Kaahumanu. Woolworths is the largest store in the complex. There are some half dozen basically fast food restaurants including Woolworths Harvest Home Snack Shop. All are moderately priced and seem adequate for a quick snack, but none is of particular note. One interesting shop is the Cycle and Sports Shop where diving and snorkeling information and equipment is available. Tour buses stop at this Center to let their passengers take advantage of the good bargains that Woolworths offers.

### KAHULUI CENTER
There are no large stores in this Center which obviously has been there for a long time. In the middle of the Center there is a tree lined mall with benches which makes a nice place for the local folk to sit and chat and watch the world go by, and based on our observation, many take advantage of it.

### KAAHUMANU CENTER
This is the largest and in many ways the nicest of the three Centers in Kahului. There are about fifty small shops, several nice restaurants, and two major department stores, Sears on the east end, and Liberty House on the west. There is a theater that shows first run movies and gives a senior citizen discount.

*Bed & Breakfast Guide*

## RESTAURANTS

**LOCAL STYLE**

**ICHIBAN-THE RESTAURANT**
At the west end of the Kahului Center facing Kaahumanu Ave. Ichiban in Japanese means "number one" so maybe they were the first restaurant in Kahului. The decor as well as the food served is pitched to the locals, but tourists are certainly welcome. It is clean and neat and the prices are low-lunch from $3 to $4. They are open for breakfast, lunch, and dinner.

**ALOHA RESTAURANT**
On Puunene St. one block south of Kaahumanu St. If you get a hankering for some real honest to goodness Hawaiian food (chicken hekka, lomi lomi salmon, kalua pig, lau lau, a bit of poi to round it all off) this is the place. When the residents really want to chow down, this is one of the places they go. Of course, you can get the same thing at any of the hotel luaus for around $25 to $30 a person, but believe us, it might not taste as good. At the Aloha it will cost 1/3 the price and no one will try to teach you the hula.

**SIR WILFRED'S**
Located in the Maui Mall. We did not get a chance to try this, but our hosts assure us it is very good.

**NOODLE KITCHEN**
At 251 Lalo Place. If you like the local style, this is a good chow down place with very reasonable prices.

-----------------------------------------------------------------

**local Style**

**MA CHAN'S**
At the front of the Kaahumanu Center. This is a good place to sample many different kinds of Oriental food. The front half of the restaurant is devoted to sit down table service while the back half is cafeteria service and hence a little lower in price. You get a good chance to look over what you are getting, which may be better for the uninitiated. We tried the shrimp tempura and although not as light and flaky as we like it, for $.75 each they would be hard to beat. Open from 6 a.m. until 8 p.m. Monday through Saturday, and from 6 a.m. until 3 p.m. on Sunday.

-----------------------------------------------------------------

**local/Tourist Style**

**\*IDINI'S DELI\***
Inside the mall behind Ma Chan's with an entrance on the parking lot side. To us this looks like a real find. They have a fine looking salad bar for $3.30 Their sandwiches looked great, served on a Kaiser roll and priced from $2.95 to $3.25. Since they are open from 8:30 a.m. until 11:00 p.m., late by the area's standards, this is a good place to eat either before or after the movie.

## APPLE ANNIE'S

On the far west of the Kaahumanu Center on the parking lot side. This is part of a Maui chain. While their menu is wide and somewhat modest in price, it is also a bit ordinary. It reminded us of a Denny's. The less adventurous would find this to their liking since it would seem familiar. At any rate, here you will get good food and you will not feel ripped off. They are open daily from 7 a.m. until 9 p.m., with a happy hour from 2-5 p.m.

## GUACAMOLE'S

Next to Annie's and as the name implies they serve Mexican food. They also have a happy hour from 2 to 5 p.m. Monday through Saturday and all day on Sunday.

## MING YUEN

At 162 Alamaha St., which runs along the east side of the Maui Mall. It is open for lunch and dinner every day but Sunday and then only for dinner. How we failed to have this in last year's book is a mystery to us since we have eaten here many times. The fare is both Cantonese and Szechun, very tasty, good service and moderate prices.

## LOPAKA'S

Located just across the street from Ming Yuen, this small restaurant opened in May of 1986. Lopaka is how you say Robert in Hawaiian. They are open from 11 a.m. until 10 p.m. with the same menu served all day. The food is reasonable and the atmosphere is O.K. They have a happy hour from 3-6 when drinks are reduced to $1.25.

## ISLAND FISH HOUSE

Just west of the Kahului Center, behind the bank. There are two Island Fish House restaurants on Maui, this one and the one in Kihei. This is by far the most elegant restaurant in the Kahului/Wailuku area and the prices reflect it. They are open for lunch Monday through Friday from 11 until 2 p.m., with sandwiches in the $5 range and entrees in the $6 to $10 range. As the sign says, dinner is served from 5 p.m. until "closing," Monday through Saturday and prices go from $10 for chicken to $20 for lobster. They almost always have local fresh fish and it is all enjoyed in a very stylish atmosphere.

## CHART HOUSE

On Puunene St. which runs along the east side of the Maui Mall, makai of Kaahumanu, the main street. This is a fairly large chain with several locations on Hawaii and the M9inland. If you are familiar with them, this one will present no surprises. They have an adequate salad bar, fresh local fish, and most of the entrees run around $15 with several chicken dishes for under $10.

## MAUI BEACH/ MAUI PALMS HOTEL

On the makai side of Kaahumanu as one enters Kahului from the airport. In the Maui Beach there are three different restaurants: Rainbow Buffet Lunch room, Red Dragon Chinese, and Prime Rib & Seafood. The Rainbow Room is open for lunch from 11:30 a.m. until 2:00 p.m. and is an all you can eat buffet at a fairly modest price. The Red Dragon Room is open every night except Monday from 5:30 to 8:30 p.m. Service is buffet, all you can eat, price moderate. Prime Rib and Seafood on the regular menu is more expensive. On Monday through Saturday the Maui Palms features the Imperial Japanese Buffet, which is excellent and the price is right. On Sunday they have the Hawaiian Buffet.

*Bed & Breakfast Guide*

## POINTS OF INTEREST

### MAUI POTATO CHIP FACTORY
At 295 Lalo St. If you haven't tried Maui Potato Chips you have missed a treat. You will really impress your friends if you stop by here and pick up a case of chips to take back home. Because of insurance liability they do not give tours.

### MAUI ZOO AND BOTANICAL GARDEN
To find take Kaahumanu St. east toward Wailuku and just before it starts to go up the hill, watch for Kanaloa Ave. on the right. Turn right on Kanaloa and go about 1/4 mile and you will find the Zoo on your right, across from the high school playing fields. While this is not much of a Zoo, it might make a nice break, especially if you have small children. They have several animals, monkeys, goats, a raccoon, and pygmy donkeys. Perhaps of more note than the Zoo is the Botanical Garden where an attempt is being made to preserve some of the plants once abundant on Maui.

### HAWAIIAN TROPICAL PLANTATION
To find go east on Kaahumanu St. to the town of Wailuku, turn left on High Street past the State and County buildings and go six miles to the town of Waikupu. You will see the Plantation just past the town on the right. This is not a bad place to shop for that gift to take home since the prices are not out of line. Every 1/2 hour there is a tour of the Plantation, which grows most of the Hawaiian crops: sugar, pineapple, papaya, banana, coffee, taro, avocado, mango, macadamia nut, guava, and even fish and prawn ponds. The cost of the tour is $5 for adults and $2.50 for children. The trolley stops half way around where fresh fruit and juice are served. We did not take the tour, but several guests have reported they found it very informative.

## BEACHES

While Kahului is not thought of as a beaching area, there are some nice spots if you know how to find them. Keep in mind, however, that the north and east of all the Islands is the windward side and that the surf, especially in winter time, can get quite rough. If you see one of the local boys riding the waves some half mile out, do not jump to the conclusion that all is safe. Off shore there are dangerous rips that can carry you away from the beach as if you were in a river. Swimming against them is useless. When drownings occur, it is usually under some such circumstances. That is not to say that one cannot enjoy playing in the surf. Also, these north shore beaches because of the prevailing winds tend to be a bit cooler than the south and west side beaches.

## KANAHA BEACH PARK
Just east of the airport. To get there take the airport road and turn left at the car rental area. Look carefully and you will see a sign pointing the way to the beach. Once you make the turn off the airport road, you should not have much trouble finding the beach. This is a great favorite with the residents of the area and on the weekends all of the tables go early. There are picnic tables, rest rooms, and showers.

## ALA KAPA BEACH
To find go east from Kahului to Ala Kapa Rd., turn makai to Laulea, turn left on the dirt road and go to the end. There are no facilities here. This is a great favorite with the windsurfers and you will see some good action at this spot.

## SUGAR GROVE BEACH
This is our name for this little secluded beach, which is much used by the residents. To find, take Nohehe Place makai to Paani St. and turn left to the Sugar Cove Condos where you will find a beach access path. No facilities.

## GOLF COURSE BEACH
Again, the name is our own invention as we have no idea what the beach is called. To find, take the road to the Maui Country Club and turn makai on Kealakai. No facilities.

## BALDWIN BEACH
Seven miles east of Kahului. This has the facilities, picnic tables, rest rooms, showers, but did not appeal to us at all.

## NIGHT LIFE

There is one theater in the Kaahumanu Center which shows first run movies and gives a good senior citizen discount. Sometimes there is something going on at either the Maui Beach or the Maui Palms Hotel. Since last year another theater has opened which shows first run movies as well as Japanese movies.

## SPORTS

### GOLF
The only course in Kahului is the Maui Country Club, which is listed as semi-private. When we visited there, we were not able to get a firm answer as to when guests could play. *Hawaii's Golf Guide* states that guests can play on Monday for a $10 green fee, $6 for a cart but not mandatory. For more information call 877-0616.

### TENNIS
There are two lighted courts at the Kahului community Park and two unlighted courts at the Kahului Salvation Army.

*Bed & Breakfast Guide*

# WAILUKU

Wailuku, the County Seat for the county of Maui, is just west of Kahului. *Wai* in Hawaiian means fresh water; *luku* suggests death and destruction. The name suggests that bloody battles were fought here, and that is exactly the case. In fact, in one big battle the river which runs through Wailuku turned red with blood from dead and dying warriors. Much more peaceful today, Wailuku gives the tourists a clearer picture of how life is lived in Hawaii today. Shops are geared for the Maui resident. Along Main St. and along Market there are many little stores with good prices. The restaurant prices also tend to be lower than in tourist areas. One must keep in mind, though, that the food is cooked for local taste.

## RESTAURANTS

**LOCAL STYLE**

SAM SATO'S
From Main St. turn right on Market and proceed north about 1/2 mile down the hill and you will see Sam's on the right at 318 N. Market St. Open for breakfast and lunch, Sam's specializes in Japanese and American with food mostly for local tastes. This is a good place to eat if you are budgeting.

FUJIYA'S
At 133 Market St. If you are a saimin lover this is your spot. Most tourists would probably take one look and walk on by, but the food is good and cheap.

YORI'S
Across the street from Sam Sato's. Some of our hosts rave about this place, maybe more about the owner than the food, although they assure us the food is good. The fare is a blend of Hawaiian, Japanese, American, really local style. You could spend the day looking at the pictures of patron's posted on the wall. If you eat there your picture will go on the wall also.

TASTY CRUST
One of our readers told us about this spot, and when we checked with our hosts they confirmed that the food, especially the Hot Cakes for breakfast, was good. The prices are very low, but do not expect a fancy atmosphere. They are open for breakfast lunch and dinner from 5:30 a.m. until 11 p.m. They are located on Mill Street just off Central Ave., which runs north off Main St.

-----------------------------------------------------------------

**local Style**

### SANG THAI
Makai of Main St. on Market St., about a block from Main. We ate here and were pleased with the prices and the food. There are several Thai restaurants on Maui now, in fact Sang Thai also has a place in Lahaina. There is an article posted on the window that says that Robert Redford ate there. Well, if it is good enough for Mr. Redford, we guess it is good enough for us.

### HAZEL'S CAFE
They have moved from their old spot, across from the old La Famalia at Vineyard and N. Church, but the move was not very far; just a few doors down Vineyard. This is a popular spot with the local folk for good reasons; the food is good and the prices are low. They are open for breakfast and lunch. Daily specials, including fresh fish at times, for under $6. While it is not much to look at, it is excellent value.

### *GOLDEN JADE*
South of Main St. at 301 Kalawi. Go one block above Market, turn left and go two blocks south, turn left and go east to Kalawi St. and turn right. To us this was the best restaurant in town for Chinese food. It is not much to look at either inside or out, and you will probably be the only tourist there. We went on a Sunday night and the place was packed, with several large banquet groups, yet the service was excellent. The servings were large and we made the mistake of ordering three dishes when two would have been ample. A good meal will run around $8 a person. They close early.

### NAOKEES
Most tourists just do not find this, which is fine with the locals; that way they don't have to wait so long for a table. If you are coming into Wailuku from the airport, just after the bridge, turn right past the market. At the next block turn right again and go to the bottom of the hill. Naokees faces the Main Street Bridge, but you enter from the back. As you enter the sign says, *Sorry, we're open.* The prices here are not as low as Hazel's and the food is not as local. Lunch for two will not be much over $10 and dinner not over $20.

### DOWN TO EARTH SNACK BAR
On Vineyard just above Central, behind the Health Food Store. Strictly take-out and for the health food eater. Prices are very low- avocado, tofu, or cheese sandwich for $2 or combine all three for $2.50.

----------------------------------------------------------------

**local/ Tourist Style**

### WAILUKU GRILL
This little restaurant located on the makai side of Main Street opened in February of 1986 and is doing very well. They are open for breakfast and lunch from 7 a.m. until 3 p.m. and they for dinner from 5-9. There prices are reasonable and the atmosphere is nice.

### CHUMS
This is a new place located on Center St. just off Main just as you cross the bridge coming into Wailuku from Kahalui. It is owned by the same people who own Ming Yeun but the menu is not strictly Chinese.

### PINTO'S
At 2065 Main St. next to the Party Pantry. They are now open for breakfast, lunch and dinner every day. Most of the food is Italian style. This is a fairly new restaurant in Wailuku which seems to attract the professional people from the area. Prices are a bit higher than most of the restaurants in town, but not as high as the resort areas. Recently they have added an early bird special of Prime Rib for $9.95.

### THE SAND TRAP
Four miles west of Wailuku, at the Public Golf course, you get there by taking Market St. off Main and driving four miles to the town of Waihee. In the center of town you will see a ball field on the right. Turn right and proceed to the end of the road. Kind of a snack/bar/restaurant, it is open from 11 a.m. until 2 p.m. for lunch, and from 2:30 - 6 p.m. for pupus (light snacks). Prices are very moderate, chicken and fries $3.95, BLT $3.75, burger with fries $2.95.

## LOWER MAIN STREET RESTAURANTS

We had a little problem finding Lower Main Street so perhaps directions will help. If you are heading east on Main St., follow the sign at the bridge which points to the right and proceed until the road dead ends. Turn left and you are on Lower Main no matter what the signs say. There are several restaurants in this area worth finding, and they are all local style. Few tourists eat in these restaurants and in our opinion many are missing a good deal, at least if the local style food appeals to you. We will list them in the order you would come to them if you were driving down Lower Main.

**local Style**

### ARCHIES
On the left side of Lower Main. Don't be fooled by the name, this is not the local pub even though it may have that look. It is local Japanese style food with several American dishes on the menu also. We recently had lunch there and enjoyed it very much. The bill was around $8 for the two of us. It is open from 10:30 a.m. until 2 p.m. for lunch and from 5 p.m. until 8:30 for dinner.

### WING SING'S
Located just next door to Archies. A very popular place for Chinese food, and although it is plain and the service unpredictable, the food is good and very reasonable. There is a large variety of items to choose from, all Cantonese style. They are open for both lunch and dinner. Depending on how hungry you are, dinner should run between $10 and $15 for two.

## TIPANAN
Located just a little way down the street from Wing Sing's on the same side of the street. If you like Filipino food you will be glad we mentioned this.

## TIN YING
On the same side as the above, open for lunch and dinner from 10:30 until 9 p.m. The food is Cantonese style, not much atmosphere, but a real experience in *local* dining.

## NAZO'S*
As you drive down Lower Main you will see a large series of buildings on your right called Puuone Plaza. Nazo's is located on the upper level. You can either park below or drive up to it. Not many tourists find this so you may be the only tourist here. Almost all entrees are below $7 and features such things as fried chicken, roast pork, corned beef and cabbage, and mahi mahi. They are open for breakfast, lunch, and dinner seven days a week.

## TOKYO TAI
In the Puuone Plaza on the lower level at the opposite end from Nazo's. This is really excellent food at very reasonable prices. Lunch is served from 11 a.m. until 2 p.m. and almost all dishes are under $6., with salad and rice included. Dinner is served from 5 p.m. until 9 p.m. and unless you want steak the bill for two will run around $12.

## MOON HOE
Just down and across from Tokyo Tai. The cuisine is Cantonese and Scezhan, the prices are modest and from the looks of things when we were there, you won't need a reservation.

## POINTS OF INTEREST

## IAO VALLEY STATE PARK
Most tourists pass through Wailuku for only one reason, to get to Iao Valley State Park and see the Iao Needle, a pinnacle which reaches to an elevation of around 2200 feet, with the Iao stream flowing at its feet. Iao State Park is about three miles west of Wailuku and is not difficult to find. Just proceed up the hill on Main St. through the town of Wailuku and when the road divides, take the one to the right and you will dead end at the parking lot for the Park.

The walk from the parking lot to the lookout at the top is about a five to fifteen minute walk, depending on how you go about it. Iao Valley is very lush and if there has been some rain, you are apt to see several water falls on the cliffs above. The best time to see the valley is in the a.m. since the needle can be obscured by clouds in the afternoon. However, the local residents say you haven't really seen the Valley until you have seen it on a clear full moon night.

When you reach the top lookout you will see a dirt trail going beyond. We took it for about a 1/4 mile but could see no reason to continue since our view was not improving. When you return to the parking lot, you might like to return by the path which goes along the stream. That will give you a better view of the many tropical plants which grow along the stream.

### KEPANIWAI PARK or HERITAGE GARDENS
Very easy to find since you pass it just before you reach Iao Valley State Park. This is a series of gardens representing the heritage of the people of Hawaii. There is a Japanese, Chinese, Filipino, Portuguese and Hawaiian garden. Since there are many picnic tables and barbecue pits, all of the tables covered in case of showers, this makes an excellent place to have a picnic. Perhaps while you are there, you will get a chance to see a wedding as the Chinese Garden is much favored for this.

### HALE HOIKEIKE
Maui Historical Society Museum. This was once the home of Edmond Bailey, a 19th Century missionary. It is not extensive and will not take long to see, including the art works of Mr. Bailey housed next door, but it is definitely worth the stop. You will see many artifacts from before the arrival of Captain Cook plus some fine examples of koa furniture which at one time was fairly common in Hawaii. It is open Monday through Saturday and costs $2.50 for adults, $1 for children.

### KAAHUMANU CONGREGATIONAL CHURCH
Since this the oldest church on Maui, it is of some note. To see the inside, however, one must attend the Sunday service as the church is not open during the week.

### HENRY ITO'S ORCHIDS
To find turn makai on Market St. off Main and go about 1/2 mile until you see the TK Supermarket on the left. Just past the market you will see Mohuhua St. Turn left and about 1/2 mile up the hill you will see Henry Ito's Orchids on the left. Some of the plants are for sale and can be shipped to the Mainland.

### WEST OF WAILUKU
If you play golf on Maui's Municipal course, you will become familiar with the four miles west of Wailuku. Most tourists, we feel sure, never venture out this way, and we feel they are missing something. Just the drive from Wailuku to Waihee four miles to the west can be quite nice. We took it for the first time trying to find a cool spot and it worked, for along this lush north west coast the trade winds do their best work. As you leave Wailuku you will be in the middle of what someday will be a huge macadamia nut orchard. Now the trees are all small.

It is beyond Waihee however, where the road really gets interesting. One can, if so inclined, drive from this point all the way around to Napili and the west shore of Maui. From Wailuku to the good paved road above the Napili/Kapalua area is 17 miles. If you take this drive, be prepared for the last two miles which are unpaved and very rutty. In fact if there have been heavy rains or it looks as if there might be while you are driving, you probably won't make it without four wheel drive. Having said all that, we still want to encourage you to take the trip, since some of the views are spectacular. Even if you do not go the entire way, drive far enough, about 12 miles from Wailuku, to get a view back to the Kahului area.

## BEACHES

West of Wailuku is a good spot for ocean views but not for ocean activities. Most of this coast line is steep and rocky, with a small beach here and there. The surf even at the best of times is strong, with dangerous rips, and at its worst, it is awesome. There are so many safe places to enjoy beaching that it would be foolish to try it along these shores.

## SPORTS

### GOLF
Waiehu is Maui's only municipal course. The green fee during the week is $15, on weekends $20. Carts are available for $11.50 for one or two but they are not mandatory. It is difficult to get a starting time here so call ahead or try late afternoons. For more information call 244-5433.

### TENNIS
There are five lighted courts at the Maui War Memorial Center that are open to the public.

*Bed & Breakfast Guide*

# UPCOUNTRY MAUI

On the slopes of Haleakala, which rises to a little over 10,000 feet, are several little towns and communities, all known as Upcountry Maui: Pukalani, Makawao, Kula, and, for our purposes, the little town of Paia, which is eight miles east of Kahului on the road to Hana.

Upcountry is the farm-ranch area of Maui where the somewhat famous Maui onion is grown. On Maui they are called *Kula Onions* and though they are expensive, $1.50 a pound, those who try them feel they are worth the price. Also grown in this area is Protea, a unique flowering shrub imported from Africa. Many of the carnations so popular for leis are grown in the Kula area. Upcountry even boasts of a winery, the Tedeschi Winery, which is known for pineapple wine and is in the process of producing grape wine.

If you go to the top of Haleakala you will go through part of this area, but you will not see it all unless you take a few side roads. When it gets too hot in the low lands, a drive up to Kula is most rewarding.

## HOSTS

**M-4**
Natalie came to Maui from the Mainland eight years after retiring from a career as management consultant with the Navy. Her home is a modern cedar chalet built on 2 acres, about 17 miles from the airport, on the beautiful green slopes of Haleakala crater in paniolo country near Makawao.
While active in community affairs, Natalie's hobbies are in music, art, and in pampering a retired race horse in his waning years whose buddy is a feisty little burro. She is sometimes available for tour-guiding since she enjoys sharing anecdotes on the history of the Island.
Her home is tastefully decorated, offering the accommodation of either a bedroom with twin beds or one with a queen sized bed, adjacent to a bathroom. A hearty breakfast is served; limited kitchen privileges, no children, and no smoking, please.
RATE: $40 single, $49.50 double.

**M-4A**
Denise and Clark offer B & B in their newly remodeled 1850 Plantation home in Upcountry Maui. The home was originally built for the doctor of the old pineapple cannery and has a long and interesting history. It is located around fifteen miles from the airport in Kahului, out toward Hana, in the midst of the pineapple fields. It is a perfect location for windsurfers who want to experience Hookipa Beach (a three minute drive) or for exploring Mt. Haleakala or Hana. Two bedrooms are offered, with a bath between the two rooms. One of the bedrooms has twin beds, the other has double. T.V in

the rooms can be provided upon request. Guests have use of the big front porch for outside sitting as well the living room with its 11 foot ceiling and the dining room where Denise serves breakfast.

The hosts are originally from Northern California. Clark now works for the Wailea Development and Denise works part time besides taking good care of her guests. Picnic lunches, laundry services, touring are some of the extras you can specially request.
RATE;   $30 single, $45 double.

## M-6

Freshly ground Kona Macadamia Nut Coffee, homemade whole wheat toast or banana bread, fresh fruit compote is a great way to start the day in this spectacular upper Kula home. It is located at about 3800 foot elevation on the slopes of Mt. Haleakala, just a short walk to the Kula Botanical Gardens. From this home it is around a 45 minute drive to the top of Maui's famous 10,000 foot high dormant volcano. The guest room provides an early morning panorama of pale pink clouds over the West Maui Mountains, stretching from the island of Lanai and Lahaina Town to the Kahului harbor. The king sized bed is covered with a goose down quilt. The white tiled private bath is not only huge, with both shower and bath, but also comes with an exercise bike for the energetic. This custom home is surrounded by 12 acres of Wattle forest and gulches. Hostess, Jody, suggests you find her place before dark, at least on the first night, and that you keep in mind the elevation and wear warm clothes, for by Hawaii standards in can get freezing up here, maybe even even into the fifties. From Jody's home it is about 15 minutes to the nearest restaurant, 30 minutes to Hookipa beach, and about 2 1/2 hours to Hana. This is a great place for those who love quiet and solitude and want to experience more of Hawaii than the beach.
RATE:   $45 single or double.

## M-6A

This Upcountry home is located on the 12th fairway of the Pukalani Country Club, at an elevation of around 1200 feet. Rob and Nilsa are eight year residents of Maui and very capable of providing information to supplement the guide books. Rob is a family counselor and certified hypnotherapist; Nilsa is a retired chemistry teacher. Both are active in community affairs. The room used for B & B guests has twin beds and the bath which is for guests only is just across the hall. Hosts observe the Island custom of not wearing shoes in the house, and they do not smoke. For those wishing to picnic, hosts can provide gear. They offer limited use of the kitchen, and for a small charge use of the laundry facilities.
RATE:   $40 single or double.

## M-8

This peaceful B & B is situated on an acre planted with huge eucalyptus trees at the 3000 foot level. Kathleen and David, the hosts, want to share their pole house all done in cedar and glass with cathedral ceilings. Kathleen has worked with the Hawaii Visitors Bureau, coordinating convention groups, since 1980, and David is a commercial fisherman in Alaska. Guests enjoy breakfast served on the 1000 foot deck and evenings in front of the fireplace. Accommodations include two rooms, one with a queen sized bed and one with two twin beds. There is a bath in between the two rooms which is used exclusively by the guests. This is ideal for two couples traveling together or a small family.
RATE:   $40 single, $45 double.

*Bed & Breakfast Guide*

#### M-12
Karl and Kuulei offer B & B in their 3 bedroom, 2 and 1/2 bath home. The view from the large deck overlooks all of central Maui from the Kihei coast to the West Maui Mountains. Located in Kula at the 3000 foot level on four acres, this is a great location for anyone looking for quiet and solitude and it is just 45 minutes to the top of Mt. Haleakala. Two rooms are used for B & B guests, one with a queen sized bed, the other twin beds. The bathroom is between the two rooms so that two couples travelling together would share the bath. Other than that it is a private bath.
  Karl is active in the Real Estate Industry. Kuulei, who works in the travel business, was born and raised in Hawaii and is a real kamaaina. The hosts have one horse and two dogs, all kept outside. Non-smoking guests only, please.
RATE:   $35 single, $45 double.

#### M-9
Rob and Clemi are former international airline employees presently watching the world go by in their own corner of Makawao, Maui, a charming town with an Old West flavor, on the slope of Mt. Haleakala at around 2000 foot elevation. Restaurants and markets are just a few minutes away and it is about a 30 minute drive into Kahului. The drive to Lahaina takes around one hour. Two of the three bedrooms are available for B & B guests. One of the rooms has a queen sized bed with built in reading lights. the other room has a single bed and a color T.V. The Hosts serve a continental breakfast on a large deck which overlooks a pasture where horses graze. For the more adventurous, there are trails which wind through local ranch country, along roads reminiscent of Ireland in the spring.
  Clemi is a writer who has a strong interest in Hawaiiana and a boundless enthusiasm for her Island of choice. Rob teaches at the local parochial school. Children are welcome.
RATE:   $35 single or double, $15 for child.

#### M-18
Dale, an interior designer who once had her own company in New York, has travelled extensively in Europe, Asia, North Africa, Mexico, and when she does travel she stays for long periods in an area, so she really gets to know a place. This gives her time to explore for artifacts, which she collects. She is a gourmet cook who makes a point of eating at restaurants known for their unique specialties. Her library is extensive and eclectic and the books are not decorative; she is an omnivorous reader. Some of her friends feel she is a bit eccentric. Could this be because she has two dogs, five cats, and four donkeys?
  Her home is a show place, situated on seven acres in a very private setting, cantilevered over gulch and stream, and has a great ocean view from the large deck. The accommodation offered is a room with a private bath and separate entrance. There is also the possibility of renting the entire home. Staying here could be that unique experience you are looking for.
RATE:   $55, three night minimum: house, $137, seven day minimum.

#### M-18A
This the last one listed in the Upcountry area but it is not last in our recommendation, at least for those who want a special experience and hang the cost. Joe, the host and the designer and builder of this unique home, has done an outstanding job of creative design. As guests enter the home their first view is a huge mural wall of a surfer catching a big one. Then there are a few stairs down to the living area, past a small interior stream and small fish pond. The bedroom used for B & B guests taxes our powers of description. It

is so cleverly built, using glass to create an open feeling, that you will feel you are nesting with the birds in a tree house, and the view is a tree-top view indeed! Guests, of course, have their own private bath, with a shower that provides a view of the Kula landscape all the way to the blue Pacific. Located above that room at the end of a circular staircase is a small room Joe calls the "moon room." It is entirely glass enclosed, hence not for day use as it is quite warm. But imagine the view of the heavens from the bed that rotates 360 degrees. Guests breakfast by the stream that runs through the home or out on the cantillevered deck which hovers over a tropical paradise. Then when guests return after a long day of exploring the Island, Joe asks them to relax in the hot tub and perhaps to share a glass of champagne. Joe is an easy going bachelor who likes to see folks smile.
RATE: $95 double for one night, $85 double for 2-4 nights, $75 double for 5 nights or more.

## PAIA

As stated above, Paia is on the road to Hana so most visitors to Maui have at least been through it. In fact, many who are Hana bound stop for a bite to eat since once past Paia there is not much civilization until one arrives at Hana. In Paia there are many little shops, most geared for tourists. We were not impressed with what they had to offer or the prices charged. But there are several antique/junk stores that are fun to browse through, and there are several restaurants mentioned below that are worth consideration. Many residents of Maui think of Paia as a Hippie type area that is getting a big economic lift from the wind surfers who come from all over the world to windsurf this coast. We could not see where things had changed much except that our favorite restaurant, Piero's Garden, is no more.

### RESTAURANTS

### LOCAL STYLE

**LARRY'S NALU-KAI LODGE**
On the left side of the Hana Highway just opposite Baldwin St. Low prices and not much atmosphere. We ate here and found the food acceptable, but not fancy. They also have over-night accommodations at low rates.

-----------------------------------------------------------------

### local/Tourist Style

**PICNICS**
On Baldwin St., which is the main street in Paia and goes mauka of the main highway, on the right hand side as one heads for Makawao. If you ask the people who live in the area where to have lunch, chances are they will say Picnics. Health food people love it for the specialty of the house, a Spinach Nut Burger, which consists of peanuts, spinach, and soy bean meal all ground together and broiled like a hamburger. We asked the girl at the

counter if it tasted like meat. She assured us it tasted like spinach and peanuts all ground up together. We had a club sandwich on a Kaiser roll and a Chef Salad, both under $4.00. They are open for breakfast, lunch, and dinner.

### DILLONS
On the makai side of the Hana Highway. Open for breakfast, lunch, and dinner. A good deal here is the early bird breakfast special from 8- 9 a.m. of Eggs Benedict for $3.85. The sandwiches and lunch specials are higher here than at Picnics, but the atmosphere and service is also a step up. While a lasagne dinner is around $8.00, most of the entrees are over $10.

### CHARLIE'S
Just past Baldwin on mauka side of highway. Especially noted for their pizzas, but sandwiches and other dishes available. Prices moderate.

### GARDEN RESTAURANT
This is a little lunch spot located where Piero's was. We did not get a chance to try it but will the next time we are in Paia.

### MAMA'S FISH HOUSE
Just east of Paia on the makai side of the Hana Highway. This is a popular spot for residents and tourists alike and often the only restaurant in Paia mentioned in most guide books. Mama's has been serving delicious local fish for about eleven years now. They are open for lunch from 11-2:30 and for dinner from 5-10 with a happy hour from 2-4. Most entrees run over $15. Some of our hosts feel their prices are just too high.

## BEACHES

### HOOKIPA PARK
Located right at the town of Paia, convenient but not too appealing. Swimming is not recommended because of the strong currents. Rest room facilities, picnic tables available. Camping allowed with a permit.

## MAKAWAO

Four miles south of Paia, up Baldwin St. mauka of Paia, is the cowboy like village of Makawao. Unless you stop here to eat at one of the places mentioned below, you will not be here long. Like Paia, there are some shops which seem to be geared toward tourists, fun to browse through and you might find the unusual gift to take home. One shop, Upcountry Down Under, has imports from New Zealand, a very different selection for Hawaii. There is also a small shop which specializes in cowboy boots, which is appropriate for this area.

## RESTAURANTS

**local/Tourist**

POLLI'S MEXICAN RESTAURANT
In the center of Makawao Town Polli's is one of the most popular spots in Upcountry and for good reason; the food is good, the portions are large, and the prices are moderate. They are open for breakfast, lunch, and dinner.

MAKAWAO STEAK HOUSE
On the right hand side of Baldwin as one enters from Paia. Nothing outstanding here, much like Chart House/Spindrifter restaurants. The food is good, nice salad bar, with most entrees between $10 and $15. They do have an early bird special for $9.95 from 5-6 p.m., but the menu is limited.

PARTNER'S-THE GATHERING PLACE
Last year this was Rodeo's. The new place opened on July 4, 1986, and is open for lunch and dinner. Food is served until mid-night, or as the new owner said, "Until the cook goes home." Their prices are moderate, chicken dinner $8.95, a 16 ounce steak for $12.95. They also have live entertainment Thursday through Saturday starting at 9 p.m. They will also prepare food to go for those who want to picnic somewhere up Haleakala. 572-6611.

## PUKALANI

Pukalani, about eight miles up the Haleakala Highway, is the first community one reaches after leaving Kahului, and unless you want to stop here to eat or play golf at the Pukalani Country Club, you will pass through in seconds.

## RESTAURANTS

**LOCAL STYLE**

Y'S OKAZU-YA
In the Pukalani Shopping Center on the right as you enter Pukalani is a Japanese cafeteria style restaurant where the local folk like to eat. A good sized lunch runs around $5, it is all tasty Oriental style food, served cafeteria style.

-----------------------------------------------------------------

**local/Tourist**

LUIGI'S PIZZARIA
Located in the Pukalani Shopping Center. They have entertainment on Friday night.

BULLOCKS
On the right as you leave Pukalani. This is a good place for a quick lunch. Prices are low and the food is not bad. The specialty of the house is moonburgers and guava shakes. They are open from 7:30 a.m. until 8:30 p.m.

GOLF COURSE
Go down the road that the shopping center faces and it will take you to the golf course, which has a nice little restaurant with modest prices. From here there is an excellent view of Kahului and the valley.

## KULA

Whether one takes the high road which continues on to Haleakala or the low road that goes to Tedeschi Winery, one is in Kula, for Kula is an area not a specific location.

## RESTAURANTS

**local/Tourist Style**

### KULA LODGE
On the right side of the Haleakala Highway. The best thing about eating at the Kula Lodge is the magnificent view of most of Maui below: from Kahului and the west Maui Mountains, to the Kihei coast line in the south. The food is nothing special, but certainly O.K., and the prices are not as high as Haleakala. They are open for breakfast, lunch, and for dinner on Friday and Saturday.

### SILVERSWORD
Across and up from the Kula Lodge, this consists of five chalet style cottages, a bar, and a restaurant. This reopened in September, 1984, with a limited menu. For lunch the specialty will be hamburgers, and not the frozen, pre-made, 1/4 pounder, we were told. We look forward to trying this on our next trip over. Sorry, we missed it again.

## POINTS OF INTEREST

### TEDESCHI WINERY
On the Ulupalakua Ranch on the southwest slopes of Haleakala, you get there by taking the lower Kula Rd. after passing Pukalani. Or if you are taking the road from Hana south, you reach it soon after you hit paved road. If you do come the Hana way, it is likely to be closed since the drive takes so long and the winery is open from 10 a.m. until 4 p.m. The Winery is already well known for its pineapple wine and will soon be making grape wine.

### PROTEA FARM
The road to this is off the upper Kula Rd. as one nears Kula Lodge. Watch carefully and you will see a sign pointing to the left. Take that road and continue on until you come to the Protea farm a mile or so up the road. On the way you will pass several small carnation farms, beautiful when the flowers are in bloom. If you have not seen protea before, you will find this an interesting stop. Feel free to ask questions as they are ready and willing to talk. You can buy flowers and they will ship them to the Mainland. Protea makes a nice arrangement either dried or fresh. They are not native to Hawaii, but they do very well in the Islands at higher elevations, and there are some that do well at sea level. At times you can buy the flowers on special for $1.25, regularly $2.00. Plants can be shipped, $20 for package of four. For more information write to Protea Farm, Rt. 1, Box 485 F, Kula, Hi 96790, or call 808-878-6015.

## HALEAKALA

To visit Maui and fail to drive to the top of Haleakala, the House of the Sun, is in our view a big mistake. In fact, do yourself a favor and go there to see the sun rise. The distance from Kahului to the summit is around 38 miles, but you need to allow around two hours for the drive, and keep in mind that sunrise at the top is around fifteen minutes sooner than at sea level. At any time of the year it can be cold, so bring warm clothes, especially in the winter, or you will wish you were somewhere else. From the rim of the crater you will view 19 square miles of awesome moon-like landscape.

Haleakala is one of the favorite hiking places in Hawaii, and short hikes down into the crater are possible. Remember, the elevation is 10,000 feet and the air is much thinner so hiking can be more difficult.

Near the top is Haleakala Visitors Center with models and illustrations of the geological history of the dormant volcano. If the day is clear, the view cannot be surpassed anywhere in the world. To check on the weather conditions call 572-7749.

## SPORTS

### GOLF

Pukalani is an eighteen hole course open to the public. Except during the height of the tourist season (January-March) starting times are not hard to get. Since the winds become quite strong in the afternoon, play is much better in the a.m. Green fees are $22, carts are $16 on a share basis, making the cost for a couple $60. For more information call 572-1314.

### TENNIS

There are two lighted courts at the Eddie Tam Memorial Center, one lighted court at Halimaile Park, and one lighted court at the Pukalani Park. All of these are open to the public at no charge.

# HANA

In spite of all you have heard about the difficulty of driving to Hana, we feel this is a must trip. A trip to Hana should be started with a full tank of gas and possibly a picnic lunch, as there are no gas stations or stores once you pass Paia. You will hear all sorts of stories about how rough the drive is, depending on how long ago the person telling you made the trip. We last made the trip in the fall of 1984 and the road had recently been improved so the drive was not all that bad. The distance from Kahului to Hana is about 50 miles. The first 20 are good, the next 15 not bad, while the last 15 gets a little bumpy and the road gets narrow. If you move right along with a minimum of stops, it will take about two or two and a half hours. Then again, if you want it to, it can take all day, as there are many places along the way to stop and sight see.

Hana itself is a delightful, sleepy little place with not much going on. Be sure to spend some time on the beach there, where the water is calm and swimming is easy. Some of the beaches both before and after Hana can be rough, especially in the winter months. Also, visit the Hana Maui Hotel, which is the center of everything in Hana.

Fifteen miles beyond Hana is the famous Seven Sacred Pools. To us the Pools were a disappointment. While the getting there was beautiful, the pools were muddy and did not look inviting; though many people swim there, it is not recommended because of bacteria from the animals living above the pools. The walk over to the pools and down to the ocean was pleasant.

Past the pools the road really gets rough, and if you are in a rented car you are not supposed to drive it. Mauians will tell you that it is no big deal and that they do it all the time in their little old whatever it might be. Well, we have good news and bad news. The bad news is that it is a big deal, and while the views are spectacular, to say the road is rough does not do it justice. We made the trip during a dry time, and we could not go much more than 10 to 15 miles an hour for the 10 miles of unpaved road. The good news is that you won't run into any traffic jams. If you tend to be timid, do not make the trip. But if you like to take chances, go for it. You might ask, would we do it again? Absolutely!

One of our readers questioned why we would recommend this road and not the Saddle Road on the Big Island. We have taken the Saddle Road and enjoyed it very much. However, if one has not driven up through Waimea or down through Volcano and around to Kona, we feel they would get the short end of things just to save a little time. If a person has already travelled these roads, then we suggest taking the Saddle Road; just don't tell the car rental places we said so.

*Bed & Breakfast Guide*

## RESTAURANTS

### LOCAL STYLE

**TUTU'S**
At Hana Bay, home style cooking, open for breakfast and lunch. Open seven days a week, prices low for plate lunch specials. You can buy it here and picnic on the beach.

------

### local Style

**HANA RANCH**
Definitely the budget spot in Hana. Open from 11 a.m. until 4 p.m., buffet style. The food is not impressive, but if you are starved and on a budget, you can have lunch for under $5.

------

### local/Tourist Style

**HOTEL HANA MAUI**
Open for breakfast, lunch, and dinner. The prices are high, but the service is elegant and the food is good.

## POINTS OF INTEREST

**KEANAE ARBORETUM**
On the Hana Highway after you pass Paia. You may want to walk around here to see taro under cultivation. The view overlooking Keanae is one of the most picturesque in Hawaii.

**HELANI GARDENS**
Located just a short distance past Waianapanapa State Park on the right. Open from 10 a.m. until 3:30, adults $2.00, seniors $1.50, children $1.00. B & B members get a $.50 discount. You can walk the lower garden, some five and a half acres of tropical and subtropical plants including a koi pond and a bamboo grove, and tour the upper garden in your car or ask a staff member to show you around. Also, there are picnic tables.

## BEACHES

### HONOMANU BAY
Located off the Hana Highway about 30 miles east of Kahului. To find take the dirt road just past Kaumahina State Park and follow it to the beach. This is a beautiful, secluded black sand beach in a tranquil setting. There are no facilities, and like many beaches on the north and east shore, not always good for swimming. Because of the high waves, the surfers love it.

### WAIANAPANAPA STATE PARK
This black sand beach is a great place for a picnic, and the swimming is O.K. if the ocean is calm. There are picnic tables, rest rooms, and showers.

### HANA BEACH PARK
At Hana Bay in Hana. As mentioned already, this is a great place to swim since the bay is almost always calm. Also, there is good snorkeling by the lighthouse. There are rest rooms and picnic tables and the snack bar is across the street.

### KOKI PARK
To get there go about two miles past Hana and watch for the loop road which leads to privately owned Hamoa Beach. You will come to Koki on the left before you reach Hamoa. This is a good place for a picnic, but do not swim there as the currents are treacherous.

## SPORTS

### TENNIS
There are two lighted courts at Hana Park that are open to the public at no charge.

*Bed & Breakfast Guide*

# KIHEI

Before Maui was developed for tourists, the Kihei area must have been one of the most beautiful in Hawaii. Located along the south west shore of Haleakala, about eight miles south of Kahului, Kihei is now one of the most developed places in the Islands, and now whenever a development is proposed for any of the neighbor Islands, protesters shout, *Are we going to become like Waikiki or Kihei?* Many people feel that what was once one of Hawaii's pristine areas has been ruined forever by poorly planned, concrete monstrosities that block the view of the shore line.

The distance from the beginning of Kihei, which starts with the Suda Snack Bar, probably the cheapest food on the Kihei coast, to the posh Wailea development on the south end, is about six miles. And in that six miles, there are more high rise condos than in any area of Hawaii save Waikiki. Still, all is not lost and there are still nice beaches and open spaces.

As stated above, Kihei ends at the Wailea Resort, a beautiful example of what the Kihei area might have looked like with better planning. Wailea is not, though, for the budget minded, whether it is golf at one of their Robert Trent Jones Jr. designed courses or accommodations at the luxurious Westin Wailea Beach Hotel. Golf, for example, is around $100 a couple, while accommodations at the Westin run from $115 to $200. Well, maybe there is a need for the Waikiki/Kihei condos after all.

Under construction at the present time and very near completion is a new hotel south of Wailea. The golf course for the hotel, the Makena Country Club, is already complete. Because this road is now paved, it is much easier to get to Makena Beach than it used to be. There is still a bit of unpaved road, but not much.

## HOSTS

### M-14
This two story home located in the hills above Kihei would be ideal for two couples traveling together since there are two large bedrooms available, each with private entrance and full bath and king sized bed. Ed and Betty, the hosts, live upstairs in the main house, while the B & B rooms are on the garden level with a view of the orchid tree and many other interesting Hawaiian plants. The upstairs deck, where breakfast is served, has a good ocean and mountain view.

Ed and Betty moved to Maui in 1980 from the Chicago area, where Ed was in government work and Betty was a nurse. Since then they have devoted their time to such diligent pursuits as spending time visiting with friends, gardening, and golfing, all of which you can do year around in Hawaii.

RATE: $50 one rate,. Three night minimum, non-smokers preferred.

### M-15
If you have never heard of "pickle ball," called in Hawaii "puka ball," Carl would be glad to tell you not only how the game is played, but, even more interesting to us, how the game was named. Then you could try a game on their pickle ball court. Carl and Barbara came to Maui in 1982 from the Los Angeles area where Carl was born and raised and retired from the L.A. Fire Department. Barbara is originally from Illinois. When they are not at home playing pickle ball, they usually can be found on the golf course.

The accommodation for B & B guests is a new 600 sq. ft. apartment complete with a kitchen and all the cooking facilities, a private bath, a queen sized bed, and a corner unit of twin beds. A barbecue is available on the lanai outside the sliding glass doors of the apartment. From their home in Maui Meadows above the Wailea development, there is a view of three islands and great sunsets. The hosts provide beach equipment. Since the apartment is fully equipped for cooking, Barbara and Carl serve breakfast on the first morning only, making it a point to spend time with their guests, answering any questions they might have.

RATE: $50 one rate, three night minimum. $10 each extra person, no smoking, no children.

### M-17
Six years ago Harriet and Tony decided that as nice as it was in San Diego, California, it was nicer yet on Maui, and since Tony is a professional tennis instructor, one of the first things they did was build two tennis courts on their property. Tennis buffs could not ask for a better place to vacation than sunny Kihei with courts available right outside their door. Tony has been a musician all his life, and he took a job playing piano part time at one of Maui's finest restaurants. Harriet works for the Wailea Development Co., driving the resort shuttle and doing P.R. for Wailea.

The accommodation is a full apartment available for B & B guests: one bedroom, private bath, kitchenette, living/dining room, cable T.V. The home has a great ocean view, and it is just a short drive to beaches, golf, and restaurants on the Kihei coast.

RATE: $45 single or double, two night minimum. $80 for 4 people.

### M-19
The accommodations offered in this owner designed home are two studio's on the garden level. Each unit is quite large, has small cooking facilities and a small frig so that meals could be fixed at home. Each unit has its own private bath with large tiled showers. The units are separate but can be connected for families or couples traveling together. Each of the rooms has T.V. Breakfast is served on the deck upstairs where guests can sit and enjoy the view of the ocean. The home is located about a mile or so up in maui Meadows which makes the beach and restaurants just a short drive away.

Joe and Barbara, the hosts, originally from Hungary came to the U.S. many years ago. They have been on Maui long enough now to be very helpful with guests on the best beaches and restaurants.

RATE: $45 single or double, $50 Dec. through March, two night minimum.

### M-25
The accommodation offered is a bedroom with an outside entrance and a private bath on the garden level of this two story Maui Meadows home. Breakfast is served on the deck upstairs, and if you are an early riser, you can watch the sun rise over Haleakala. From the west deck the view is of Kahoolawe, Molokini, and Lanai, and the beautiful sunsets of the south Maui Coast. The bedroom has twin beds.

The hosts, Willard and Mary, moved to Maui in 1980. Originally they hail for So. Dakota, but that was many years ago, and more recently they lived in the Bay Area of California. Each year they spend five months in the California Sierras, so their home is only available for seven months out of the year. Mary is a retired teacher, who enjoys gardening, sewing, knitting, and she does volunteer work for R.S.V.P. ( Retired Seniors Visiting Program). Willard is a retired contractor and an avid golfer, so his location in Maui suits him fine. Golf courses are close by.

RATE: $30, single or double, 3 night minimum, no smoking, please.

### M-27
This home is located in Maui Meadows, just about one mile from the beach. Ann, the hostess, is an active Realtor and also operates a large condo cleaning business, which takes her all over the Island, so she knows Maui well. At the present time two of the bedrooms in her three bedroom home are available to B & B guests. Each room has a sliding glass door to a large wrap around deck where guests can sit at watch the sun set. Each of the rooms has a double bed, and guests are welcome to use the sitting area for T.V. viewing in the evening. The home is surrounded by a lovely tropical garden with several patio areas which guests are encouraged to enjoy. There is a bath room between the guests rooms for the exclusive use of guests.

RATE: $40 per room, three night minimum.

### M-31
This comfortable Maui Meadows home above Wailea Resort overlooks the ocean and is less than five minutes from Maui's most beautiful beaches. The huge lawn surrounding the home is perfect for sunning or guests can sit in the shade under the trees and relax in the cool. The master bedroom offered for guests use has a private entrance through an enclosed courtyard. This wing has its own lavatory/shower room, vanity dressing area, and walk in closet. It has a king sized bed and a color cable T.V. The "den" bedroom is very spacious and airy with 14 feet of sliding window with an ocean view. The new Simmons queen sofa bed, swivel rocker, and cable T.V. make it ideal for sleeping and

lounging. The adjoining private bath has a tub/shower. The shady lush courtyard has a small frig for guests to use and is an ideal lounging area where breakfast can be served.

The hosts, Dave and Jackie, have lived on Maui for over 12 years. They are originally from New Jersey where Dave worked as a physicist for the Federal Government. They migrated to Hawaii after Dave took an early retirement. Travel has always been one of their great loves, along with gardening and ocean activities.

RATE:   $40 single or double, 3 night minimum, $75 for couples traveling together, both rooms.  Non-smokers, please.

## M-10

Since this one bedroom condo on the ground floor of a small complex does not have a host living in the home, it is not really B & B. We have it for our members at an attractive rate, just in case they need more than a room in a home. The condo is fully furnished, all the appliances and material for cooking, color T.V., washer-dryer. There are two pools and a tennis court for guests to enjoy. The unit could accommodate a family since there is a queen sized bed in the bedroom, and a queen sized sofa bed in the living room, and a roll away bed for a fifth person.

RATE:   $45 for two, $10 each additional person.

*Bed & Breakfast Guide*

## RESTAURANTS

**LOCAL STYLE**

**SUDA'S SNACK SHOP**
You will see this on the left as soon as you reach the Kihei area. Very low in price, heavily frequented by locals. This is a good place if the budget is tight, or you like the local style food and are not looking for atmosphere.

-----------------------------------------------------------

**local/Tourist Style**

**SAND-WITCH**
At Sugar Beach Resort, the first resort you come to in Kihei. Good home cooking, sandwiches, at reasonable prices.

**POLLI'S ON THE BEACH**
Upstairs by the fitness center at Kealea Beach Club (see Makawao for details about menu and prices).

**HONG KONG**
Next to Suda's Snack Shop where Robaire's used to be. Open for lunch and dinner specializing in Cantonese style food, moderate prices. We liked the food and the service.

**IDINI'S DELI**
This is owned by the same people who have Idini's in Kahului, one of our favorites in that area. They have just opened up in the Menehune Shores Condo, where Hong Kong used to be. We feel sure they will be a success.

**MAUI LU RESORT**
On the mauka side of the main road as you enter the Kihei area. There are two restaurants here, a coffee shop in the front for breakfast and lunch, and a large dining room called Jessie's for lunch and dinner, which offers entertainment as well as food. On Monday, Wednesday, Friday, and Saturday they feature the Hawaiian luau. On Thursday they have a special Hawaiian luncheon, also with entertainment. Also, they have been offering early bird specials for under $10.

**CHUCK'S STEAK HOUSE**
In the Kihei Town Center. Prices here are reasonable and the food is good.

**KIHEI SEAS**
On the mauka side of the highway upstairs at the Rainbow Mall. They have an early bird special from 5-7 p.m. for $8.95 or a super special of steak and lobster for $11.95.

**PASTA & PIZZA RESTAURANT**
At the back of the Rainbow Mall, open for lunch from 11-3:30 and for dinner from 5-10. This is a cute little place where the prices are not too high.

### KIHEI'S PRIME RIB HOUSE
At the Kai Nani Village above the La Familia. The good deal here is the early bird prime rib for $7.95 between 5-6 p.m. Other than that this restaurant is much like Mainland places, salad bar, with entrees between $10 -$16.

### ISLAND FISH HOUSE
In the south Kihei area on the mauka side of the main road. This is a good splurge place. The prices are high but the food, service, and atmosphere are excellent.

### LA FAMILIA
Originally located in Wailuku on Vineyard St., they have since closed that one to concentrate on the one in Kihei. If you like Mexican food you will enjoy this. The food is good and the prices are moderate, in the $6-$8 range.

### INTERNATIONAL HOUSE OF PANCAKES
In the Azeka Shopping Center. Like IHOP's everywhere else, its strong point is that the food is familiar, reasonable, and they are open Sunday-Thursday from 6 a.m. until midnight, and on Friday and Saturday from 6 a.m. until 2 a.m.

### SAILMAKER RESTAURANT
On the highway at the Azeka Center. This is in the Apple Annie chain with a full nautical atmosphere. They have a breakfast special at $2.99 and an early bird dinner special between 4-6 p.m. at $5.95.

### OUTRIGGER MAUI
At 2980 So. Kihei Rd. They have an early bird special from 5-7 p.m. for $8.95, with a happy hour from 3-5 p.m. They are open for lunch from 11-2:30.

### OCEAN TERRACE
On the ocean in one of the condos on the south end of Kihei just before you get to Wailea. The setting here is the nicest in the Kihei area in our opinion. They are open for lunch and dinner, with lunch between $4 and $6, and dinners between $8.95 for spaghetti and $15 for steak. They also have an early bird special between 5:30 and 7.

### SAND CASTLE
In the Wailea Shopping Mall. This is not low priced but the food, service and setting is good, all first class as one would expect in a resort of this caliber.

*Bed & Breakfast Guide*

# BEACHES

As you drive the six mile stretch of the Kihei coast you will see many beaches that in the morning offer the calmest, warmest water in all of Hawaii, with a great view of the little Islands of Lanai and Kahoolawe. Since several of them are County Parks, showers, change rooms, rest rooms, and picnic tables are available. What will not be as obvious are the beaches developed by Alexander & Baldwin, the developers of the Wailea Resort, and since turned over to the County. Easy access is available by paved road and parking is ample.

### MOKAPU/ULUA/WAILEA BEACH
These three beaches are controlled by Maui County. Access to them is easy once one arrives at Wailea.

### MAKENA BEACH
This is one of the most spectacular beaches in Hawaii. To get there, go through the Wailea development past the golf course, and then through the new Makena development and that golf course to where the paved road ends. Continue on past the road which goes to the left to the Makena Golf Course. Go about one third of a mile and you will come to a road which goes makai to the beach. You will know you have arrived when you see all the cars. There are no facilities so if you intend spending time here, bring food and drink.

# SPORTS

### GOLF
At Wailea there are two eighteen hole courses, both championship caliber. The green fee for non-guests is $50, cart included and mandatory. For more information call 879-2966. The Makena Golf Course is located south of Wailea. Green fees are $32, cart included and mandatory. Call 879-3344.

### TENNIS
There are fourteen courts at Wailea which are open to the public.

# LAHAINA

At one time Lahaina was a haven for whalers, and during the winter months it is still a great place for whale watching. Located on the south shore of the West Maui Mountains, Lahaina is fully protected from the winds that often whip the Kaanapali/Napili area. It is fairly teeming with tourists and with shops and restaurants to serve their every need. It is from Lahaina that one can catch a glass bottom boat that gives a good glimpse of the coral reef, rife with sea life, or hop on a sail boat to cruise to one of the nearby Islands. You will find whatever you like here for Lahaina lives for and on the ubiquitous tourist.

We won't mention every restaurant and shop, for to do so would be close to a book in itself. As you walk down the main drag, appropriately called Front St., you may be a little overwhelmed by shops, many having sales, and after a while the next store tends to look just like the one you were just in. And yet if you are really looking for bargains, Lahaina, because of the intense competition, is a good spot.

Restaurants, however, are another matter. Almost all restaurants in town cater to tourists. That and the fact that rents are astronomical (one shop keeper told us it was not uncommon for a new shop located on Front St. to pay up to $60,000 to the landlord just for the privilege of opening the door) work to keep the prices up.

## HOSTS

### M-2

This is for those who want to be where the action is since Don and Odette's home is right in Lahaina Town in a quiet residential section, one block from the beach and only a short walk to all the shops and restaurants. One would think this home was designed for B & B. The accommodation offered is a large, cheerful room just off the courtyard garden, with a private entry and patio for the guests to enjoy. Next to the room the hosts designed a bathroom with a shower in an atrium setting, which guests share with the tenant in the other garden bedroom. In the room is a wash basin, a small refrigerator, and either twin or full king sized bed.

Odette and Don are from Washington and Alaska respectively and have been in Hawaii for over fifteen years. Odette is a Field Director for the Girl Scouts for the Molokai, Lanai, Lahaina area and is also active with aerobics. Most of Don's time is spent working in his "only in Hawaii" outdoor workshop or drawing plans for someone's dream home. Just ask Odette where her favorite beach is and Don where his favorite disco is and before you know it they will tell you where the best place to eat is.
RATE: $40, single or double.

### M-3

Situated on a quiet cul-de-sac in a residential section above Lahaina, this home looks down on Lahaina's wharf and out beyond to the islands of Molokai, Lanai, and Kahoolawe. The hosts, who designed and built this home, offer a 275 square foot studio completely separate from the main house. The unit has a kitchenette for light cooking, a queen sized bed, color cable T.V., and a private fully tiled bath. The studio opens on to a large lanai where guests are welcome to use the BBQ and the spa. Guests are also welcome to use the laundry facilities. The home is located just 1.1 mile from the ocean and the center of Lahaina.

The hosts, Tom and Ana, have lived on Maui for over three years. Tom is an accountant and Realtor, while Ana works part time with the Lahaina Restoration Society and also has her own housekeeping business as well.

RATE: $50, one rate, 3 night minimum requested, $45 during off season.

## M-7A

Enjoy the grandeur of a Haleakala sun rise, or moon rise, in the privacy of your own cliff cottage on Maalaea Bay. While this is not right in Lahaina, in fact it is seventeen miles before you reach Lahaina, between Kahului and Lahaina, we choose to put it in this section so guests did not miss it. The setting is choice; just a few feet above the ocean on a small cliff side setting. While there is no beach right at the house, there are plenty of beaches in the neighborhood. The accommodation offered is a small studio fronting the ocean, small kitchenette, private bath, and a private lanai. The studio is not ornate but it is certainly adequate. Since there is a king sized bed and a single bed, the studio could accommodate a family of three. There is also a bedroom in the home that is available that has a private entrance, queen sized bed, and a private bath.

Billie, the hostess, has a large interest in music and may even plunk out a song or two on her guitar as guests relax in the evening.

RATE:   $55 for the cottage, single or double, $10 extra for 3rd person.  $40 single, $45 double for bedroom in house.

## RESTAURANTS

### LOCAL STYLE

**SUSHIYA DELI**
On Prison St. off Front. A definite two scoop rice place where you will get filled up for low cost. It is clean and if you like local style, you will feel right at home.

**NAOKEE'S TOO**
On the far west end of Lahaina on Front St. When we put this in last years book we put it in the Tourist section since we judged in by its name. This year we stopped for a visit and decided to change the category. The setting is the best thing about this Naokee's's although anyone really stuck on LOCAL food will enjoy eating here.

-----------------------------------------------------------
**local Style**

**GOLDEN PALACE**
In the shopping center off Front St. at the west end of town just before Longi's restaurant and  across from the Post Office. Open for lunch from 11-2 and for dinner from 5-9. They specialize in Cantonese food. Prices are moderate.

THAI CHEF
   In the shopping center mentioned above. Since we are fond of Thai food, we had lunch hear and found it very good.

FUJIYAMA'S
   In the rear of the shopping center mentioned above. Those who enjoy Japanese food tell us this is the best value in town. The food is good and the prices are moderate. They are open for lunch and dinner and do a brisk business with the local crowd.

-----------------------------------------------------------

local/Tourist Style

** LONGI'S **
   On the mauka side of Front St. on the west end of town. In spite of the prices, this is our favorite spot in Lahaina. Not only is the ambience good, the food and service are great. Do not be surprised when the waiter grabs a chair, turns it around backwards, plunks himself down, and proceeds to rattle off the menu, which is all in his head.

PIONEER INN
   Stop by here even if you've eaten, for it is more than an Inn; it is an institution. Recently we heard a visitor comment that it was like staying in a museum. Old and funky, yes, but as a fine wine it seems to improve with age. The main restaurant, located on the south east end of the Inn is open for breakfast, lunch, and dinner. The prices are moderate. Do not give up if there is a crowd. They are used to that and can handle lots of people. For dinner you can enjoy the Boiler in the Inn's courtyard. You better like the cooking; you do it yourself. During the day you can get a snack in the courtyard: roast beef sandwich for $2.95 or turkey for $2.50.

GREENTHUMBS
   On the makai side of Front St. in the center of town. This is listed as a Mexican restaurant, but we would be more inclined to call it health food. No hamburger here as everything is vegetarian. The setting is nice and our hosts assure us the food is good.

OCEANHOUSE
   We had this in last years book because they had an early bird special that made them a good deal. Unfortunately, this year they have dropped that. We have kept them in the book, however, as they have some interesting Cajun dishes including the famous blackened red fish. We were there just before lunch and could sniff the aroma of a spicy roux. Next time we are in Lahaina we intend giving this place a try.

ALEX'S HOLE IN THE WALL
   On Wahie Lane, an alley that runs off Front St. in the 800 block. They are open for dinner every day but Sunday. Their prices are high except for pasta, which was what we enjoyed for around $8.

GERRARD'S
   Several of our hosts rave about this spot. The prices are fairly high but if it is as good as they claim, it is worth it.

## SPLURGE RESTAURANTS

### LA BRETAGNE
Across the street from Lahaina Shore Village, facing Maul-ulu-o-lele Park. There are several French restaurants on Maui, and we have been told that this is the best. If you are in a splurge mood and do not mind spending between $50-$100 give this place a try.

### CHEZ PAUL
This excellent French restaurant is located east of Lahaina right at the 15 mile marker. We had dinner here and even though the was in the neighborhood of $100 for two, we feel it was worth it. Let's face it, though, this is not the place to bring the kids and you have to be in an expansive mood.

## POINTS OF INTEREST

Not only is Lahaina swollen with tourists of all ages, since it was the State Capitol until 1843, it is full of valuable historical landmarks. The East Indian Banyan Tree, just across from the Pioneer Inn, is the oldest and perhaps the largest in Hawaii. The building in front of the tree, once the Courthouse, is now the Police Station and the Center for the Lahaina Art Society.

Lahaina Boat Harbor is filled with private and commercial craft of all sizes and descriptions and any number of purposes from glass bottom sight seeing to whale watching in a sailboat to a dinner cruise on a larger boat or a catamaran to one of the smaller islands. While not as famous as the Kona Coast for marlin, plenty of big fish are brought in to the Lahaina Harbor.

Baldwin House was the original home of Medical Missionary Dr. Dwight Baldwin and his family. He was responsible for saving the people of Maui from the small pox epidemic of 1853. Now completely restored, the home is open for tours from 9 a.m. to 5 p.m. There is a small admission fee.

Hale Paahoa, which translates *Stuck in Irons House*, is located aptly on Prison St. Behind its stone walls were thrown the town drunks and other wayward souls.

### DAN'S GREENHOUSE
Located on Prison St. one block off Front St. Don't miss this, especially if you have kids that are getting a little hot and tired of all the shopping and sightseeing. We are sure this place will pick up their spirits. Hopefully, Coco, Dan's triton cockatoo, will be sitting on his perch outside and in the mood for a conversation. Coco has delighted visitors since 1978.(When we visited this year Coco was not there. He had been sent to Oahu for some R & R.) But coco is only one of the many wonders at Dan's, so even if you have left the little ones at home, stop by so you can tell them about it.

## TAKE HOME MAUI
At 143 Luakini St. around the corner and west of Dan's. Stop by and get a sample of local pineapple and perhaps you will decide that the folks back home might like a little taste. If so, no problem, they will sell it to you there and make sure it is ready for you at the airport when you are ready to depart, or you can have it mailed to the Mainland. You will pay more per pound than if you were to consume it on Maui, but keep in mind that all fruit sent to the Mainland has to be specially treated.

## WO HING TEMPLE
On the mauka side of Front St at the west end of town. It is open Monday through Saturday from 9 a.m. to 5 p.m. and on Sundays from noon to 5 p.m.

## BEACHES

### LAHAINA BEACH
There are no facilities here, in spite of the fact that except for Kaanapali beaches, this is the most frequented in the area. To find, go north from the middle of Lahaina until you come to Puunoa Place. Turn makai to the beach. Swimming is good on any beach in the Lahaina area; snorkeling is fair and very easy since the water is shallow along this coast.

### WAHIHULI STATE PARK
There are picnic tables, rest rooms, and showers here and a little lawn too. Located just north of Lahaina off the main highway.

### PUAMANA PARK
Two miles south of Lahaina, this is a good place for picnicking, not so hot for swimming or snorkeling.

### LAUNIUPOKO STATE PARK
Since there is little beach here, this is more a place for picnicking as there are tables and rest rooms. Swimming is safe but not appealing. It is located about a mile south of Puamana.

Bed & Breakfast Guide

# KAANAPALI/NAPILI/KAPALUA

As you leave Lahaina heading north, you enter the area that many Mainlanders consider the premier spot in the Islands. Long ago if you took this drive you would have looked down on seemingly endless white sand beaches. The beaches are still there, of course, but hidden behind the many hotels and condominiums that line this area. At one time this was the dumping ground for the waste product (bagasse) of the Pioneer Sugar Mill.

There is excellent swimming and snorkeling at the Kaanapali beaches. On the rare occasions that the surf is too high for safe swimming, the hotels fly a red flag to warn their guests. Since private beaches are not allowed in Hawaii, feel free to stop by and enjoy the water whether you are a guest of the hotel or not. Some people think a stop by the Maui Hyatt is a must.

Keep in mind that this area is totally devoted to tourism so restaurants and shops reflect that. Hotels in this area are all on the posh side, starting at Kaanapali, where there are several hotels, and ending at the elegant and expensive Kapalua Bay Hotel. We would venture to say that there were no bad restaurants here, and no doubt some are excellent. All are going to be more expensive than they would be if they were in another location. We have not spent as much time in this area as we have elsewhere since it is not really a Bed and Breakfast area. At the present time we have no host homes here. A few of the restaurants we have tried and liked are mentioned below.

## RESTAURANTS

**EL CRABCATCHER**
Located in the Whalers Village at Kaanapali. Full dinners go for around $14, light supper around $10. They are open for lunch from 11-3 and dinner from 5:30-10:30, with the happy hour from 4:30-6:30. There is Hawaiian and contemporary music from 9:30-12:30 at night. Reservations are usually needed. Also, in the Whalers Village there is a free Tahitian show every Wednesday and Sunday at 6 p.m.

**ORIENT EXPRESS**
Located at Napili Shores, they feature an extensive menu of Thai and Szechuan cuisine. They have an Early Bird special every evening from 5-7 p.m., which consists of a complete five course dinner. They are expensive, but if you love this kind of food, it is worth it.

### DOLLIES
Located in the Kahana area which is between Kaanapali and Napili. It is a little sandwich place, order at the counter and take to a table. We felt that the sandwiches priced between $5 and $6 were not a very good deal compared to what you can get at the Grill and Bar mentioned below.

### THE GRILL AND BAR
Or as the locals call it *the Gorilla Bar*. Whether for lunch or for dinner this is good value. Not only is the setting great, the service excellent, the food good, but the price is right. We had a good lunch, couple of beers included for around $13. It is located at the Kapalua Bay Golf Course.

### PINEAPPLE HILL
This is a former plantation manager's home in a lovely setting high up behind the Kapalua Golf Course. The view is spectacular, looking over to Molokai and Lanai. The prices are high. We suggest that you at least stop by here for a cool drink. They open at 4:30.

## BEACHES

### KAANAPALI RESORT BEACHES
Access to this long stretch of beach is through any of the hotels. Swimming and snorkeling are ideal especially at the north end in front of the Sheraton Maui. All of the equipment can be rented at the beach.

### NAPILI BAY
The easiest access to this beach is through the Napili Kai Resort. Swimming and snorkeling are good here.

### D.T. FLEMING PARK
About ten miles north of Lahaina, this beach has all the facilities other than food. Most of the time swimming is good, but from time to time the surf gets a little rougher than at Kaanapali or Kihei. The main problem we experience every time we go north of Kaanapali is wind.

### NORTH OF FLEMING PARK
There are several beaches beyond Fleming that are beautiful to behold, but none have facilities and all are a little difficult to get to. Also, swimming can be tricky when the surf is up. For privacy, however, they are tops on Maui for obvious reasons. The first, Oneloa, is about a mile north of Fleming Park. Stop at a safe place off the road and hike down the steep trail to the beach. When you have gone three miles north of Fleming, watch for a dirt road which will take you to Ponakupile Beach. Snorkeling is great here when the sea is calm. Around six miles north of Fleming you will come to a rocky little beach called Honokolau.

For most visitors who even get this far, the road stops here, but for the really adventurous, going beyond this point might prove irresistible. (see *WEST OF WAILUKU* in earlier section). If the weather is nice, we urge you to continue. For two miles you will think you are crazy and that we are crazy for suggesting it. Then you will come to a fairly good road, sometimes paved, sometimes dirt, that will take you all the way to Wailuku.

## SPORTS

GOLF
There are four courses in this area, two at Kaanapali and two at Kapalua. The Village course at Kapalua, finished in 1975, was designed by Arnold Palmer. At the Kapalua Bay Course Palmer assisted architect Ed Seay. Green fees here are $48 for non-guests, with carts $12 on a shared basis, a mere $120 for husband and wife. At either the Royal Kaanapali North or South, fees are $37, and carts for two are $26. For a couple it would be $100.

*Chapter VIII*..................................................................KAUAI

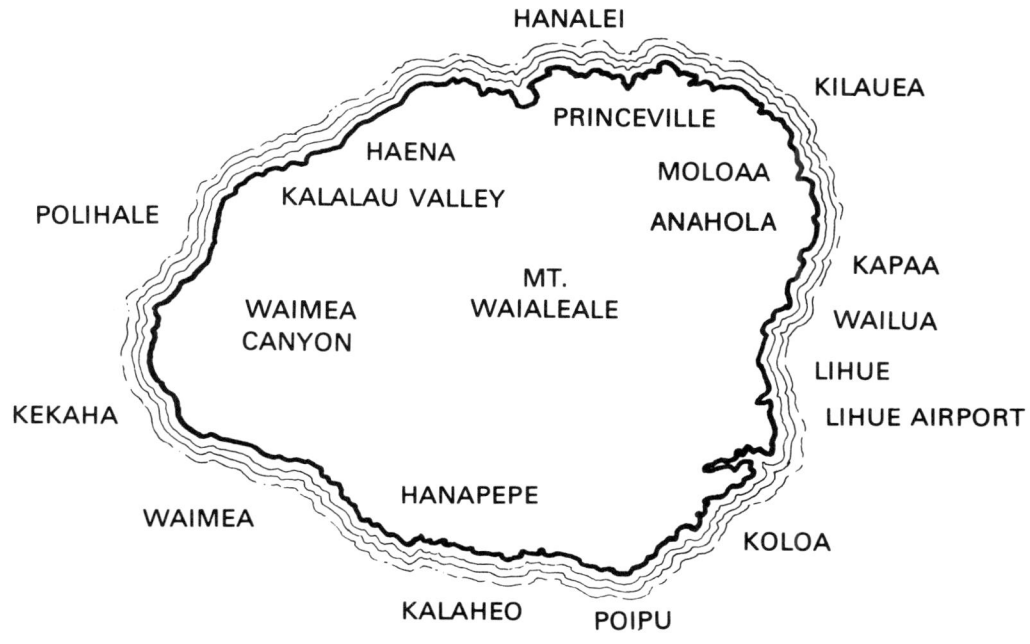

# KAUAI......THE GARDEN ISLAND

### .....DRIVING TIMES....

From Lihue Airport to: (approximate)

Wailua.......................7.5 miles, 15 minutes
Kapaa......................... 9 miles, 20 minutes
Hanalei..................... 35.5 miles, 45 minutes
Poipu..........................12 miles, 20 minutes
Hanapepe....................17 miles, 40 minutes
Kalalau Lookout...........45 miles, 90 minutes

# KAUAI

That Kauai is called the Garden Isle is no surprise to anyone who has been there, and yet the name is in one sense of the word a misnomer. It really depends on what one imagines when one hears the word *garden*. If one comes to Kauai expecting to see a profusion of flowers neatly arranged in some sort of a nursery fashion, disappointment will be inevitable. Often we have been asked the question, "When do the flowers bloom?" The first time we heard this question, we were surprised since flowers are always in bloom on Kauai: bougainvillea, plumeria, African tulip, hibiscus (the State flower), just to name a few. But what really strikes any visitor to Kauai is the lushness. Perhaps it should have been called the Emerald Isle, or as Mark Twain once suggested for Oahu, Rainbow Island.

Located north and west of Oahu, Kauai's beauty seems never ending. Whether one prefers the lush verdant tropics of the Hanalei Valley or the stark, sharp beauty of the arid Waimea Canyon, or the many-meadowed valleys of the Na Pali Coast, beauty is never lacking. Nowhere in the Islands are beaches more plentiful or more beautiful.

At the center of this Jewel rises Mt. Waialeale, which means *rippling on the waters*, where rainfall is not measured in inches but in feet. Can you believe an average rainfall of thirty-seven feet? And just a few miles away, in the Waimea/Kekaha area, desert conditions prevail. If any tourist has had a stay on Kauai during one of its rainy spells, it would be hard to convince him that those of us who live here do much more than grow moss. We remember one particularly rainy time when we were having lunch at the Sheraton Coconut Beach Hotel. The rain came down so hard that the pool overflowed. Suddenly the Fire Department rushed in, dropped large hoses in the pool, and began pumping the water toward the ocean. Seeing this Evie exclaimed, "Kauai is the only place they call the Fire Department to put the water out." Yes, we do get a little rain on Kauai, and yet since most of the rain comes at night or in the early morning, one need not be too concerned. Visitors can be assured they will see more shades of green than they thought existed, and there are few days the sun cannot be found.

Since much of Kauai cannot be seen from the main highway, which traverses three quarters of the way around the Island, we recommend visitors take a helicopter ride. Such a trip is not inexpensive, around $106 ($20 discount for B & B members); however, our recommendation is to take the ride, for unless one is a strong hiker, much of the Na Pali Coast, Waimea, and Waialeale cannot be seen. The hike to Hanakapiai Beach, the first two miles of the Na Pali Coast, is not that strenuous and should be attempted unless walking is a problem.

Kauai is, for that matter, a hiker's paradise, with many miles of trails not only along the Na Pali Coast but in the Waimea Canyon and Kokee State Park and in the interior of the Island above the Kapaa area. Hiking to the top of Sleeping Giant is far more ominous in appearance than in reality, but the reward at the top is not diminished.

Ever the land of enchantment and romance, Kauai was and still is in some people's minds the home of the Menehunes, that diminutive race of people who never took a task they could not complete in one night. It is the Menehunes who are credited with the construction of the Menehune Fish Pond outside of Lihue and the Menehune Ditch off the Waimea River. Legend has it that the Menehunes are still living on Kauai, deep in the valleys along the Na Pali Coast.

How much time one takes to explore Kauai depends on how one goes about it. Our first visit was two weeks, and that did not give us the time we needed. We have lived on Kauai since 1979 and are still discovering our new home. After all, we have not even been able to catch up with the Menehunes, yet.

## KAUAI'S LUAUS

This year we are including this section on luaus on Kauai since so many of our guests are interested. Next year we hope to have the same information for every Island; however, any of the hosts can supply guests with information about luaus on their Island.

### SHERATON COCONUT BEACH
This luau is held every day but Monday. At 10:45 a.m. they hold the Traditional Hawaiian Imu Ceremony. At 7 p.m. there is a Tropical Shell Lei Greeting and the bar is open from 7-8 p.m., with the buffet starting at 8 p.m. At 8:30 entertainment by the Victor Punua Polynesian Revue begins. Adults $33, children under 12 $20. For reservations call 822-3455, ext. 651.

### KAUAI RESORT
Every night except Monday and Saturday. At 6 p.m. they have the Imu Ceremony and the Shell Lei Greeting, the bar is open from 6:15 to 7:15 and then dinner at 7:15. The Polynesian Revue starts at 8:15.

### TAHITI NUI
We give a lengthy description of this luau in Hanalei Restaurant section and we suggest you check it out as this is our favorite luau spot on Kauai.

### POIPU SHERATON
Every Sunday and Wednesday there is a luau and Polynesian show. The Buffet features American, Hawaiian, Japanese, and Chinese cuisine and starts at 6:30 p.m. The show starts at eight. The tab is $26 a person.

### SMITH'S TROPICAL PARADISE
Located just south of the Wailua River. There is a luau every Tuesday, Wednesday, and Thursday. the cost is $33 for adults, $20 for children and includes the entrance fee to the park, a luau, cocktails, and a Polynesian show. Everyone we talked to who has gone has felt they more than got their money's worth.

# LIHUE

In the early 1800's there is no record of the name Lihue, which may have meant "cold chill," and there was little activity in the area. It was not until one of the early missionaries, Reverend Dr. Lafon, moved to Lihue from the Koloa area to start a church and school in 1839 that Lihue began to grow. In 1854 William Harrison Rice, a former missionary, took over as manager of the fledgling Lihue Sugar Plantation. Due to his efforts, mainly the digging of an irrigation ditch to bring the plentiful mountain waters to the Lihue sugar fields, the Lihue Plantation became one of the most successful in the Islands. Rice died of T.B. in 1862 at the age of forty-nine, but the success of the Rice family was assured, and they played a major role in the development of Kauai.

Now all visitors to Kauai know about Lihue; it is the place you have to go through after you leave the airport to get to wherever it is you are going, and as one drives from north to south and south to north one again goes through Lihue. To those of us who live on Kauai, however, Lihue is the center of things, for it is the County Seat as well as the center for State Office Buildings on Kauai. It is also the shopping center for Island residents, since Kukui Grove, one of the largest shopping centers on the Neighbor Islands, has most of the big stores: Penney's, Sears, Liberty House.

The newest development in the Lihue area is the Kilohana Center located just south of Lihue in Puhi, just next to the Community College. This is part of the old Wilcox estate and was built in the 1930's. This beautiful old plantation home has been restored and now houses many little shops that specialize in Hawaiian products. There are also two restaurants, Gaylord's and Plantation Cookout, mentioned in the restaurant section.

Since Lihue exists for residents, it is an excellent place for visitors to discover a truer picture of local life. Stores and restaurants, while delighted when tourists visit, are not dependent on the tourist trade. A good place to pick up bargains is at Gem Department Store in the Foodland Shopping Center. While not a full line department store, they have a good selection of things and prices are lower than shops in resort areas. Also, if you are going to camp on Kauai, you will need to secure a permit in Lihue. It is possible to obtain a permit through the mail so you could have it before your arrival. Write to the Division of State Parks, P.O. Box 1671, Lihue Hi. 96766. You will need to send a copy of your driver's license, name of camp site, and dates of use. There is no charge for a permit. For more information call 808-245-4444.

*Bed & Breakfast Guide*

HOSTS

### K-8
SAIL B & B HAWAII
We have plenty of great B & B homes but let's face it, this one is just a little special. Bed and Breakfast on a 90 foot sailing ship? This might just be the ultimate tropical experience. This ship is meticulously hand crafted using 22 varieties of wood which recreates Hawaii's sailing heritage. The ship has a full kitchen, dining room and lounge, as well as two bedrooms and two bathrooms with fresh water showers, and a spacious deck. The friendly hosts, John and Cheryl with their crew await your visit. During the winter months the ship berths at Nawiliwili Harbor in Lihue. In the summer months Hanalei Bay is home. Several options are available for B & B guests.
1.) overnight only- $50 single, $70 double. 2.) sunset cruise and overnight- $100 single-$150 double. 3.) half day sail and overnight- $125 single-$200 double. 4.) all day cruise and overnight- $175 single-$300 double.

### K-35
Paul, the host, is an instructor in Business Management at Kauai Community college. To accommodate B & B guests he offers a second floor bedroom in his two bedroom, one and a half bath condo. There is a pool and lanai available, and guests can share the TV and the kitchen. Paul also has snorkeling gear for the guests to use. Since this unit is in the center of Lihue it would be suitable for a person who did not want to rent a car. The bedroom has a double bed and Paul has no objection to smoking.
RATE   $25 single, $30 double.

# RESTAURANTS

## LOCAL STYLE

### HAMARA'S SAIMIN
2956 Kress St., which runs off Rice St. They serve probably the best saimin to be found in the Islands.

### MA'S PLACE
4277 Halani St., which runs off Kress St. Good food at low prices, mostly Hawaiian food. Tripe stew is a specialty of the house.

### TOMI'S
4252 Rice St. Easy to find. Very LOCAL, low priced.

### LIHUE DELICATESSEN
On the highway near the old theater, next to the barber shop. Box lunches at low price, very tasty.

### JUDY'S OKAZU & SAIMIN
We discovered this through a B & B guest. When the guests were doing their laundry in the Foodland Shopping Center, a local lady gave them some flowers and wished them much aloha. As they talked she told them she had the little restaurant next door. Several days later they decided to give it a try. The owner remembered them and gave them a warm greeting. After they finished their lunch, which they especially enjoyed since the food was new to them, the owner refused to let them pay. With people like this in Hawaii, the aloha spirit is in good hands. Needless to say we recommend eating here.

### FREDDIES
Located behind the Shell Station on the makai side of the main highway. Each day there are several different specials, very Local style and low in price. We did not sample the food but it looked good.

### SAMPAGUITA'S
Located a few miles north of Lihue on the makai side of the highway, just past the gas station. Filipino take out. Very ethnic, an interesting place to visit.

---

## local style

### *KIIBO'S*
2991 Umi St. This is our favorite spot in Lihue for lunch. Japanese food at low prices. Open for lunch 11-1:30, dinner 5:30 - 9 p.m. Beer and saki served, 245-2650.

### KAUAI CHOP SUEY
Located in the Harbor Center across from the Kauai Surf. This is high on the list for the local folks. You get lots of food for a modest price. Cantonese style. Open every day for lunch from 11-2 except Sunday and every day for dinner from 4:30-9:30.

## Bed & Breakfast Guide

**HO'S**
3016 Umi St. off Rice St. Not bad Cantonese food at modest prices. Open for lunch Monday-Saturday from 10:30 to 2:30, and for dinner every day from 4:30 to 9:30.

**BARBECUE INN**
2962 Kress St. off Rice St. Open Monday-Saturday for breakfast, lunch, and dinner. This is where the county takes the jurists; either the prices are right or the judge is a silent partner. Wide variety of entrees, modest prices.

**TIP-TOP CAFE**
3173 Akahi St. off Hardy. Great ox-tail soup and excellent macadamia nut cookies.

**DANI'S**
4201 Rice St. across from Pay and Save. Heavily frequented by locals, but some dishes to appeal to all. Modest prices

**LIHUE CAFE & CHOP SUEY**
2978 Umi St. off Rice St. Cantonese style food but also some Japanese food served. Not much atmosphere but the food is good.

---

**local/Tourist Style**

**THE OAR HOUSE**
At one time they served full meals here, but now it is a bar that serves sandwiches and hamburgers. It is located at the foot of Rice St., just across from Harbor Village and right next to the entrance of the Kauai Surf, which is closed for remodeling at the present time. We had lunch at the Oar House and liked both the food and the atmosphere.

**EGGBERT'S**
4481 Rice St. across from the Foodland Shopping Center. As the name suggests, breakfast is the specialty and at one time when they were called The Egg & I that is all they served. Now they have enlarged and serve all day. Prices are modest for this category and the entrees will all be familiar to you, 245-9025.

**\*CLUB JETTY\***
Located at the end of Rice St. down in Nawiliwili Harbor. Open for dinner only Monday-Saturday. This is another of our favorites in Lihue. The food is tasty, the atmosphere is nice, right on the water, and the service is friendly. Most of the food is Cantonese but there are American dishes available, 245-4970.

**CASA ITALIANO**
2989 Haleko Rd. off Rice St. Open for lunch and dinner every day. Nice atmosphere in what was once an old plantation house. Dinner prices are high for this category ($13-$17) unless you opt for a pasta dinner which if you like Italian food is excellent. Lunch prices are much lower ($5-$8), 245-9586.

**J.J.'S BROILER**
2971 Haleko St. Dinner only. They specialize in Slavonic steak, which we have been told is very good. Otherwise, a very typical broiler-lots of steak, fish, lobster, 245-3841.

## BULL SHED
In the Harbor Center. If you have tried any of the broiler types (Chart House, Spin Drifter) you will know what to expect. Prices in the $10-$20 range, 245-4551.

## *HANAMAULU RESTAURANT & TEA HOUSE*
In Hanamaulu two miles north of Lihue on the mauka side of the highway. This is almost in a category of its own. If a local family is having a special occasion they would probably have it here, since the Tea House can handle groups up to 300. The food is a mixture of Chinese and Japanese with a few other ethnic dishes thrown in. For plenty of atmosphere, make a reservation for the Tea Room, where you can sit on the floor Japanese style. They are open for lunch from 9 a.m. to 1:30 p.m. and for dinner from 4:30 to 9:30, 245-2511.

## MILE-TWO
As the name suggests, this place is located at the two mile marker as one drives north toward Kapaa. They are open for lunch and dinner. The prices are modest and the specialty of the house is ribs.

## GAYLORD'S AT KILOHANA
This is newest addition to Kauai and we think it is here for a long time. The setting is delightful, along the patio and garden of the Wilcox home. At the present time it is open only for lunch. Our only complaint was they gave us too much to eat. Not only was the sandwich we had amply but we had a choice of soup or salad. Lunch for two was about $15.

## PLANTATION COOKOUT
This is also located in the Kilohana Center and is open just for dinner. We had mixed feelings about our experience here. There is a somewhat limited choice: chicken, fish (mainly halibit or salmon), or beef, each entree around $14. What we liked best was their salad bar which is pretty extensive. We were a little surprised at plastic glasses for the wine and not pleased with the styrofoam cups for the coffee. In keeping with the *cookout* theme, dinner is served at picnic tables and patrons sit on benches.

## KUKUI SHOPPING CENTER RESTAURANTS

### FAMILY KITCHEN
Located in the Kukui Shopping Center on the north side. The food is served cafeteria style and is mostly local fare but also hamburgers and sandwiches.

### KUKUI NUT TREE
In the Kukui Shopping Center. Modest prices, good sandwiches, Mainland style. Open from 7 a.m. to 8 p.m. every day but Friday when they stay open until 9 p.m. and Sunday when they close at 3 p.m.

### GREAT GOURMET
In the Kukui Center just behind Liberty House. They have recently started serving soup, salad, and sandwiches in this gourmet food shop. For a quick snack while you shop either this or the one below would be our recommendation. Also, if you are craving some good cheese, this is about the only place you will find it.

### RAINBOW COFFEE
In the Kukui Center. No heavy meals here, but great for a light snack or a tasty dessert. They also have all kinds of coffee. Since it is located in Rainbow Books, you will have plenty of reading material while you snack. Behind the book department is an interesting art gallery.

### JONI-HANA
Located in the Kukui Shopping Center. Sit down or box lunches to take out. Low prices, interesting Japanese dishes, but beef chop suey is also served. (can you see the problem with labels?).

### ROSITA'S MEXICAN FOOD
A Mexican restaurant in the Kukui Shopping Center which we believe is run by a couple from California.

### BRICK OVEN PIZZA
Same owner as the one in Kalaheo, which is our favorite spot for pizza in Hawaii. It is open from 11 a.m until 11 p.m.

## POINTS OF INTEREST

### KAUAI MUSEUM
4428 Rice St. Open Monday-Friday, and starting May 1986 on a trial basis, they will be open on Saturday from 9:30 a.m. to 1 p.m. Adult admission $3.00, children free. A good collection of natural history, with changing exhibits. They have a self-operated film that gives a good introduction to Kauai. Also, a gift shop and book store, which carries most of the books about Kauai. For information call 808-245-6931.

### GROVE FARM HOMESTEAD
There is a two hour guided tour every Monday, Wednesday, and Thursday starting at 10 a.m and 1:15 p.m., which gives a flavor of early plantation life. Since the tours are limited to twenty people and by reservation only, call or write in advance. (P.O. Box 1631, Lihue, Kauai, Hi. 96766: 808-245-3202). It is located on the south side of Nawiliwili Rd. Admission is $3.00 for adults, $1.00 for children 12 and under.

### MENEHUNE FISH POND
To get to the Fish Pond overlook take Rice St until it dead ends at the Harbor, turn right and proceed on the road that goes by Matson which will be on your left. You will go across a one way bridge and the Fishpond overlook is a mile or so up that road. There are many fishponds in the Islands but I believe this is the largest. Legend has it that this one was built by the Menehunes, a diminutive race that lived on Kauai prior to and with the Hawaiians.

### MENEHUNE GARDENS
Located just behind the Banyan Harbor Condos at Nawiliwili. There are better botanical gardens all over Hawaii and several on Kauai, but this is a fun place to go and worth the $2.00 to meet the people who run it. They have many tropical plants and what they claim is the largest banyan tree in Hawaii.

### SUNSHINE MARKET
Held only on Friday starting around 3 p.m. We think this is a must see if you are interested in Island life. Here local people bring their garden goods and offer them for sale. Some of the produce you may not be familiar with unless you know Filipino and other Island food. Located at Vidinha Stadium.

### KAUAI SURF JAPANESE GARDENS
(CLOSED UNTIL REMODELING IS COMPLETE, PROBABLY LATE 1987)
Within the grounds of the Kauai Surf Hotel. This is a peaceful, beautiful place to wander around for a little while, a kind of get away spot which does not get as much use as one would expect.

### KAHANA KII FINE ARTS GALLERY
3878 Kuhio Highway, in behind the Shell Station and Freddies restaurant. Owned and operated by Carl and Dawn Steinhart, who moved to Kauai from Stockton, Ca., in 1979 to open this gallery. Since they feature many of the local artists (Dawn is an artist) a visit here is worthwhile.

## THE KAPAIA STITCHERY
Just north of Lihue at the bottom of the hill past Wilcox Hospital on the mauka side of the highway. If you have an interest in hand made crocheted items at very fair prices, stop here. Run by the Yukimura family, they have been selling things made by the family and other local people for many years.

## WAILUA FALLS
To get here take the highway from Lihue north. When you pass the hospital, you will start down the hill. At the bottom of the hill, watch for the sign on the left that points the way to Wailua Falls. Take this road about four miles where it ends at the falls. If you get tempted to hike to the bottom of the falls, forget it! It is far too dangerous. Also, crossing the river above the falls is very dangerous. One slip and you better be in a barrel.

## HANAMAULU MUSEUM
Right in Hanamaulu, you can't miss it. No charge to see this. Some artifacts, but mainly the sugar story. Since none of the sugar mills on Kauai allow tours, a stop here will answer some of your questions.

# BEACHES

## KALAPAKI BEACH
Right in front of the old Kauai Surf Hotel. You can get access to it by parking at the Oar House and walking between the shops. Kalapaki Bay is very calm, and while the water is not as clear and blue as in some other places, swimming is good.

## HANAMAULU BAY OVERLOOK
This is not a beach but an interesting ocean/bay overlook. To get there take the airport road and go past the airport where the road ends at the overlook. In hot weather, this is a great place to catch the cooling trades. You are bound to see local fishermen trying their luck.

## HANAMAULU PARK
When you reach Hanamaulu, around two miles north of Lihue, watch for Hanamaulu Rd., just beyond the Shell Station. Turn makai and this drive will put you right at Hanamaulu Bay, where you can swim, picnic, and fish.

## NIGHT LIFE

POLYNESIAN SHOW AT KAUAI SURF
(CLOSED FOR REMODELING)
Every Monday, Wednesday and Friday night starting at 8:30 at the Planter's Bar there is a Polynesian Show which is about as good as any you will see on the neighbor Islands. There is no admission charge, and while drinks are available, they do not hustle you. After 10 there is dancing in the lounge on the 10th floor.

CLUB JETTY
Disco/Rock N' Roll music every Thursday, Friday, and Saturday night and they sometimes go until 4 a.m. It gets pretty lively when the cruise ships are in.

PARK PLACE RESTAURANT AND NIGHT CLUB
Located at 3501 rice St. This could be listed under restaurants but mainly it is a disco spot with dancing until 4 a.m. They do have a pupu menu and a seafood bar. For more information call 245-5775.

LIBRARY
Located on Hardy St. Every Tuesday night from 7 to 8 there is a free movie on some facet of Polynesian life or on a subject appropriate to Hawaii. For more specific information call 245-3617. (see Poipu section for the one in Koloa Town).


## SPORTS

GOLF
(CLOSED FOR REMODELING)
The Kauai Surf has an eighteen hole course that is open to the public. Until 3 p.m. the green fees are $30 for eighteen, $15.00 for nine, cart included. After 3 p.m., a cart is not required and the fee drops to $10.50 making this a good deal. For starting time call 245-3631 and ask for the Golf Course.

TENNIS
Public courts with no charge are located at the War Memorial Convention Center just past Wilcox School on Hardy St.

WATER SPORTS
The best place to rent equipment is at Kalapaki Beach where one can rent from Kauai Windsurfing. Such things as windsurf boards, glassbottom kyaks, surf boards, wave skis, rubber raft, Hobie Cat are available. From Aqua Bikes you can rent aqua bikes, snorkeling gear, and boogie boards. Lessons on the use of any of these are available.

# WAILUA

## WAIPOULI/KAPAA/ANAHOLA

To the ancient Hawaiians Wailua was an important area, a place special to the Alii, those born of Royal blood. Commoners lived here at the behest of the chiefs. When chiefs from the other Islands visited Kauai, they most often came to the Wailua area, where there were several sacred temples and special places of worship.

Now, except for Lihue, Wailua is the main business center on Kauai as well as being a major tourist area. The oldest major hotel on Kauai, the Coco Palms, is a Kauai landmark for most people who have visited here. The newer Plantation Marketplace, a tourist shopping mecca, houses the Sheraton Coconut Beach Hotel, the Beach Boy Hotel, and several condo complexes. There are also many small eating places and several large restaurants.

From the Wailua river to the end of Kapaa, a drive of about four miles, there are about forty restaurants, which run the gamut from the posh spots at the Coco Palms to funky little Sharon's Saimin, where lunch is under $3.00. Excluding fast food and resort restaurants, we cover most of them. With this many restaurants, competition for business is keen, and restaurant owners keep prices down in an effort to attract customers. To some extent the same is true for the little shops. Because of location, they cannot command the same prices as the more heavily used shopping centers.

Kapaa town seems to be a curious mixture of the old, the older, and the oldest. Like many small towns in America, Kapaa Town has no where to go but up, but it does it very slowly. Yet progress is being made and not at the expense of historical considerations, since the buildings that have been built and restored are in keeping with the old Hawaiian architecture. Let us hope that as Kapaa Town modernizes it does not lose its charm.

## HOSTS

**K-2**
We call this "our little old Hawaiian grass shack." Since it is located right on the beach in Anahola, five miles north of Kapaa, it is just right for guests who want to get away from it all and enjoy a more rustic vacation, swimming, snorkeling, or just basking in the sun. The home is modest and the setting is lovely. The hostess and her sons are anxious to share their home with you. Since there is only one bathroom, the guest and the family share. Either double or single beds are available.
Originally from Minnesota, this hostess has been on Kauai for twelve years now, with an eight year stop over in California in between. Since being a good mother is the most important thing in her life right now, most of her time is devoted to that pursuit.
RATE: $17 single, $22 double, two night minimum.

**K-3**
This home is located four miles from the central area of Kauai's *Coconut Coast*. The hosts, Bev and Bud, are originally from California and moved to Kauai in 1982. Bev's interests are gardening, knitting, crocheting, and playing cards (bridge, pinochle, cribbage, etc.). Bud is an avid golfer and since Kauai is a golfer's Paradise, Bud says he has died and gone to heaven.
The accommodation offered is a studio that is attached to the rear of the main house. It has a private entrance, a lanai (screened in porch), a private bath, color cable TV, and a complete kitchenette. It has most of the comforts of home for long or short stays. Since it has a double bed and two punees, it can sleep a family of four. Use of the washer and dryer is available at posted prices.
RATE:    $39 single or double; from April-Dec.15 $35 single or double, $7.50 each additional person.

**K-4**
Your hosts from K-3 also offer the master bedroom in the main house. It has a private bath and dressing room, color cable TV, and a double bed.
The room looks out over a part of the garden that reflects Bev's interest. The garden includes trees of all kind: coffee, golden bamboo, all-spice, papaya, avocado, banana, and more. You will also find a rose garden, azalea garden, oriental garden, orchids, ginger, anthurium, bougainvilla, and many more flowering plants. The home is located on a dead end street in a quiet residential area. A group of six could combine K-3 and K-4.
RATE:   $30 single or double; from April-Dec. 15 $27 single or double.

**K-4A**
Arlecia and Newton have built a large Hawaiian style home overlooking the north fork of the Wailua River, complete with koa floors and wall papered walls giving their new home an old fashioned look. Moving from busy Honolulu, they chose a quiet residential subdivision three miles above the Coco Palms Resort. The accommodation offered is an oversized bedroom with a queen sized bed and a full private bath with a private entrance, which nicely accommodates a couple. The home has a lovely garden with many tropical plants.

Newton and Arlecia, who are half Hawaiian half English, were born and raised in Honolulu. Since Newton has been a merchant seaman for thirty-five years, he has been all over the world. Arlecia, who has worked as a secretary most of her life, loves gardening, sewing, working with stained glass, and quilting. She has made several large quilts for her family. She enjoys reading and is a great cook. Smokers O.K. They have two pets, a dog, Ilio, and a conure, a parrot-like bird.
RATE:   $35 one rate, no small children.

### K-5

*Hale Makano* is the home of Kauai born Ronald and his wife Marjorie, who is originally from Massachusetts. Both are now retired and live on a peaceful, tropical 1/2 acre property with a separate B & B accommodation. Guests are welcome to use the pool and the patio area, which overlooks the beautiful Wailua River Valley.

The accommodation offered is a separate cottage with a large veranda that sleeps four comfortably. The bedroom has a king sized Simmons bed and there are two punees in the sitting area. There are light cooking appliances, dishes and flatware as well as a small frig which makes it ideal for snacks and light meals. Breakfast is served each morning in the main house. Three night minimum. Non-Smokers, please.
RATE: $30 single, $15 each additional person up to four, plus 4% excise tax.

### K-5A

This home is located in the Wailua Homesteads behind Sleeping Giant, overlooking miles of pasture to Mt. Waialeale, the wettest spot on earth. Kay, a lively lady in her seventies who enjoys cooking, golf, gardening, bridge, travel, and mystery stories has made available three bedrooms: 1.) Plumeria, twin beds and stall shower, 2.) Orchid, king bed and stall shower, 3.) Ginger, queen bed and tub/shower. Also, a large living room, a T.V. room, an extensive library, and a lanai are provided for the guests to enjoy. Teenagers are welcome and Kay has no objection to smoking or social drinking.
RATE:   $30, single, $35 double.

### K-5B

This charming brand new one bedroom cottage overlooks acres of pasture land and affords an excellent mountain view. The accommodation offered consists of a bedroom with a double bed, a living room with a queen sized sofa bed, a full private bath, and a kitchenette complete with microwave, dishwaser, refrigerator stocked with breakfast fixings, and all the things needed to prepare meals if that is desired. There is also a lovely lanai area with outdoor furniture that guests are encouraged to enjoy.

The hosts, Larry and Susan, hail from Texas. They moved to Kauai to open a fast photo business, but the real love of their life is horses and Larry is quite a Polo player, while Susan roots him on. Recently Larry has become interested in drama and got rave reviews playing the sheriff in *The Best Little Whorehouse in Texas*. Since the hosts live in the main house, guests have plenty of privacy.
RATE:   $30 single, $40 double, $50 for 3, $60 for four.

### K-9

The best way to describe Iris is that she is an American, Swiss, Australian and world-traveled. Born in Australia, she has lived in many parts of the world, managing hotels in Switzerland, Australia, and Africa. There is not much Iris doesn't know about hospitality. She is an avid gardener and each Monday, Wednesday, and Friday Iris treks on down to the Sunshine Market to sell her fruits, flowers, and organic produce. She is also a gourmet cook. She prefers non-smokers.

Her home is located about one and a half miles above Kealia Beach in Kapaa Heights. The accommodation offered is a new, separate, cedar building at the front of the home, private entrance, private bath, small refrigerator, radio, with phone in the room, and has a choice of either twin beds or king sized. Iris always makes sure there are boogie boards, beach mats, ice chest, blue ice for the guest to use. Smoking outside, please.
RATE: $35 single, $40 double, $5 extra for one night.

### K-33
This home is located about eight miles north of Kapaa on Moloaa Beach in one of the most beautiful settings in Hawaii. Denny and Debra, the hosts, are sure they have found Paradise and want you to experience it with them. The accommodation offered is a little rustic cottage, not at all fancy but nice, with a full kitchen, queen sized bed, private bath. There is a cool spring that Denny and Debra have made into a shower outside the cottage that is very nice after one returns from the beach. Pick this if what you are looking for is a beautiful, secluded beach spot, but not all the amenities of a resort hotel.
  Denny and his family, who were all born and raised on Kauai, have a big interest in the old Hawaiian songs and the art of slack key guitar playing. Sometimes the family gets together for an old fashioned luau, and when they do guests are always invited to join in. If you really want to get away from the hustle and bustle and enjoy the "real Hawaii" this is the place.
RATE: $38.50 single or double, two night minimum.

### K-41
Nestled under the eyebrow of the Sleeping Giant is a studio apartment where guests can sleep cool and quiet. This Island hidaway is very private. The apartment has two twin beds that can be put together to form a king sized bed. There is a refrigerator, color TV on cable, private bathroom with shower, and a hot tub. Guests here have the best of both mountain and sea since it is just steps from the Nonou Trail for hikers, close to horseback riding, and yet just minutes away from Lydgate Park where snorkelers can feed the fish by hand.
  Earle and Joy, the hosts, love their Island home and are anxious to share it with B & B guests. Since Earle is a shell collector, they love to comb the beaches and know all the best spots. Joy's great lovwe is orchid growing.
RATE: $30 single, $40 double, $240 a week double, non-smokers only.

## RESTAURANTS

**LOCAL STYLE**

**SHARON'S SAIMIN**
In the center of Kapaa Town just past the Ono family restaurant. Closed Monday. Twenty-one varieties of saimin at low prices.

**HIGASHI'S**
Next to the Bank of Hawaii in the center of town across from the ball field. Very LOCAL, lots of rice, low prices. Some of the locals think they have the best teriaki beef on the Island.

**ALOHA DINER***
In the Waipouli complex on the mauka side of the highway. All Hawaiian food (chicken hekka, lau-lau, lomi lomi, poi). You will get the same food here that you would get at a luau for a much lower price. This is a good place to try out Hawaiian cuisine.

**BIG SAVE**
In the shopping center in Kapaa. Inexpensive plate lunches. This spot is popular with locals.

**FAST FREDDIES**
A few doors up from Sharon's Saimin. This used to be Nat's but is now under new management. We tried the Chicken Teriaki and it was pretty good, plenty of rice and potato salad for $5.50. It's not much on atmosphere but very clean and comfortable.

------------------------------------------------------------
**local Style**

***EL CAFE***
The old place next to the Roxie Theater is closed they are now open at their new location just around the corner on Kuhio Highway, next to the motorcycle shop. Norbert is running things as before so we would imagine that the food will be as tasty as before. They are open for lunch and dinner and this is a good place to get a good meal for a low price.

**RESTAURANT SHIROMA**
In the Waipouli Complex, which is between the seven and eight mile marker. Open for breakfast, lunch and dinner. Very low prices and for what you pay the food is good, but fixed to please locals.

## WAIPOULI
In the Waipouli Shopping Center behind Mac Donald's next to Foodland. Very similar to Shiroma's in most respects.

## ONO'S CHARBURGER
In Anahola north of Kapaa next to the little store. Take out only. Very good hamburgers at a modest price. There are a few tables under the Royal Poinciana tree.

---
### local/Tourist

## WAILUA MARINA
Located at the mouth of the Wailua river where the boats to Fern Grotto dock. This defies a label since almost everyone eats here. When we first visited Kauai, we stopped here for breakfast one morning and someone in the party asked for an Irish coffee. "I'm sorry," the waitress replied, "we only serve Yuban." They are open for breakfast, lunch, and dinner. Prices are moderate to low for a place that has so much tourist business.

## AL & DON'S
This is a little hard to find. It is located in the Kauai Sands Hotel, which is just south of the Plantation Marketplace. Open for breakfast and dinner only. About the only tourists who find this are the ones staying at the hotel, but the locals have found it because it is such a good deal. The atmosphere is good, right on the water, and the prices are even lower than they were in 1985. The menu has changed slightly; it is not quite as extensive, but there is plenty to choose from and the highest price on the menu is shrimp at $7.75 with full dinners for as low as $4.95. A full liter of wine goes for $5.75, up $1.00 from last year. 822-4221.

## BULL SHED
The entrance road is just across from Mac Donald's in Kapaa. Very nice setting, right on the ocean, especially if you have a window table. Open for dinner only. This has long been a favorite with tourists. Broiled steak and fish, and prime rib, salad bar included with all meals. All entrees except chicken over $10. Reservations accepted only for parties of six or more.

## RIB & TAIL
In the Big Save Shopping Center in Kapaa. If you can't get in the Bull Shed try here, since the food and prices are very similar. Also, there is dancing here. 822-9632.

## *ONO FAMILY RESTAURANT*
In the center of Kapaa on the makai side of the highway. Open for breakfast, lunch and dinner. Moderate prices, good food. Good spot for a fresh fish dinner under $10. Be sure to try their Portuguese bean soup.

## KOUNTRY KITCHEN
Toward the end of Kapaa, about a mile past Ono Family Restaurant on the mauka side of the highway. Open for breakfast, lunch and dinner. Moderate prices and good food, much like a Mainland cafe. Home made corn bread.

### TROPICAL TACO
In the Big Save Shopping Center in Kapaa. At one time this was limited to takeout, but it has been remodeled and enlarged and now has plenty of seating room. This is a good place to get filled up at a low price.

### **KINTARO**
Across the street from the Coco Palms as you enter the Waipouli/Kapaa area. More expensive than most of the other places in town but we think it is worth it if you like Japanese food. Excellent sushi and sashimi and other authentic Japanese dishes. Since last year they have expanded and now offer Tappanyaku style (food cooked in front of you). The decor is interesting and the service is good. 822-3341.

### KAPAA FISH AND CHOWDER HOUSE
At the north end of Kapaa on the mauka side of the highway, across the street from Otsuka's Furniture. This was formerly the Kauai Gardens. When they closed, the Chowder House, which had just opened in Koloa, took over, did a lot of remodeling without destroying the garden setting, and are now quite well established. They are open for lunch and dinner, with entrees in the $12-$18 range. 822-7488.

## POINTS OF INTEREST

### KAMOKILA HAWAIIAN VILLAGE
This is a restored ancient Hawaiian village located on the north bank of the Wailua River on the site of an old village. Guided tours are provided and visitors get a chance to see some of the old Hawaiian crafts. To find take Highway 580 toward the mountain and watch for the sign on the left just opposite the falls. The charge is $5 for adults, $1.50 for children between 6 and 12. They are open from 9 a.m. until 4 p.m. Monday through Saturday.

### FERN GROTTO
To get to the Fern Grotto one must take one of the river cruises from the mouth of the Wailua River, either Smith Boat Cruise or Waialeale Cruise. It costs $7 and some people feel it is too touristy but we have enjoyed it the two or three times we have done it. Try not to get on a boat with all Japanese tourists because the guides will speak Japanese.

### OPAEKAA FALLS
Take Route 580 from the Coco Palms and go about two miles up the hill. You will see a large parking lot on your right. Once there be sure to cross the street to look over the Wailua River and the valley below.

## ALEXANDER'S NURSERY
Continue up Route 580 for another mile or so and you will come to the nursery on the right. It is closed Sunday and Tuesday. It is lots of fun to look around here at all the tropical plants. Richard and his wife are very helpful in answering questions.

## STATE PARK
If you continue up 580 for another few miles, past the University of Hawaii Experimental Station, you will come to the Wailua River up near its source. You will be about seven miles from the Coco Palms. Depending on the rainfall, the river will be going either under or over the road. Most of the time it is safe to drive to the other side of the river to the parking area. This area is not kept up as it once was, and yet it is a great place to enjoy some of Kauai's natural beauty. You can walk down along the river bank, and, if you like, you can swim in one of the swimming holes along the way.

## COCONUT PLANTATION SHOPPING CENTER
Retrace your route down to the Coco Palms. At the main highway turn left and go about one mile and you will see the entrance to the Marketplace on the makai side. On Thursday, Friday, and Saturday, starting at 4 p.m., there is a free hula show. There are all kinds of shops and restaurants. One shop you should not miss is the Kahn Gallery, which features many of the local craftsmen. While many of the items they carry are expensive, the quality merits the price. Not everything in the store is high priced. There are koa chop sticks by Troy Lydgate and baskets by Theo Morrison, but even here the quality is obvious. When you visit here, be sure to have Angela show you some of her sculptures.

## SUNSHINE MARKET
Every Wednesday starting at 3:30 local folk sell produce (see Sunshine Market under Lihue section). To find, take route 581 (Kukui St.) and head mauka for a few blocks. You will come to a park and some tennis courts on your right. The sale takes place in the parking lot.

## SLEEPING GIANT
When we first visited Kauai, we felt that the top of this mountain was inaccessible. In reality it is not too strenuous a hike, with the trail beginning on either side of the mountain. To hike from the east side, turn mauka just north of the Coco Palms on Haleilio Rd. and continue toward the mountain, bearing to the right until you come to the trail head marker. To hike from the west, go mauka on 580 until you reach 581, turn right and drive a little over one mile where you will see the trail on the right.

## FRUIT FARM
This is the best place to buy papaya, banana, and pineapple, especially if you are here for a long stay. To find, take Kauaihau Rd., which runs into the main highway at the north end of Kapaa, and drive a little over three miles. Just after you pass the ball field on the left, watch for a driveway on the right which may have a keep out sign. Ignore the sign, drive in past the house to the garage where you will see all the fruit. If no one is around, weigh the fruit and leave the money on the bench at the back of the garage. The cost is $.20 a pound.

## BEACHES

### NUKOLII
Starting behind the Wailua Golf course and going south, almost to Hanamaulu are beautiful, almost unused, white sand beaches. If you walk along here, yours may be the only footprints you will see. This is a good place for beaching and getting away from crowds, and maybe doing a little fishing, but it not so good for swimming. Waves tend to be rough with lots of rip tides.

### LYDGATE STATE PARK
Just past the Wailua Golf course you will come to the Kauai Resort. Turn makai at the resort and go past it to Lydgate. Once a place of refuge and sacred to the ancient Hawaiians, this is a great spot if you have children. Many residents bring their children here where the water is safe. If you are a beginning snorkeler, this is the place to start.

### COCO PALMS BEACH
Just across from the Coco Palms, parking can be found at either end. Swimming is good and safe if you do not venture too far out. At times you can watch the surfers at the north end. If you walk around the point at the north end, you will come to a secluded section, good if you want to be alone.

### KEALIA BEACH
Just past Kapaa you will come to one of the most beautiful crescent beaches in Hawaii. Be careful here, for the waves can be awesome and the rips treacherous. At the far north end of the beach is a little cove used by locals and a safer place to swim. This is also an excellent place to body surf.

### DONKEY BEACH
Closed to all but those who have a Lihue Plantation sticker.

### ANAHOLA BEACH
North of Kapaa, just before you reach Anahola as you go down the hill, you will see a Hawaii Visitors Bureau marker on the right. Take this road and after one half mile you will see a sign pointing down a dirt road to the beach. Swimming is fair here, but if the surf is up, best to stay out. Beachcombing here is excellent. If you are early enough or lucky you may find a glass ball off one of the Japanese fishing boats. These are getting rare as other material is being used to make the floats, mainly plastic. If you miss the first road, you can take the road just past the store. Watch that you do not swim into the coral at the left side of the river. You can also find beach access by turning makai at the 14 mile marker on Aliomanu Rd. and going about 2.3 miles. This is a good place to go if you really want to get away from it all. Just past the 15 mile marker on the main highway you will come to the other end of Aliomanu Rd. Don't get confused, the two roads no longer connect. If you turn makai here and go about two miles to Kukuma Rd. and then left for about .2 of a mile you will find access to a very small, secluded beach.

## **MOLOAA**

We think this is the most beautiful beach in Hawaii. Swimming is safe here unless the waves are very big on the north shore. To find, turn in at the fruit stand which is on the makai side of the highway just past the 16 mile marker. Take the road behind the stand which goes off to the left and proceed for 1.2 miles until you come to Moloaa Rd. on the right. Take that road and proceed to the beach. There is not much parking, but few people use this beach. When you come out you can get back to the main road by continuing on Koolau Rd. for 2.3 miles. The road is a little rough but certainly driveable.

### NIGHT LIFE

#### COCO PALMS
Every night starting at 7:30 there is a torch lighting ceremony at the Coco Palms. There is no charge. Everyone who comes to Kauai should see this at least once, if for no other reason than to hear the talk that goes along with it. People react differently to the ceremony, but see it for yourself. To some it is the highlight of their trip.

#### VANISHING POINT
The Kapaa disco, it sometimes jumps until 4 a.m., much to the discomfort of those staying at Kapaa Shores condos across the street. Heavily frequented by locals, it is not used much by tourists.

#### BEACH BOY
Located in the Marketplace, there is sometimes some action here.

#### KAUAI RESORT HOTEL
Sometimes the Kauai Resort will feature entertainers from Honolulu. To find out what is going on, call 245-3931.

#### PLANTATION CINEMA
At the south end of the Marketplace. There are two small theaters here which show first run movies. On Thursday night admission is $1.00.

*Bed & Breakfast Guide*

## SPORTS ACTIVITY

GOLF

Wailua golf Course, County owned and operated, is one of the best deals in Hawaii. Green fees for non-residents are $10 weekdays, $11 on weekends and holidays. Carts are available, both hand and power for $3.00 and $11.00, but not mandatory. Clubs can be rented from the pro shop located next to the sign-up window. Larry Lee Sr. and Larry Lee Jr., the pros, are most helpful. They also handle the hand cart rental. If you rent clubs, a hand or power cart is mandatory. The driving range is open every day until 10 p.m. Small buckets are a $1 and large buckets are $1.75. Golf Digest rated Wailua one of the best ten Municipal courses in the Nation. For a starting time call 245-2163.

TENNIS

The Coco Palms has courts which are open to the public for $6 for one confirmed hour and longer on a space available basis. Public courts with no charge are located in three places in the Kapaa area. 1.) Wailua Houselots, just past the Coco Palms take Haleilio Rd. until you come to Nonu St. on the left. Turn on Nonu and go several blocks to the courts. 2.) Kapaa Town, turn mauka on route 581 (Kukui St.) and go about 1/4 mile and you will see the courts on your right. 3.) Wailua Homesteads Park, take 580 mauka for a little over two miles, turn right at 581 for about 1/2 mile and you will see the Park on your right.

WATER SKIING

At the mouth of the Wailua river on the north side. To get there go up 580 one block and turn left to the river. For more information call 822-4274 and ask for Pete Fisher.

DIVING & WINDSURFING.

In the center of Kapaa is Sea Sage Dive Shop. Equipment is available for purchase or for rent and dive trips are available.

BICYCLE RENTING

Bikes can be rented at the Sheraton Coconut Beach Hotel or at Aquatics Kauai, which is on the highway north of the Foodland Shopping Center.

# NORTH TO HANALEI

Several years ago *Sunset Magazine* did an article on Hawaii in which they said, "It is the Hanalei Valley that most people see when they close their eyes and dream of Hawaii." The drive from Kapaa to the end of the road at Kee Beach, especially the ten miles past Princeville, is one of the most scenic in Hawaii. The question of how long this drive takes is a difficult one to deal with since there are many little side trips to take to get the full impact of this area.

The first town you come to after you leave Anahola is Kilauea Town, and unless you pull off the road, you will go right past it. Kilauea is mainly a residential area so you will not find much here in the way of shops or restaurants, and yet one of the most interesting shops in Kauai is here, Kong Lung's, or, as the sign in the window used to say *Gumps in a Cane Field*. We were told that one of the Gump family happened to see the sign and asked that it be removed, so it was changed to *Gifts in a Cane Field*. Another interesting business in this town is Jacques' Bakery, which has bread so good that most of the better restaurants on the Island use it. What used to bring most people to Kilauea was the Slippery Slide from the movie *South Pacific*. Several years ago the land was purchased and rumor was that it was going to be developed into a tourist destination spot. The present owner submitted plans to the Planning Department of Kauai but as of this writing he has not been able to get approval of his plans. It seems that many of the people who live in Kilauea are against development of the area. It will be interesting to see if he is able to get approval in the future or if he even tries. At the present time the slide is closed to the public.

Just past Kilauea, as you go down the hill and just before the bridge that crosses Kalihiwai Stream, look to your left and you will see a fairly sizable waterfall. One can judge from this how much rain is falling in the high country. If you park by the bridge, you will get a good view of Kalihiwai Valley.

At about the twenty eight (28) mile marker, just past the Princeville Airport, you will come to the entrance to Princeville on the right. This planned development is made up of many homes, condo complexes, the Hanalei Bay Resort, the new Sheraton Hotel, and the Princeville Golf Course, a twenty-seven hole, Robert Trent Jones Jr. designed course that has vistas unsurpassed anywhere. One does not need to be a golfer to enjoy a walk or ride around this course. In March the LPGA holds the Kemper Open here.

At the present time Princeville is developing a whole new phase and as one drives in one sees on the right a huge excavation that is going to be a man made lake for the golf course that is under construction. To some of us who live on Kauai, all of this development seems a little premature since Princeville even in the busy season never seems to be short of space to accommodate visitors. But tourism on Kauai is growing and while we are all for that, we know that even those who visit Kauai do not what wall to wall condos, especially half empty ones. One point we would stress, however, is that there is no indication that what happened on the Kihei Coast of Maui will be allowed to happen on Kauai. While development does go on, the Planning Commission makes sure projects are tastefully done and no high rise buildings are permitted.

Just past Princeville is the overlook for Hanalei Valley, where fields of taro grow in all stages of development. It is from taro that poi, a staple to the Hawaiian people, is made. When you reach the bottom of the hill, you can drive into this area to get a closer look. A very good dirt road goes only a few miles.

Next is sleepy little Hanalei Town nestled between the Hanalei River and Hanalei Bay. Change comes slowly here and is sometimes resented by the long time residents. The most recent change is the addition of Ching Young Village, made up of Big Save Market, a number of little shops, and several small restaurants all vying for the tourist dollar.

The seven mile drive from Hanalei town to the end of the road is of unparalleled beauty and charm. One crosses a number of one-way bridges, where small streams flow to the sea. The road rises and falls and constantly there are beach vistas hard to believe. One passes what is perhaps the most famous beach in Hawaii, Lumahai, or Nurse's Beach from the movie *South Pacific*. All of this ends at Kee Beach, the setting for the love scene in. *The Thorn Birds*.

*KAUAI*

## HOSTS

### K-6
Strictly speaking, this is not a B&B home since there is no host present. This is a condo located in the Princeville development, in Hanalei Bay Resort and is offered to B & B members at a reduced rate. This one bedroom condo can be rented for $65 a night for the entire unit or for $50 for the studio. The bedroom has two double beds and the studio has two couch beds so the unit could handle a family of six. The amenities include tennis, swimming, movies at night, a bar and a dining room, with a view of Hanalei Bay. There is a $25 cleaning fee.
RATE: Studio $50, entire unit $65, $390 a week.

### K-12
This home is in Kilauea, just a few miles before one reaches Princeville and the Hanalei area. It is just a few minutes drive to the Kilauea Lighthouse and bird Sanctuary. Kilauea is both a farming and a residential community and was one of the main areas on Kauai for pineapple. This three bedroom, one bath home with separate shower room, is an old plantation worker's home. The home is modest and down to earth as are its owners, Donna and George, who always make a guest feel right at home. Two bedrooms are offered: one, the Pink Room, has a double and single bed, the other, the Blue Room, has a queen bed.

The hosts, both in their sixties, are non-smokers and avid runners who enter marathon races whenever possible, usually accompanied by their dog, Waggers, who so far has entered forty five races, including two marathons. So into running are Donna and George that in 1985 they are traveled to Liechtenstein to run the entire country. Donna substitute teaches and George makes children's toys as well as drives the school bus. Their home is a short distance to a secluded beach. They can take families. Smoking outside, please.
RATE: $15, single, $20 double.

### K-14
Janie has been doing B & B for about five years now, and guests love not only the location but the excellent accommodations, a fully furnished studio apartment with a double bed and studio couch. Everything is very modern and convenient, completely separate from the main home, so guests have lots of privacy if desired. The unit has full cooking facilities and the makings for breakfast are provided (fruit, rolls, juice coffee or tea) and guests can dine at their leisure. The studio has color T.V., is within walking distance of the golf course, swimming pool, tennis, with beaches just a short drive away.

Janie moved to Kauai from Denver about six years ago. She was reared in Oklahoma and attended prep school and college on the east coast. Now she enjoys gardening and just relaxing on the beautiful Garden Island.
RATE: $45 double, $1000 monthly, 3 night minimum, breakfast is not served.

### K-14B
Surrounded by the lush green fairways of the Princeville Golf Course, Howard and Lorraine have a large Condo, which they wish to share with visitors. The room provided is fully furnished with its own bath and a private entrance. Guests are encouraged to enjoy the living area of the home as well. Laundry facilities are also available.

Howard and Lorraine are recent residents of Kauai, having moved from California, where they operated their own business. Now they have a mail service business on Kauai.
RATE: $40 April through November, $45 December through March.

### K-16A
This home is secluded, peaceful, attractive, and on the Golf Course at Princeville. The host, a former Honolulu resident, offers a two room deluxe apartment adjacent to her home. It is a stucco building with sky lights and an etched glass Italian Tile shower. There are twin beds in the bedroom and a double bed in the living room. The apartment is furnished with a small refrigerator, toaster oven, coffee maker, and blender so light cooking could be done. There is also a good selection of books and magazines. The home is close to shopping, restaurants, tennis, golf, and beaches are just a short drive away.
RATE: $50 double, $12.50 for extra person, two night minimum.

### K-21
Lillian offers to share her beautiful home right on Anini Beach with visitors in the event she is "on Island." Since she is a world traveller, she is not always available. She recently returned from a trip to Africa and Israel and then made a trip to the Far East. It is her love of travel that makes B & B interesting to her as she has a natural affinity for travelers.

Her home is halfway between Kilauea and Hanalei just a few steps from the ocean at Anini Beach. The room offered has an ocean view, and a double bed. There is a large covered porch for relaxing and viewing the magnificent sunsets of the North Shore. Smoking outside, please.
RATE: $36 one rate, two night minimum.

### K-28
This B & B accommodation, hosted by Florence, is about five miles from the end of the road past Hanalei Town. There are two rooms available for guests so that a small family could be accommodated. Since her home is right on the beach, it makes a great place to start a day of shelling and swimming. One of the bedrooms has a double bed, the other has a single bed. Breakfast is served on the deck in tropical splendor.

Florence has been in Hawaii for many years. She has owned and operated a successful business and is now retired. One of her hobbies is antiques. She is also on the Board of Directors of Serenity House.
RATE: $35 for single room, $40 for double room, 2 night minimum.

### K-30
We call this *Taro Patch Cottage* as it is located in the middle of a taro patch in the Hanalei Valley. The cottage is fully furnished and is set up for short or long stays. There are two bedrooms, one with a queen bed, the other with a single bed. Since there is no host for this one, breakfast is not served.
RATE: $62.50 double, $74.50 for three, three night minimum.

### K-32

Steve and Sarah are somewhat new to living on Kauai, but they have visited here for some years. They bought their home a few years back, but it took a little while to get it all together to settle in Paradise, and that is what they feel the North Shore of Kauai is. Sarah works in a tourist-related business, while Steve works in real estate.

Their home is located just steps from Hanalei Bay, which suits them fine since one of the things they enjoy most is shell collecting and just hiking on the beach. The room offered has a private bath. Breakfast is served on the large deck.

RATE: $33 single, $38.50 double, two night minimum.

### K-50

Located in the little town of Kilauea just minutes from Hanalei Bay and the north shore beaches, Manya and her husband have built a large tri-level home that is just perfect for B & B guests. The upstairs has two two separate rooms, each with a private entrance and kitchenette. Each room has a full private bath and each has twin beds. The kitchenette has a small frig, tiled counter and sink, a toaster oven, dishes and flatware, great for preparing lunches or snacks. Manya serves breakfast in the dining room down stairs or for those who prefer she leaves breakfast fixings in the kitchenette. Non-smokers, please, as the hosts are allergic to smoke.

RATE: $35 single, $40 double, $5 extra for one night.

### K-51

This B & B accommodation is for the adventurous and for those who really want quiet and solitude in a tropical paradise that the hosts have created out of what was once a kukui nut forest. Now coconut trees, ginger, and hibiscus line the stream and path that runs through the property to a secluded beach. This path also leads to a cottage that is fully equipped with a refrigerator and hot plate, and all the cooking equipment one would need. The bedroom of the cottage has twin beds, plus there are twin beds in the living/dining area for extra people.

The hosts, Frank and Enes, have a vegetable garden, citrus trees, and even some chickens, as well as a big friendly doberman who watches over the property and will tag along if guests decide to do some hiking to waterfalls nearby.

RATE: $65 double, $10 extra person.

### K-52

Beyond Hanalei on an ocean road almost to Haena is King Hale. The backyard is the beach where the diving and windsurfing are perfect, ocean conditions permitting. The front yard is an immaculate private tennis court. The accommodation offered are very versatile. A large three bedroom, two bath duplex complete with kitchen, cable TV, double beds, outside shower, and a comfortable living room. One of the bedrooms has an outside private entrance and a private bath. This is a large area and can be rented separately. It comes equipped with a coffee maker, toaster oven, and a small frig.

Larry and Julia, the hosts, live in the adjoining duplex. Both are very active in the happenings on Kauai. Larry is instrumental in the promotion of the Kauai triathelon events. Julia is the editor of the Garden Island newspaper.

RATE: Total unit can accommodate three couples available for $120 a night, $650 a week, $1500 a month. Separate bedroom $50 per night. Two bedroom unit $80 a night.

## RESTAURANTS

### MOLOAA FRUIT STAND
Just past Anahola and before Kilauea, you will see it on your right. It is possible to get a sandwich or a cold drink here.

### KILAUEA SNACK SHOP
Behind the Post Office and behind the 76 Gas Station in Kilauea Town. Take-out only. Some LOCAL STYLE plate specials as well as hamburgers and other sandwiches. They are open from 5:30 a.m. until 3:30 p.m. Monday through Friday, and from 8 a.m. until 3 p.m. on Saturday and from 8 a.m. to 2 p.m. on Sunday.

### CASA 'D AMICI
This is the newest restaurant on Kauai and from what our hosts who live in this area tell us, they will be very successful. The fare is Italian and the prices are modest especially for pasta.

## PRINCEVILLE RESTAURANTS

### CHUCK'S STEAK HOUSE
Prices are moderate to high and the food is what one would expect in a tourist restaurant, that is, very reliable. They are open for breakfast, lunch, and dinner, 826-6522.

### BEAMREACH
To find, turn in at Princeville and go past the golf course to the last condo complex on the right. Open for dinner only. The food is good, their prices range from $12 to $20, 826-9131.

### BALI HAI
This restaurant is located at the Hanalei Bay Resort. At our last visit, prices were reasonable. The outstanding thing here is the fantastic view of Hanalei Bay, 826-6522.

### LANAI RESTAURANT
Located above the Pro Shop at the Princeville Golf Course. This used to be Godfrey's. It is owned and operated by the same people who own Chuck's Steak House mentioned above. We have not had a chance to try it but since Chuck's is very reliable our guess is that this will be too, 826-6226.

TORTILLA FLAT
Located in the Shopping Center in Princeville. This is fairly new and we have tried it several times. They have Mexican dishes and they have standard American dishes also. The food is moderately priced by Princeville standards, but it lacks the atmosphere of The Lanai, Bali Hai, or the Beamreach, 826-7255.

## HANALEI RESTAURANTS

LOCAL STYLE

HANALEI MUSEUM SNACK SHOP
Behind the museum on the mauka side of the road when you enter Hanalei. Take-out only. Plate lunch specials including fresh fish when available for under $4. Hamburgers and other sandwiches are offered.

THE VILLAGE SNACK AND BAKERY SHOP
In the Ching Young village. Good food at low prices, try the home made pie.

-------------------------------------------------------------
local Style

FOONG WONGS
In Ching Young village, on the second floor. Cantonese style, with plate lunch specials of a Hawaiian flavor. It is the plate lunch specials that make this a good deal. If one orders several dishes a la carte as we did, their price will be high for what you get, 826-6996.

HEALTHY JONES
In the Ching Young Village. Sandwiches to keep you fit at fair prices.

BLACK POT LUAU HUT
This is located just east of the Ching Young Village in a small shopping center, this restaurant has been open since May of 1985. Most of the dishes have a local flavor and the prices are reasonable. Fresh fish is served when available for around $7.00. They recently opened a full bar, 826-9871.

WAINIHA GENERAL STORE
Past Hanalei between the thirty four and the thirty-five mile marker. Closed Monday and Tuesday. Hamburgers and sandwiches for take-out. Good food at low price.

-------------------------------------------------------------

### local/Tourist

**PAPAGUYO AZUL**
This used to be called El Cafe but has recently changed hands and we were told that the menu would change also. All of the dishes will be made with fresh ingredients imported from California. The food is take out only but there are a few little outdoor tables provided.

**WEST OF THE MOON CAFE**
This is a new little restaurant just next door to Black Pot. Mostly they serve sandwiches with prices between $3-$6. It is cute and clean, 826-7460.

**\*\*TAHITI NUI\*\***
In the center of Hanalei. The Tahiti Nui really defies description and in spite of the enlargement and modernization it remains a unique spot in Hawaii. We are not great promoters of the Hawaiian luau, but if it is a luau you are looking for, this is the most interesting we have been to. The price is up to $20. and drinks are not included. There is a good sampling of Hawaiian food and plenty of dessert. The show is the best part of the evening and always a special treat is hearing Louise Marston, the owner-operator of the Nui, sing one of her Tahitian songs. The entertainment is very "local" and can be a delight. To quote one of our guests, "This luau had a family flavor. The songs were mostly about the North Shore, Hanalei, and the beautiful scenery of that area." Luaus are held on Wednesdays and Fridays, but call ahead for information. If not a luau, stop by for lunch or dinner, or just a cool drink in the bar, 826-6277.

**THE DOLPHIN**
On the makai side of the highway as you enter Hanalei. Open for dinner only. Good food, with prices in the $12 to $18 range. The setting is nice, right along the Hanalei River, 826-6113.

**SHELL HOUSE**
On the highway just past the Tahiti Nui. Open for breakfast, lunch, and dinner. If you have tried this before and were not pleased, give it another try, as there is new management and the food is very good and the prices are not too high. We recently had lunch there and were pleased. They have started serving blackened fish for dinner, and as far as we know they are the only ones on Kauai who have. 826-9301.

**CHARO'S**
Past Hanalei between the thirty-five and thirty-six mile marker at the Colony Resort. This used to be called the Sandgroper but has since been purchased by Charo, completely remodeled and in many ways improved. We had lunch there and the food and service was very good. Especially good was the clam chowder. It is located right on the ocean in a very pleasant setting. We were told that Charo spends as much time on Kauai as she can and when on Island visits her restaurant daily, taking much care with the menu, 826-6422.

## POINTS OF INTEREST

### THE LIGHTHOUSE
Take the main road into Kilauea and go past Kung Lung Store. The Light House area is a sanctuary for a large number of marine birds (the Red footed Booby, the Frigate, the Albatross). There is a small museum in the Light House that has pictures of all the birds. It is also possible to borrow binoculars to watch the turtles. The gate to the Light House opens at noon and closes at 4 p.m.

### CHRIST MEMORIAL CHURCH
This stone edifice is not as old as it looks. It was built during World War II in 1942. The church is left open so visitors can enjoy viewing the hand-carved altar and stained glass windows imported from England. There is also a small graveyard behind the church that is interesting to visit.

### HANALEI MUSEUM
In the center of Hanalei Town. Fee for adults in $1.00, children free. The museum has a small collection of artifacts.

### WAIOLI HUIIA CHURCH
On the mauka side in Hanalei Town. This church is over a hundred and forty years old and holds services every Sunday. The unique thing is that the hymns are sung in Hawaiian.

### WAIOLI MISSION HOUSE
Built in 1836, this old home gives one an idea of life long ago. There is no charge and visiting hours are from 9-12 and 1-3.

### WET & DRY CAVES
Near the end of the road past Haena Beach Park. Legend has it that this was once the home of Madam Pele, the volcano goddess. When the caves filled up with water, Madam Pele, liking a warmer clime, moved on to the Big Island.

### KALALAU TRAIL
The trail head begins at Kee Beach on the mauka side of the road. Hiking the entire eleven miles is strenuous and should only be done with planning. Usually this hike takes a couple of days in and out and a camping permit is required. The two mile hike to Hanakapiai Beach, however, is not that tough. In fact, the hike from Hanakapiai Beach to Hanakapiai Falls, a distance through the valley of about two miles, is also not that hard. We would urge anyone who is a good walker to at least try the first two miles, and if they felt up to it to try the hike to the falls. Under no circumstances should anyone try swimming at Hanakapiai Beach as the rip tide is fierce. Strong swimmers have been swept out and drowned at this spot. It may look inviting but it is a definite no-no!

*Bed & Breakfast Guide*

## BEACHES

The North Shore of Kauai is one beautiful beach after the next. People debate which beach is best. In actuality they are all "best" depending on weather conditions, wave conditions, one's mood, or whatever. We would encourage you to spend some time at one of the less accessible beaches to get that "away from it all" feeling. Also, none of the beaches mentioned below are difficult to get to, and if hiking is involved, it is very little. It is possible that at some of the beaches you will be the only ones there.

### **KALIHIWAI BEACH**
Just past Kilauea, before the road descends, you will see Kalihiwai Rd. on your right. Once on this road you will see a "No Outlet" sign. That means that the road dead ends at the beach. The swimming here is safe, especially in the lagoon where the river meets the ocean. Things can get rough way off to the right as you face the ocean. If the surf is up, be careful. There are no facilities here, so if you intend to stay awhile, pack a lunch.

### ANINI BEACH
About one mile past the first Kalihiwai Rd., you will come to another Kalihiwai Rd. At one time they were connected by a bridge over the lagoon. Once again you will see a "No Outlet" sign. As soon as you can, turn left on Anini Rd. and proceed to the beach. You can stop anywhere along here you like, but a mile or so up the road you will come to a public park where there are picnic and rest room facilities. The water is shallow, making this a perfect place to snorkel, especially for the beginner. Also, windsurfing is good here.

### HANALEI BEACH PARK
Hanalei Bay is surrounded with beach, but the most popular place is by the pier on the far east side of the Bay. To find, turn makai off the main highway at the Tahiti Nui and go one block, turn right and this road will take you to the park. There are picnic tables, rest rooms, and showers.

### LUMAHAI
Near the thirty-seven (37) mile marker, at an obvious vista point, you will find a small trail leading to the beach. Unless the waves are small and the ocean is calm, this is not a good place for swimming.

### TUNNELS BEACH
This beach is located near the end of the road, just before you reach the wet caves. Watch for the beach access sign, turn makai and the beach is about 100 yards ahead.

From Hanalei to the end of the road at Kee Beach there are numerous other beaches to enjoy such things as sitting in the sun or shelling. No doubt you will see surfers at various points. Do not conclude that this beautiful water is perfectly safe. North Shore water on each Island can be dangerous. There are so many safe places to swim on Kauai that it is silly to take chances in dangerous places. Keep in mind that this is an isolated area and should one get in trouble, it would take some time for help to arrive. Kee Beach at the end of the road is safe for swimming and snorkeling in the summer months, but when the surf is up, do not venture out here or your next stop might be Mid-Way Island.

## NIGHT LIFE

There used to be music at the Hanalei Bay Resort, and perhaps when the new management takes over they will have some evening activity in the Happy Talk Lounge. The Tahiti Nui has shows when they have a luau and sometimes even when there is no luau they have music in the bar. Also, often there is some special thing going on and these will be mentioned in the Garden Isle newspaper.

### KILAUEA THEATER
Located a few doors from the Kong Lung Co. Store. They started out showing old movies but lately have started to show some first run movies.

### BRIDGE
On the first and third Thursday of the month there is a duplicate bridge game. For information call Lolita Horney, 826-6805.

## SPORTS

### GOLF
Princeville Golf course at the Princeville development is one of the most photographed courses in Hawaii, and a favorite with many of Kauai's visitors. Were it not the most expensive course on Kauai, it would be much more popular. Unless one is staying within the Princeville Development, green fees are $40 and the cart, which is mandatory, is $26. A husband and wife would pay $106 for a round of golf. These are the kinds of prices that convince many visitors that Hawaii is only for the rich. If money is no object, the course is worth it, for there are vistas unsurpassed. For those staying at Princeville, the fee is $27 plus $26 for a cart. Since B & B has four accommodations within the Princeville development, B & B members who choose these could play Princeville for a total of $80 a couple, a savings of $26 a round. On Tuesday and Thursday after 3 p.m. a cart is not required and the green fee for nine is $23 for those not staying in Princeville and $15 for Princeville guests. For more information call 826-3580.

### TENNIS
There are courts open to the public at the Princeville Golf and Tennis Club, $4 per person per hour, court rules. There are also courts at the Hanalei Bay Resort.

### POLO
In the spring and summer months there are Polo games held at Anini Beach Park.

## SOUTH TO POIPU

Most of the tourist activity on Kauai takes place in the Poipu area, on Kauai's south side, about twelve miles from Lihue, where beaches are big and the sun shines brightly. The first place you come to after you leave Lihue is the little community of Puhi, where Kauai Community College is located. Across the street from the college, on the makai side of the road, is Mike Masaki's fruit stand. Stop by here for a visit or to pick up some fresh papaya or pineapple, or maybe an orchid spray or a few anthuriums.

A few miles south of this you will see a sign pointing to the left for Kipu. If you take this drive, do not expect to come to a town or anything resembling a town. Two and one-half miles after leaving the main road you will reach a monument to William Hyde Rice, who died in 1924. He was the son of William Harrison Rice, one of the first managers of the Lihue Plantation. William Hyde Rice was born and grew up on Kauai and had a great knowledge and love of the people and legends of the Hawaiians. Not only did he speak Hawaiian, it is said he understood it on a multiple meaning level that even some of the Hawaiians failed to grasp. His book *Hawaiian Legends* is considered one of the most important of its kind. The monument in his memory was erected in 1925 by his many Japanese friends. You can drive past the monument on dirt road and all you will see are some little Hawaiian homes and plenty of cats and chickens.

Perhaps during your stay on Kauai you will hear about the tunnel in this area that goes to the Poipu/Koloa area. Local folks insist that if you try to go through this tunnel carrying pork your motor will stall and you are apt to see Madam Pele. We have been through this tunnel, but alas no Madam Pele appeared. Since this is private property, belonging to one of the sugar companies, we do not recommend using this route.

When you return to the highway, you proceed south to one-half mile past the six mile marker where you will come to the road to Koloa. The first part of this road is called the *Tunnel of Trees* because of the huge eucalyptus trees that line the road. Before the hurricane these trees were so thick they blocked the sun, hence the name. This is a much safer tunnel to use to get to Poipu/Koloa. We have heard of Madam Pele making appearances here too, but usually after mid-night, and by then we are fast asleep. At the Tunnel of Trees, turn left and three miles later you arrive at Koloa Town, the oldest plantation town on Kauai.

Recently Koloa Town has been receiving a face lift, making it an attractive tourist center. When you turn right as the road dead ends in Koloa, you will see a cluster of small shops on your left. At the back of this mall there is a display of pictures depicting the devastation of Hurricane Iwa in November of 1982. Poipu was the hardest hit by Iwa.

After you make the jog in the road at Koloa town, you proceed three miles and you are in Poipu, the tourist mecca of Kauai. Poipu is an area, not a town, and in a sense the center of Poipu is Poipu Beach Park at the foot of Hoowili Rd. off Poipu Rd. Just west of Poipu Beach are the hotels: the Waiohai, Poipu Beach Hotel, the Sheraton, and the Kiahuna with its complete tennis complex and an eighteen hole, Robert Trent Jones Jr. designed golf course. To the east are a series of condos, available for vacation rentals. To the north of these condos is Poipu Kai development, made up of four condo complexes with many lots for private homes. Much care has gone into the planning of this area, and while there are one or two unattractive condos just above Brennecke's Beach, when this area is compared with others in Hawaii, it is obvious that someone deserves credit for making sure Poipu stayed attractive.

## HOSTS

### K-1
This new, custom home is located about 1/2 mile from Poipu Beach park in a quiet residential neighborhood. The entire lower level is the private accommodation offered and includes a large bedroom with a queen sized (baffled) water bed and a full bathroom. In the living area there is a double bed for one or two extra people or a family traveling with children. There are light cooking facilities, dining area, and a private covered lanai.
A breakfast of homemade bread and freshly ground coffee along with tropical fruits are served by your host and hostess on the upper level overlooking a mountain view. The hosts, Jim and Carolyn, have two small children, so naturally they do not object to families with children. Carolyn's job is the home and children. Jim works out at Barking Sands.
RATE: $45, one rate, $10 for extra adult, $5 for child, two night minimum, no smoking in the house.

### K-20
Located within walking distance of the Poipu Kai development and Poipu Beach Park in a residential neighborhood. Carol Ann was born in Honolulu and is a third generation Hawaiian (her grandfather fought in the Hawaiian Revolution and her father was born under the Monarchy). Carol Ann teaches part time in the public schools. She is a full time painter and photographer. She has three grown children and seven grandsons. Walter, an engineer, was born and raised in San Francisco and has lived in Hawaii for almost twenty eight years. He is an avid tennis player and windsurfer. They both enjoy travel, classical music, and theater.

*Bed & Breakfast Guide*

The accommodation offered is on the ground floor of a two story home. There are two bedrooms available so four people could be accommodated. The main bedroom used features a king sized bed and a private bath, the other room has twin beds. Carol Ann and Walter live on the second floor with their two dogs, Brandy, an eleven year old Irish setter, and Sam, a four year old part Lab. Since Carol Ann is allergic to smoke, no smoking in the house, please.
RATE:   $40 single or double, $55 both rooms.

### K-22
The accommodations offered are one of several bedrooms in a large, fifty year old Plantation Home, located about one block from Poipu Beach. Each bedroom is roomy and has a private bath. The home is two story, and the hosts occupy the garden level apartment. Guests are welcome to use the large lanai for reading, sunset watching, or just relaxing.  The home is situated on an acre of beautifully landscaped property. At the present time there are four self contained units behind the home, and by January of 1987 there should be five more. The hosts provide beach equipment: snorkels, fins, mats, coolers, boogie boards.
RATE:   $40 single, $50 double.

### K-22B
This three bedroom home is several houses up the street from K-22. Since this home is fully furnished and occupied only by B & B guests, there is no host to serve breakfast. While this home is best suited for long stays with monthly rates available, short stays are also possible. Only one couple at a time in the home unless couples are traveling together, so this is ideal for the ones who want plenty of privacy.
RATE:   $60 one couple, $80 two couples, $1500 a month for one couple, $2000 for two couples.

### K-23
The accommodation offered is a separate, fully furnished apartment on the garden level of K-22B. The bedroom has an extra long double bed.  There is color cable T.V. in the living room. Also, the couch in the living room makes into a bed so a small family could be accommodated. From this home it is just a short walk to Brennecke's and Poipu Beach or one can walk in the other direction to Shipwreck Beach. For those who want to enjoy ocean activities, snorkels and boogie boards are available as well as plenty of beach mats. As in K-22B, there is no host so no breakfast is served at the home.
RATE:   $40 single or double, $5 for extra person over two

### K-24

This is Al and Evie's Poipu Plantation, what they hope is to be a culmination of their B & B Hawaii dream. At the present time there are four units available, each a roomy one bedroom, fully contained apartment. The view from each unit, both mauka and makai is good and the view from the upper units is outstanding. Eventually five more units will be constructed: three one bedroom and two with two bedrooms and two baths. Already there is a large deck for sunning and barbecuing and soon a hot tub will be added. We stress the fact that while these are available to B & B members, no breakfast is served, since the units are self contained, and can you imagine serving breakfast, even a continental one, to nine or ten couples? We can imagine it also, that is why no breakfast is served.

RATE:  $50 for garden view, $60 for one bedroom ocean view, $80 for two bedroom ocean view.

### K-25

This location would be hard to beat since it is right on the ocean just a few doors away from Spouting Horn on Kauai's sunny south side. Bob and Gloria, the hosts, have furnished their home with antiques, creating a very cozy atmosphere. Breakfast is usually served on the large deck overlooking the ocean. The accommodation offered is a bedroom with a queen sized bed with a separate entrance by the koi pond. The bath is shared. If two couples are travelling together, Gloria moves to the Tea House and makes available two queen rooms with the bath between.

Bob is a psychologist who continues his practice on the Mainland and he manages to get to Kauai quite often. Gloria is employed in Lihue.

RATE:  $50 per room, $45 during off season.

*Bed & Breakfast Guide*

## RESTAURANTS

**LOCAL STYLE**

**BIG SAVE**
In the Big Save Market at the east end of Koloa Town, you get lots of chow down food at low prices.

**\*SUEOKA'S MARKET\***
Just to the right and alongside Sueoka's market. Every day is bargain day at this little take out stand. Hamburgers are only $.70 Feed one to the kid and if he makes it, order up. Just kidding, the food is very good for the price. Try the plate lunches, tasty and cheap. Or for a snack, seven won ton for $1.00.

---------------------------------------------------------------
**local Style**

**\*TAQUERIA NORTENOS\***
Next to Kukuiula Store. The owners describe this food as *Sonoran style Mexican*. Morgan, who moved to Kauai from Tucson, Arizona, was raised by a Mexican Nanny, who taught her that style of cooking. The service is take out only. Lots of food for a low price. Open every day accept Wednesday from 11 a.m. until 11 p.m. This is about the only place in the area that you can get a snack after 10 p.m.

**KOLOA ICE HOUSE**
At the east end of Koloa Town, just before Big Save. Very good sandwiches for a modest price. Also special dishes such as chili & rice for under $2.00. Shave ice served. When you see shave ice with beans, do not worry, it is not the ones they use in chili.

**\*KOLOA BROILER\***
In the middle of Koloa. If you do not like the cooking, there is no one to blame but yourself since you are the cook. There is a good-sized broiler in the room where one can broil a steak, fish, beef kabobs, or a hamburger. This along with a salad bar with rice and beans, priced between $6 and $8 makes this one of the livelier spots in the area. It can be crowded, but be patient, they eventually get everyone served.

---------------------------------------------------------------
**Tourist**

**FEZ'S PIZZA**
In the center of town behind the liquor store. They have a little salad bar and a few other things available: pasta, sandwiches.

**HOUSE OF SEA FOOD**
In the Poipu Kai development, formerly called Kona's. We have tried this several times and each time it improves and now we recommend it highly especially to seafood lovers. They have come up with some really interesting seafood recipes. Most entrees run between $15-$20 and salad is included. The setting is nice, 742-6433.

### BRENNECKE'S
Right at Poipu Beach Park, open for lunch and dinner. Mainly tourists eat here. All of the entrees come with pasta in a white sauce. Very good fresh fish starting at $13. What we like here are the "starters;" ie., cerviche, tomatoes and onions vinigarette, etc. We often make a meal of just starters. Also, since it is right on the ocean, it is an excellent place to watch the sun set. They have a long happy hour in the afternoon and the drink prices are reasonable, 742-7588.

### COURTSIDE RESTAURANT
This fine little restaurant is at the Kiahuna Tennis Club and plenty of tourists who would love it unfortunately never find it. They are open for breakfast and lunch, and lunch goes to pretty late in the afternoon. Every day different specials are offered at modest prices. We feel sure that even those who are not tennis buffs will like this spot.

### KIAHUNA CLUBHOUSE RESTAURANT
At the Kiahuna Golf Course. Open for breakfast and lunch from 7 a.m. until 3 p.m. and for dinner from 5:30 to 9 p.m. 742-6055.

### THE BEACH HOUSE
On the road to Spouting Horn. The original Beach House was destroyed by the hurricane but they have built it back bigger and better than ever. The setting is perfect, right on the water. They are open for dinner only and a reservation is suggested. The food is O.K., very much what you would expect, and the service is good considering the crowds they handle. Prices range from $13 to $20, 742-7575.

### THE AQUARIUM
It is a little hard to find as it is on a dead end street which runs off Hoone Rd. alongside Nihi Kai Villas just east of Brennecke's Beach. The specialty here is Italian cuisine. Full dinners can be ordered, ie. salad, antipasta, pasta, or ala carte. We usually order one full and one ala carte and there is more than we can eat. Unless you have a pasta dinner, figure around $15-$20 a person, 742-9505.

### KOLOA FISH AND CHOWDER HOUSE
This is a new restaurant in Koloa and as anyone who has visited Poipu at the height of the tourist season knows, restaurants in this area are sorely needed. Needless to say the specialty here is seafood, but that is true of almost all the tourist restaurants in the Poipu/Koloa area. The decor is very nice and the service is good. Entrees are around $15-20 and come with salad, 742-7377.

### KEOKI'S PARADISE
This restaurant opened in early 1986 and is located in the new Kiahuna Shopping Center at the entrance to the Kiahuna Golf Course. They are open for dinner only. We enjoyed our dinner very much and the prices are quite reasonable, with some dishes under $10. The only thing we didn't enjoy was the tape of the frogs croaking. Friends tell us they have dispensed with the frog tape, 742-7534.

### POIPU BEACH HOTEL
Next door to the Waiohai Hotel, in fact the same owner, but not nearly as expensive for either food or accommodations. At lunch time you can broil your own hamburger by the pool.

## PLANTATION GARDENS

Located in the Kiahuna development next to the Waiohai. If you are looking for the nicest restaurant in the area, this is probably it. The atmosphere is excellent, the service is good, and the food can be great. Price wise, it will be around $20 to $30 a person depending on wine and dessert choice. Everything is extra, but for a special occasion this would be our choice.

## POINTS OF INTEREST

### SPOUTING HORN

To find, just stay to the right on Poipu Rd. after you pass Kukuiula Store and you will come to it. We enjoy seeing and listening to Spouting Horn since it is always a little different depending on the mood of the ocean. It is fun to calculate which swell is going to produce the highest fountain. One of our friends dubbed it *the god's bidet*. This is a good spot to pick up a gift for someone on the Mainland as the vendors are pretty competitive. At one time these vendors paid no rent, but now they are controlled by the County and bid for their spots.

### PLANTATION GARDENS

At the Kiahuna, all around the Plantation Garden Restaurant. At one time there was a charge to go through these gardens, but no longer. Unlike some botanical gardens, you won't always know what you are looking at, but it is all beautiful. Of special interest is the cactus garden.

### OLD KOLOA TOWN

Koloa is the oldest plantation town on Kauai. Some time around 1835 Ladd & Company, made up of three men, William Ladd, Peter Allen Brinsdale, and William Hooper, started a sugar plantation in Koloa. Hooper was made the manager of the operation and in spite of his lack of knowledge about sugar, the plantation became successful, and no doubt this success encouraged others to go into the production of sugar. Koloa was also a place for whaling ships to stock up for their long journeys to and from the North Pacific. The newest addition to Koloa town is a small shuttle bus that runs from Koloa to Poipu Beach and through the Poipu Kai development. At the present time there is no charge to ride this bus, but we understand that when they are approved by the PUC there will be a small charge.

### FARMERS MARKET

This got started in July of 1986 and is a welcome addition to the Koloa area, since residents had to drive all the way to Lihue before. The market is on Monday, starting at noon at the ball park next to the Fire Station in Koloa.

## BEACHES

### KOLOA LANDING
To find, take the middle road where Poipu Rd. divides just past the Kukuiula Store. Watch for a dirt road on the right. This is not really a beach, but if the ocean is calm and you are a confident swimmer, this is a good place for snorkeling. Often the dive shops bring people here for lessons or for certification. This is the spot where ships docked and cargo was loaded and unloaded in the early days.

### POIPU BEACH PARK
With little doubt, this is the most popular beach on Kauai and for good reason. First, it is almost always sunny, and if a shower comes, do not panic and leave, just wait a bit and very likely the sun will return. Also, the facilities are excellent: picnic tables, rest rooms, showers, a store and a snack bar across the street. Then, the swimming and snorkeling is excellent. The best snorkeling is in the cove to the right, out around fifty feet. It is only three to five feet deep in most places and many varieties of fish can be seen. Surfing is out in front of the Poipu Beach Hotel.

### BRENNECKE'S BEACH
Once known as the best body surfing beach is Hawaii, Brennecke's was damaged by Hurricane Iwa. It is, however, coming back and hopefully its reputation will be restored. It is located a hundred yards or so east of Poipu Beach Park.

### SHIPWRECK
To get to this beach it is necessary to drive through Poipu Kai. Continue on Poipu Rd. into Poipu Kai until the road becomes a dirt road. About a half-mile into this cane road you will see a dirt road that goes makai. Take this to the beach. Although this beach is beautiful and great for sunning, it is not so good for swimming. Many of the expert body surfers who once used Brennecke's now use Shipwreck. If you beach here do a little exploring east of the beach. There are some beautiful little coves along these cliffs. Look for the petroglyphs along these cliffs.

### MAHAULEPU
East of Shipwreck about three miles. Just continue on the cane road from Poipu Kai until you come to a road lined with power lines. Turn right. Do not take the forks to the right or the left. When this road turns sharply to the left, you are almost there. Drive straight ahead until you see a parking area. This is where the locals go to picnic and fish and enjoy a day of relaxing. There are no facilities so if you intend on staying, pack a lunch.

## NIGHT LIFE

**POIPU BEACH HOTEL**
After 9 p.m. there is a band for dancing. Since the band is not there every night, call ahead at 742-1681.

**SHERATON HOTEL**
Sometimes the Sheraton has entertainment but it is not on a regular basis so it is best to check in advance. They offer a luau with the usual show attached. 742-1661.

**THE LIBRARY**
On Wednesday night starting at 7 p.m. the library in Koloa shows the movie that Lihue showed on Tuesday. (see Lihue section).

**BRIDGE**
Every Tuesday night starting at 7 p.m. there is a bridge game under Kona's restaurant in Poipu Kai. It is a very low key game of Chicago or Country Bridge. You do not need a partner since if there is an odd number, they will make up a team of three or have the dummy play with the spare. Coffee is served.

## SPORTS

**DIVE SHOPS**
The Full Fathom Dive Shop in Koloa offers boat dives every day and they rent all kinds of equipment. There is also a little store at Poipu Beach that sells and rents equipment.

**TENNIS**
The only public court is on the left as you enter Koloa on the Tunnel of Trees Rd. The Kiahuna has courts for $6 an hour, unless you are staying at the Kiahuna and then they are "free." Poipu Kai also has courts at $6 a person a day, court rules. It is best to call ahead to reserve a court. They also rent rackets for $3 each (742-6464). Also, there is a court at Poipu Sands in the Poipu Kai development that is seldom used.

**HORSEBACK RIDING**
· A new and welcome addition to the Poipu area. For reservations and information call CJM Country Stables, 245-6666 or evenings 338-1314. There are all sorts of rides available, from one hour for $16 to weddings and celebrations on horseback at quoted prices.

**GOLF**
You can't miss the Kiahuna Golf Course as you drive down Poipu Rd. The fee is $45 for eighteen, cart included and mandatory. For more information call 742-9595.

# KALAHEO

Kalaheo, a thriving residential community, is little visited by tourists since there are seemingly no attractions in this area. However, we will be pointing out several things we feel all visitors should see, and since these will take you off the the main highway, we suggest you take a little time and enjoy the scenery.

When you get to the center of Kalaheo, turn makai on Papalina St. and go up the hill until you see Puu Street on the right. This road will take you through some of the residential and farm area of Kalaheo and will return back to Papalina St. at the entrance to the Kukuiolono Golf Course. Along this drive you will get some good views of the south Kauai Coast, all the way to Niihau, the so-called Forbidden Island.

When you reach Papalina St., if you turn left you will return to the main highway. If you turn right and go down the hill you will come to Waha Rd., a left turn will take you to Lauoho where you turn right to get back to the road that runs between Koloa and the main highway. Most of the locals who drive from the Poipu-Koloa area use this road as a short cut to the golf course.

## HOSTS

### K-10

Clarence and Pat have lived all over the world, and when they decided that Kauai was the place for them, they constructed a beautiful home in the hills of Kalaheo, which Pat designed. Pat, who is originally from England, has a great love and knowledge of animals and has cats, dogs, and horses. Pat is also quite an artist, as many of her guests have mentioned, although she is somewhat modest of her talent. Clarence, a retired Brigadier General of the U.S. Army, has worked in real estate on Kauai and keeps up to date with what is happening on the Island. Pat and Clare, as he likes to be called, are avid bridge players.

The accommodation is a large studio apartment, kitchenette, full bath, T.V., private lanai, with a full mountain and ocean view. There is a queen sized bed and one single bed. Their home is located about five miles from Poipu Beach and a mile or so from Kalaheo. The rural and very private setting takes one away from the hustle and bustle.

RATE: $49 double, $10 extra for child, $15 for adult.

### K-18

Lorraine was born in Oklahoma, raised in Portland, Oregon, and has lived in San Francisco, New Orleans, Caracas, and for about the last twenty years in Hawaii. Before Lorraine retired, she worked for the Government at the Pacific Missile Range. What she likes most now is taking long walks with her dog, and also indulging in her main hobby, photography.

Lorraine's home is located between Lawai and Kalaheo. The accommodation is a large sleeping and sitting area with a separate bath and lanai. Up a few steps from the sitting area is a comfortable dining area with a sink and a refrigerator.

RATE: $45 one rate plus 4% tax.

### K-29

Originally from So. California, Norm and Bobbi came to Kauai in the middle '70's. Their custom designed home is elegantly finished in koa wood, one of Hawaii's most beautiful hardwoods. The richness of it color enhances the beauty of this comfortable home. A large living area offers a panoramic view of the ocean. There are two patios for relaxing, one with a hot tub. Two guest rooms, one with a queen bed, the other with two double beds, are available. There is an extra large tile bath with a dressing area for the guests use.

After Bobbi and Norm stayed in a B & B home on the Big Island, they decided they would enjoy sharing their home with others. What better way to meet interesting people? Their home is just a short drive from the main highway and close to Kukuiolono Golf Course.

RATE: $33 single, $38.50 double.

### K-40

There are panoramic ocean and mountain views from this immaculate and spacious two bedroom apartment. Janice and Ken, who own a construction company, recently finished building and landscaping this 1200 sq. ft. apartment with B & B guests in mind. The apartment has two bedrooms, one with a queen sized bed the other with twin beds. The couch in the living room makes into a bed making this a perfect accommodation for a family. There is a private bath, of course, and a fully furnished kitchen complete with microwave. There is a color TV in the dining/living room. The white rattan furniture, Roman Shades, and Oriental rugs add a touch of elegance.

The hosts and their two daughters, Ronda and Raquel, live in the main house on the property. The girls are interested in beaching, body surfing, and jazz dance. Both are in high school and help with the B & B hosting. Ken and Janice are avid golfers and are just three blocks from the Kukuiolono Golf Course. Janice moved here from Lake Tahoe and originally hails from Missouri, while Ken is from New Castle, California. Two baby sitters are available to those travelers with children.

RATE: $55 double, $65 for family of four, $75 two couples, $85 for six.

## RESTAURANTS

**local Style**

BRICK OVEN PIZZA
If you like pizza be sure to eat here. Maybe we have been in Hawaii too long, but we think this is the best pizza we have ever had anywhere. Try their whole wheat pizza with the garlic rubbed crust, topped with Portuguese Sausage.

*GARDEN BROIL*
On Papalina Rd. and open for breakfast, lunch, and dinner. This was formerly Joshu's Grill but has since been taken over by a Korean family. The food is very good if you like this ethnic type food. The prices are very modest, around $6 a person. The specialty of the house is Kalbi ribs which happens to be one of our favorites. Since they do not serve alcoholic beverages, you are welcome to bring your own wine. There is a liquor store just up the street.

LAWAI RESTAURANT
This is located on the main highway just before you come to Kalaheo, in the town of Lawai. The owners of this restaurant used to run the Waiapouli Chop Suey in Kapaa. The food is Cantonese style, moderately priced (most dishes under $5), and in our opinion pretty tasty. As in most local style restaurants, it is possible to get Japanese dishes also. The atmosphere is local.

BURGER INN
Don't be fooled by the name. This is a very local style place with plenty of plate lunch specials for reasonable prices. It is located on the main highway, just west of the stop light in Kalaheo.

## POINTS OF INTEREST

### KUKUIOLONO GOLF COURSE
Be sure to visit here whether you golf or not. The Japanese garden here is delightful. Nowhere on Kauai, unless you climb Sleeping Giant, will you get better views, from the Poipu shoreline all the way to Kekaha and Niihau beyond. The gate closes at 6:30 p.m., so if you are there to watch the sunset, keep one eye on the clock or you may spend the night.

### OLU PUU GARDENS
Located about a half mile beyond Kalaheo on the mauka side of the main highway. There are guided tours every Monday, Wednesday, and Friday starting at 1:15 and 3:15 p.m.. The tour lasts about two hours and the charge is $6.00 per person, $4.00 for senior citizens. For information call 332-8182.

### PACIFIC TROPICAL BOTANICAL GARDENS
This is a guided tour by appointment only on Mondays, Tuesdays, and Thursday starting at 8, 9, 10:30 and 11:30. The charge is $10.00. Since part of the tour is by Jeep on narrow dirt roads, the tours are called off if it is rainy. For more information call 332-8131.

## SPORTS

### GOLF
If Wailua isn't the best deal for golf then Kukuiolono is. It is a nine hole course and not quite as nice as the other courses on the Island, but it is still a challenge. As stated above, the setting and the views make one forget the dubbed drive or the missed putt. Daily green fees are $5, but for those on extended stays, a six months ticket can be purchased for $50 which allows unlimited play. For more information call 332-9151.

# HANAPEPE

As you drive in to Hanapepe, just as the road forks, look to the right, up the hill, and you will see a rainbow of bougainvillea. Hanapepe is a most colorful little town. At one time, when pineapple was king, it was a thriving, bustling community with several hotels, a movie house, and even a taxi service. All of the buildings, some now in a state of disrepair, housed profitable businesses.

While not quite the same since the demise of the pineapple industry on Kauai, Hanapepe is not dead yet. Recently it was used by the makers of *The Thorn Birds* as the setting for the honeymoon scene. If you look to your left just after you enter town and start to round the first corner, you will see the Dungloe Hotel, which formed the main scene. As you drive through town, keep in mind that the movie makers had to work hard to make Hanapepe look older.

There are several art galleries in town. One is located in the hotel mentioned above and is owned and operated by James Hoyle, a local artist of some note. Finding any of the galleries open at any given time is another matter. After all, these are artists first and business people second.

Whatever you do in Hanapepe, be sure to stop at the Feed Store located at the end of town after you cross the bridge. Mr. Shimonishi is a grower of orchids, and if you walk behind the Feed Store you will see orchids of every size, color, and type. In fact, Mr. Shimonishi has created at least one type of orchid, we have been told. Some, but not all, of the orchids are for sale, and you can not beat the prices. Most of the orchids you see displayed at the hotels or for any special occasion come from Mr. Shimonishi.

The new rage in Hanapepe is Lappart's Ice Cream, which is located on the main highway on the mauka side in the middle of Hanapepe. Now there are several outlets for this very tasty confection and we wouldn't be too surprised to see franchises popping up on the Mainland. At any rate, this might be a good place to stop for an afternoon refreshment.

# RESTAURANTS

## LOCAL STYLE

### SAIMIN CORNER
You may not find this no matter how hard you look, and if you do it probably won't be open. The Corner is owned by a little old man who is more or less retired and opens now only on Friday evening and some weekends when he feels like it. Only saimin is served. We have heard it is tasty and very cheap.

### LINDA'S
In the center of Hanapepe on the makai side of the street. Open from 7-1:30 for breakfast and lunch, with breakfast served until 10 a.m. Good local food at low prices, a good spot for lunch either going to or coming from the Canyon.

### LEEWARD DINER
On the main highway, on the mauka side. It is owned and run by Gladys Fuji. It would be easy to miss as it is very small, but try hard to find it because for the price it is hard to beat. The specialty of the house is ox-tail soup.

---
## local Style

### MIKE'S-CONRAD'S-WONG'S
Hold on a minute, what is this three in one stuff? Are we trying to condense? No way, Jose, that is just the way this one comes. Got a group that can't decide between Chinese, American, Japanese, Korean? No worry, take them to MCW's. "But," you say, "we got one guy who wants Mexican." So, they have that, too. It is located on the main highway on the makai side, you can't miss it. It is open from 7 a.m. until 9 p.m. every day but Monday when the hours are shortened to 10 a.m. until 2 p.m. If you get there at the right time, you may see about 150 people rush in at once, since this is used by the large tour bus companies as their lunch stop. Have no fear, though, they can handle you too, as the place is huge. Prices are moderate and we have found the food good.

### KAUAI KITCHEN
Across the street from Conrad's. Low prices, tending toward local style food.

---
## local/Tourist Style

### GREEN GARDEN
Probably more has been written about this restaurant than any other on Kauai, and it has long been a favorite with locals and tourists alike. They are open for breakfast, lunch, and dinner, closed Tuesday evening. There is a very nice garden atmosphere. Keeping in mind that this is considered a "tourist" restaurant, prices are not too high and the portions are ample. We have been getting some great reports lately, especially about their mahi mahi. One of their specialties is box lunches, called bento in Hawaii, for those who would like to picnic in the Kokee area, 335-5422.

## POINTS OF INTEREST

### HANAPEPE VALLEY LOOKOUT
After you pass Kalaheo and start toward Hanapepe, you will come to the lookout on the right. There is quite a bit of farming done in the Hanapepe Valley.

### PORT ALLEN
To get to this turn makai at the Eleele Shopping Center and drive right out to the pier. Sometimes in the afternoon it is possible to buy a fresh fish from one of the local fishermen.

## BEACHES

### SALT POND
As you reach the west end of Hanapepe watch for a road on the makai side of the highway with a sign for Salt Pond. About one-half mile down this road you will see a sign pointing to the right for Salt Pond Park. Swimming here is very safe. Rest rooms, showers, and picnic tables available.

*Bed & Breakfast Guide*

# WAIMEA/KEKAHA

It is from either Waimea or Kekaha that one goes to Waimea Canyon and Kokee State Park. Since both of these towns are mainly residential and not tourist oriented, spending a little time here gives the visitor a truer picture of life in Hawaii than some of the more familiar tourist areas. Waimea is the larger of the two, and you might find it interesting to walk around. If you do, visit the Waimea Fish and Flower Store, which may seem like a strange combination; they were once very successful selling both, then their concentration was on flowers. Now we understand they sell neither, but their shop is still there. Check the Thrift Store and you might get a great buy on an aloha shirt. You might also enjoy a picnic at the park located at the mouth of the Waimea River. To get there, turn left on Ala Wa just after you cross the bridge.

In Kekaha it is fascinating to watch the huge sugar cane trucks unloading at the Kekaha Sugar Mill. As the cane goes into the hopper, it is washed, and before it is ground it is washed again. What comes out the side and is dumped into the trucks is called ofalla and is used for cattle feed or for fertilizer. The syrup from the cane is processed into a brown sugar, unrefined, stored in a huge tank which you can see from the road. It is then sent to Lihue, where it is processed into molasses to be shipped to California for refining.

You may also enjoy browsing through Kauai's Hidden Treasures, a gift and curio shop, where you may find an Island souvenir. While it is a bit of a tourist trap and somewhat garish, they do have Niihau shell necklaces at lower prices than you will see in the stores. The quality of Niihau shells varies greatly, however, and lower price is not always best value.

**HOSTS**

**K-27**
Ron and Kathryn offer guests a rustic separate studio at Kokee with full bath and a queen sized futon. The yard is is filled with colorful flowers and vegetable gardens. Breakfast is served in the main house in the hosts large kitchen. When the hot tub is heated, guests are welcome to indulge.
Kokee is a haven for hikers and bird watchers, with trails to mountain water falls and along the ridges of the Na Pali Coast. Ron, who has lived here for seventeen years, is very familiar with the area and can point you in the right direction, or is available for hire as a guide. Ron and Kathryn also arrange Fantasy weddings for Mainland visitors, and offer a highly personalized tour of the back roads of Kauai in a luxury, air conditioned Jeep Cherokee.
Kokee Lodge, which serves breakfast and lunch every day and dinner on Friday and Saturday, is within easy walking distance on the home.
RATE: $40, one rate. One nighters are welcome.

## RESTAURANTS

### LOCAL STYLE

**\*YUMI'S\***

In Waimea on the right side of the main highway if you are heading west toward Kekaha, just past the twenty-three (23) mile marker. The specialty here is home made apple, pineapple, and coconut turnovers, as good as we have eaten. Get there early as they usually sell out by noon. Also, the owner makes excellent sushi. All of the food is low priced.

**BIG SAVE**

In the Big Save Market. Local food, low priced, plate lunch specials.

---

local Style

**TRAVELER'S DEN**

In Kekaha on the makai side of the highway just past Kekaha Sugar Mill. For the most part this is a local bar, but they do serve lunch and it is a good place to stop for a beer, if you are so inclined. Lunch is served from 11-2 p.m.,( or as Robin the waitress told us, "When the girl comes to cook."). Their specials are roast pork or meat loaf for $3.25, or fried chicken or hamburger steak for $2.25. Happy hour is from 3:30 p.m. until 6 p.m., when beer is lowered from $1.25 to $1.00 and mixed drinks to $1.15. Pupus are served.

---

local/tourist

**\*WRANGLERS RESTAURANT\***

Located in the center of Waimea on the makai side of the main highway. This is a new restaurant and from our experience there, it should be around for a long time. The menu is quite extensive, from plate lunch to Mexican to sandwiches, with very good deals on their plate lunch specials. Their dinner prices are for the most part under $10 with just a few over. 338-1218.

## POINTS OF INTEREST

### RUSSIAN FORT
Located just before you cross the Waimea River, you can't miss it. One needs a little imagination for this, as there is little left but piles of stone, attesting to the fact that the Russians tried for a foothold in Hawaii in the early 1800's. In actuality all of this was the work of one man, Georg Scheffer, an employee of the Russian American Co., who acted on his own without the sanction of the Russian Government.

### MENEHUNE DITCH
You will see signs for this in the center of Waimea. Perhaps one needs an engineering degree to see the significance of this ditch, which runs along the Waimea river. Legend has it that the Menehunes built the ditch in one night. More fun to us is the little foot bridge which spans the Waimea River.

### NIIHAU
No place on Hawaii causes more wonderment that the little island of Niihau, the so-called *Forbidden Island*. The simplest explanation for Niihau is that it is privately owned, hence visitors must be invited. In 1863 a family headed by a widow, Elizabeth Hutchinson Sinclair, bought the Island of Niihau for the price of $10,000. With her were her two daughters, Helen Robinson and Jean Gay. With Helen was her son Aubrey Robinson. Jean had married Thomas Gay, a widower with a five year old son. At the time they purchased the Island, there were about 300 Hawaiians living on Niihau. The importance of this extended family on the history of Kauai is significant and too extensive to be covered here. A good book for further study would be *Kauai, A Separate Kingdom* by Edward Joesting, University of Hawaii Press and Kauai Museum Association, Limited. Now some 250 people, almost all pure Hawaiians, live here. There are no modern facilities: no T.V, washing machines, in fact no electricity. The children of Niihau are educated on Kauai and have the advantage of speaking both English and Hawaiian.

### WAIMEA CANYON
Called "the Grand Canyon of the Pacific," the beauty of the Waimea Canyon can hardly be over-stated. Take Canyon Rd. from Waimea and proceed up the mountain. Be sure to stop along the way before reaching the Canyon to enjoy the view of Kauai's west shore. From here you will get the best view of Niihau you are likely to get. There are two official lookout points where you park the car and walk to the lookout. Along the way there are several unofficial lookout spots, no guard rail, so be careful.

### KOKEE STATE PARK
A little ways past the last Canyon lookout you will come to Kokee State Park, where there is a small restaurant, gift shop, and museum. From this point there are many hiking trails: out to the Na Pali coast overlook, into Alakai Swamp, to Waimea Canyon overlooks, and down into the Canyon. Or one can simply enjoy being around the Park, picnic on the lawn and watch the wild chickens cavort.

## KALALAU LOOKOUT

Several miles past Kokee is the Kalalau Lookout. No matter how foggy it might be, spend a little time here. One of the most beautiful sights in Hawaii is the fog invading and retreating in Kalalau Valley. Too often visitors see the clouds and decide it is the wrong day, when just a little time later all the clouds might be gone.

## BEACHES

There are beaches all along the south coast and they are little used except by surfers. The waves along here are big and rough and the undertow and rip tides can be extreme. Playing in the surf may be O.K. when it is not too rough, but swimming is very dangerous.

## POLIHALE STATE PARK

To find, go to the end of Highway 50 and you will see a sign pointing to the left for Polihale. You will go about five miles on cane road but do not give up. You will end up at the Park. There are picnic tables, rest rooms, and shower facilities here but no food, so stop by in Kekaha or Waimea to buy food. The swimming is fairly safe in the summer months, but dangerous in winter or when the surf is up.

## Bed & Breakfast Guide